THE MAN UNDER THE BED

Turn Up The Bass

Flashbacks from the 90's North East Rave Scene

Contents

1

Hardcore

Adie Scott never saw God on Ecstasy, but he did see someone who claimed to be the Devil. It was 6a.m. and he was coming down heavily in a rave, teeth grinding and sweat drying tight on his face, hair matted. Where as earlier he could not put his hands together as some mad force pushed them apart as he brought them close, now his palms could touch and it was deflating. The magic was fading fast. It was then he appeared. Off to the side, looking on intently with a wicked Jack Nicholson intense grin. Adie didn't know if it was someone pretending to be the Devil, or auld Nick himself, but it freaked him out. He quickly averted his gaze down towards his trainers, but when he glanced up, the Devil was still there, through the darkness and the moving arms of the crowd, leering at him. Adie tried to concentrate on the music, the crashing cymbals and pounding drums, the basslines that rumbled up through his body and made every nerve-end tingle, but he couldn't get the Diablo out of his clouded thoughts. What the hell did he want with him? He walked away from the barrier he'd been leaning on, nervously twisting the cap on the bottle of water he was carrying, and when he quickly flashed his eyes across, the Devil was gone.

A surge of relief raced through his body. He tried to dance, but his feet were heavy and plodding, his arms stiff and disjointed. And when he looked over again, he was back. A twisted smile and dark eyes piercing right through him. He instantly froze up and looked the other way. He was definitely after him.

No denying it, the Devil was following him about full of evil intent. Projecting menacing messages embedded in the repetitive metallic bleeps and squelches of the Acid House tracks into his mind. Adie was freaking out big style; gasping for breath as his chest tightened, waves of panic chilling the beads of sweat running down his back. A girl with black pig-tailed hair, chewing hard on some gum, appeared through the fog belching out of a smoke machine like an industrial chimney and squeezed his wrist.

"Are you OK? You look a bit done in?" she said.

"My head's mashed," he replied. "The Devil's been following me about," he said, angrily jerking his thumb back in the direction of the fallen angel. Her dark eyebrows knotted as she frowned across at him, then her eyes gleamed brown and wide.

"It's a mirrored wall, you nutter!" she laughed.

It can't be denied that the chemical MDMA (3,4-methylenedioxy-methamphetamine) had a massive impact on the North-East's traditional cultural nightlife by the early 1990s. When people first started dropping pills instead of downing copious amounts of alcohol and staggering around the Bigg Market and the Quayside spewing and fighting, the atmosphere definitely changed. While the street marketing for the drug saw it dubbed many names including white lightnings, doves, dollars, or the capsule rhubarb and custards, it was a word-of-mouth culture shared among small groups of friends that created a different scene. Watch out for the slammers, they're very heavy - full of Ketamine, people would warn each other. Ecstasy was fairly exclusive and certainly wasn't cheap when it first arrived in the North East and at around £25 a pill, the cost could have fuelled a massive night around the pubs with the likes of Scottish & Newcastle breweries favourites of Newcastle Brown Ale, McEwan's Export and Exhibition all being less than £1 a pint at that time. Many people will recall boozers in Working Men's Clubs and gloomy wooden bars at the time saying that they would pack in the drink when it went over a quid. Heavy drinking had long been the mainstay of the weekend in the area. The frothy white head on a dark pint of McEwan's Best Scotch being set down in front of men with craggy, lined hardened faces in flat caps knocking on tables with their dominoes; old women in snugs wearing shawls knocking back gin and cackling, blokes in grimy boilersuits off shift at graft, their bait bags by the brass foot-rail. Putting on tweed jackets and ties for comedy nights and turns at the club, hair combed back with Bryclreem. The Miner's strike in 1984/85 and the pit closures changed a way a life in the rows of colliery villages throughout the Durham and Northumberland coalfields that had been going for a century, washing down the black dust with ale on a Friday and Saturday night. Go and see the Pitman painter's exhibition at the Woodhorn Colliery near Ashington and you'll see a life of hard work, wheel heads, pigeon duckets, leek shows, washing ringers and pantries, the light from pubs shining out onto dark pavements and football simply and realistically recorded on canvass. The decline of heavy industry in the region certainly marked the start of a long, drawn-out transitional period from a mechanical towards a digital age marked by unemployment, ram-raiding, riots on estates and a sense of hedonism that the North East is renowned for. Construction workers, lorry drivers, care workers and nurses all going out on a Saturday night to get pissed up and have fun under a solitary glitter ball in their denim or leather jackets with loud Heavy Metal and Hard Rock or Disco music blaring from a jukebox - the eternal weekend Night Fever. To slap on some Hi-Karate or Brut and a gold chain and get out there with your bleach-tipped mullet hair. Down ten pints, spill the salad from a kebab on the pavement, punch some kid in the jaw and wobble away home with a girl you've pulled in high white stilettos under the moonlight on cold, wet, empty streets. Seemingly stuck in a cycle of beer, chips, nothing flash, just that prevalent ethic of going out and getting yourself a trade and getting away to the match on a Saturday.

Newcastle United was in turmoil both on and off the pitch in the late 1980s. The 'United Supporters for Change' group were attempting to get Chairman Gordon McKeag to sell up and were boycotting the games at St. James' Park. The ground wasn't the plush all-seater affair that graces the city today; the grey concrete hulk of the Gallowgate that rose into a peak in the corner and the section under the large scoreboard with its dancing electronic men when a goal was scored was the noisiest, most popular end. It sloped away behind back down towards the Strawberry bar with open concrete wall urinals that stank of piss from full bladders being emptied on the way in while, if you were unlucky enough to be stuck firm on the swaying, packed, terracing, you could end up with a 'hot leg' as somebody rolled up their programme like a funnel to piss down as they couldn't get back out while the match was on. The stench from the brewery drifted over the ground from beyond the high stacks of the floodlight pylons and churned the guts of those in the grip of a hangover. The small corner of the Leazes End terrace housed the visiting fans and gangs of lads in paisley shirts and Stone Island with curtains haircuts would get up to the dividing fences to shout abuse, chant and chuck coins back and forth. The wooden benches under the high cantilever roof and seats of the East Stand where the people rose in anticipation every time the black and white shirts went over the half way line.

With home crowds down to around 15,000 due to the boycott, you'd see older football lads around the town in Eldon Square or on Northumberland Street and they'd say to each other: "You're not going to the match are you? You'd better not be!"

Mike and Adie had travelled into Newcastle on the bus and after their regular ritual of getting dinner upstairs at the Eldon Food Court – satay beef for Mike and chicken curry for Adie – they'd wandered up to the ground out of habit as much as anything, just to see what was going on. It was half time and the crowd was emptying out of the metal gates from the Corner out by the red brick turnstiles in their hundreds. The temptation proved too much and they pushed in past those coming out to get into the ground. A watching policeman laughed as they made their way up the steps against the flow. "Please yourselves, lads," the copper said with a grin. "They're 3-0 down to Coventry City."

Subsequently away games became a massive deal, especially for those involved with the Supporters for Change, and organised coaches ferried the Magpies fans around the country in their thousands. Filling eight-pint plastic containers with ale at chucking out time in a local pub after a full night of drinking and waiting under the blue neon star in the darkness before getting on a bus to visit the South coast; watching dodgy imported Dutch porn movies and wedging a bin between the back seats for a toilet that was emptied out of the emergency exit when it was full and sloshing about. The Union Jack flags hanging in the back of other coaches on the motorways proclaiming where they were from and flashing the Vs and banging excitedly on the windows as you went past, cars and work vans full of lads on the road cheering in recognition as they drove by.

Ian was a big United fan who followed the club around the grounds, the fine drizzle whipping down and dripping off the rusted lip of an old cantilever stand. Going mental as the ball hit the back of the net, feeling the full heaving force of the surge of bodies behind him, the stale smell of drink, tobacco, body odour, wet denim and boiled onions filling his flared nostrils. He soaked up the animal roar that rolled around the dark empty roof space and echoed back off cold concrete as he jumped up and down, grabbing hold of the man in fronts' coat and shouting in his face. He grinned back, not caring, he'd seen him around. Ian clambered up on a barrier and was hanging onto the caging screaming obscenities at the pissed-off looking home fans across the dividing lines of fences and police. He struggled to snort whizz, his nose was that broken across the bridge. He punched the air and gave the fingers to their element, mocking them, his black leather jacket gleaming with the wet. Ian recalled a trip down to Plymouth when he'd gone into the wrong end with his mate Charlie after they'd followed the green shirts up to the ground from a session in a local pub.

"Newcastle had a green and yellow away shirt at the time and we thought nothing of it," he said. "We came up onto the top of their Kop and looked over the pitch to see a sea of black and white at the other end. We gave started chanting 'United!' and they just poured down on top of us. The police had to come in and drag us out. As they were taking us around the pitch, big, bearded Brian 'Killer' Kilcline was waiting to take a throw in and just shook his head as we went by. We were literally covered in spit by the time we got into our end where the lads were all laughing and cheering as they chucked us in the cage. Saturdays were a big deal. You work all week and want to let your hair down on a Saturday, be it at the match, in a club or at a rave."

Ian was arrested at St. James' in April 1990 for invading the pitch. Visitors West Ham were awarded a dubious penalty in a highly-charged atmosphere and around 250 -including Rob, Charlie, Mike and Adie - spilled out of the paddock onto the turf to charge the East End fans in the nearby small corner section of the Leazes. Ian was jumping up on the advertising hoarding just a couple of feet away from the Hammers when he was lifted.

"They chucked me in the small cells under the Gallowgate then took me down to Pilgrim Street nick," said Ian.

"What I'll always remember is I was number 581. More than 581 people were lifted that day, ten to a cell, lads from North Shields, South Shields, Jarrow, the West End, all over the city. It's hellish, really, fighting at the football, and all a bit daft now looking back."

In November 1988 six travelling Mags had been lifted in London when the police found CS gas, baseball bats, pool cues, a smoke bomb, Stanley knifes and blades in their hired car at King's Cross station ahead of a game against Millwall. Mike saw Manchester United's Red Army in action on Barrack Road in Newcastle as large numbers of hooligans clashed with chair legs and baseball bats as bar stools and pint glasses flew through the air. The rave scene was still pretty much underground at the time and Ian remembered pulling into small towns all over England on the way back from games to drink and seeing gangs of lads and lasses in floppy hats and baggy dungarees in the back rooms of bars getting ready to receive the location and head away on the motorways in a convoy of battered Fiestas and Escorts for Acid House parties in abandoned warehouses.

"We were at an away game across in the North-West and the North Shields boys in the back of the bus produced a little plastic bag of Es as we pulled into Blackpool on the way back. They handed them out and were pissing themselves laughing when one of the older lads who was a big drinker started stripping naked and dancing on the tables. He just couldn't handle it at all. He lay down in front of the bus starkers and we had to bundle him back on board with his clothes rolled up so we could get home. Mental," laughed Ian.

The spread and subsequent popularity of the drug throughout the country had been so rapid that by the time of the World Cup in Italy in the summer of 1990, New Order had initially tried to name the England team's song 'It's E for England' before it was vetoed by the FA and changed to *World in Motion.* The establishment weren't as quick to catch on when The Shamen were dancing about on prime-time Thursday night TV at Top of the Pops in 1992 with wide Cheshire smiles, black PVC and BDSM gear, and Mr C chanting; "E's are good! E's are good!" and getting away with it simply by the play on words in the song *Ebeneezer Goode.*

MDMA earned its reputation as the 'love drug' across in the United States where it was legal until 1985 and had been used by therapists in psychotherapy sessions as an empathogen in the 1970s before becoming hugely popular as a recreational drug called 'Adam' (MDEA was 'Eve') at a Dallas, Texas nightclub called Starck in 1984. The drug had found its way across to the Spanish holiday island of Ibiza by the following year.

Ecstasy had essentially been illegal in Britain since 1977 as a modification to the Misuse of Drugs Act 1971 extended the definition of Class A drugs to include various ring-substituted phenethylamines that act on the central nervous system as stimulants or hallucinogens, into which chemical compounds such as MDMA, MDA, MMMA, PMMA, MDEA and similar structures fell. But the drug had been around since its inception in a German chemical lab in 1912 by Anton Kollisch of Merck, who was working on a compound to stop abnormal bleeding.

In mid-80s Britain the view of street drugs had been tempered by a smacked-out Zammo Maguire's descent into the dirty, seedy world of heroin addiction in the children's TV show Grange Hill. With AIDS leaflets from the Government also dropping through the door, intravenous needles and chasing the dragon were certainly seen as a dark and unattractive world and a dangerous urban underbelly. Fear was a prevalent emotion with the threat of nuclear destruction from the Cold War, unemployment, and even sex seemingly harbouring imminent doom.

Ecstasy at least promised some joy, an escape into wonderfully tactile sensations and a loss of inhibition, a dancing, grooving, grinning day-glo world all from ingesting one little white pill. With LSD (acid, trips, strawberries, window panes, purple ohms, test tubes, flying keys, microdots), amphetamine sulphate (speed, Billy Whizz), cannabis resin (tack, squidgy black, hash,) and amyl nitrates (poppers) also included in the raver's chemical arsenal, the party was about to get started. Temazepam (wobbly eggs) was later added to help them take the edge off all the stimulants and try and get some sleep. While drinking was frowned up as the loud and lairy staggering of 'beer monsters' was an anathema to the blissed-out vibe that E brought about, alcohol was still a popular psychoactive and was continuing to fuel violent clashes before the rave scene really took hold.

"Everyone was off their heads and they were getting involved in the new order. Ecstasy was a big thing, and it was like 'where do you get it from?' You'd seen some of the lads going from big fat louts to skinny nutters. They were nutters anyway, it didn't matter what they were doing, drinking or taking pills, but they were friendly nutters, if you know what I mean?" said Ian.

"There were five lads I knew and they got off the bus at King's Cross on a trip to London. They headed off up to Whitechapel up the East End and went up to the Queen's Head at Plaistow, where the ICF used to drink, and they waited outside until about 12 o'clock then took a fire extinguisher and smashed the door off with it. Kicked off in their own boozer with them. Just five of them. Nutters. Absolute nutters," he laughed.

"There was a hairy one when 'Boro, Newcastle and Chelsea were all in London one Saturday. It was a bad bit of policing really. The whole lot came together at King's Cross. West Ham joined up with Chelsea, and Newcastle joined up with 'Boro. Now I'm not being funny, but I know which fucking side I'd be on! 500 lunatic 'Boro and 700 Geordies? Just stand your ground, you're ganna be alright. They came up the Tube station and I was a bit frightened, if I'm being honest. You heard them. Chelsea. It was the Headhunters. Bad mistake. Newcastle and 'Boro ran them across the concourse, man. They weren't frightened of them one bit. Fucking Headhunters?"

"London was always a good trip, I liked getting away down to London. I also liked going to the Potteries, Port Vale or Stoke, they always had a big army. The Midlands was good because you could drink all the way down and all the way back and it was in striking distance so you could get back in time for the Bigg Market or the nightclubs, the likes of Walkers. Port Vale were headcases – there was a big old concourse right outside the ground and they ambushed the Geordies there. Bad mistake again, because it was over Christmas, and the Geordies like a bit of a holiday over Christmas, so they'd brought about 5,000! Stupid mistake, they got ran all over their own town. Unbelievable, but it was a bit lairy."

Newcastle's trips around the country weren't just all about violent clashes, though, and there was a sense of adventure and fun as well.

"We missed one game at Stoke City because Catweasle, the driver, bottomed the bus! That was the end of that one. We went down to Brighton one day and Little Tommy was off his head on pills. We went past a place called Preston Park where they were playing rugby. They took a line-out and Little Tommy ran and grabbed the ball and ran the full length of the pitch with two rugby teams chasing him. It was fucking brilliant! He was faster than them, he was neater than them, and like an American footballer he did a scoring dive beneath the posts! You've got to laugh at that, man."

A new crew of young hooligans were making their name in Newcastle at that time. The Gremlins were hatched in around 1985 from the football casuals who wore gear like McKenzie jackets, La Coste polo shirts and Ivan Lendl Courts as the city became increasingly designer-label and fashion conscious. You'd see the Gremlins congregating at Grey's Monument or Eldon Gardens in the city centre to hit the shops or head away down to Trax in a group of half a dozen or so to pick up tickets for a rave. Many of the Gremlins were also instrumental in organising coach travel away to music events, and they could sort you out with anything you needed. Entrepreneurial, sharp, and increasingly influential on Tyneside's night life, the gang were often involved in violent clashes with nightclub doormen. One night the Gremlins, around 60 of them, literally picked up a car and wedged it in the doors of a club where they'd been having bother with the bouncers on the door. Another night chipping the rim of pint glasses on a wall as they ran down as a mob to fight with the hard-men in their black suits that were unregistered and unregulated then as one of the crew was getting hassle. They were also involved in football violence, of course.

"I remember one day and it must have been either the start or the end of the season, because it was sunny, and loads of the Gremlins were down drinking outside a bar opposite the Central Station," said Ian.

"They were knocking back bottles and stashing their empties so when the away fans landed and were escorted out of the station, there was bottles flying everywhere and shattered glass all over the street."

The buzz of a football riot is something akin to a rave; a controllable mass of pure energy which swirls around a calm epicentre, unpredictable chaos directed by DJs or leading thugs, a low rumble and indescribable electric tension that sets your heart racing. The Gremlins; it was always a great moniker. The 1984 Hollywood movie of the same name obviously influenced its choice, the carnage and bedlam left in the wake of the Mogwai that had eaten after midnight reflecting the devastation that the lads could leave behind them. During the Second World War the Americans had graphic posters declaring slogans such as 'Gremlins think it's fun to hurt you' and 'The Gremlins will get you if you don't watch out' as little menacing characters pulled pieces of airplane engines apart and pulled knifes.

"I was lodging in a new town in south-east Northumberland and doing a computer training course at the time," said Mike.

"I met a lot of decent lads at the college and was still going to the odd Toon game. Some of the lads were connected to the Gremlins and Select 125 - we swapped stories, and my mate Daz told me how Select 125 had steamed the 'Boro Frontline in Kings Cross when the two firms had met after games in London. I don't know how true it was, but he was a handy looking lad though!"

In the May of 1989 United were staring relegation from the old Division One in the face and were rock bottom of the table when the notorious Millwall made the long journey north. Only 14,731 bothered to go into the game. There was a full-on riot after. Police horses and dogs trying to disperse the baying mob, groups of people huddled on traffic islands as the police charged, lumps of concrete and debris strewn on the empty road behind the lines as they forced the crowd back. The disturbance continued down Northumberland Street as a mob of around 3-400 lads led by the Gremlins continued kicking off with the Police as they made their way down towards the Central Station to attempt an attack on the visiting fans. As Mike and Adie ducked off into a side street to avoid getting lifted by a snatch squad, a white transit van pulled up and a group of vicious, scarred and wild-eyed blokes jumped out.

"Are you fuckers Geordies?" one shouted in an aggressive Cockney accent.

"Aye," they replied, in resignation rather than bravado. We're about to get bushwhacked by the Bushwhackers. Fuck.

"We nearly shit a brick, but they smiled and said: 'Only joking, lads!' They were Geordies, and off they went presumably looking for Millwall. I heard they found them later," laughed Mike. The main body of the mob continued on and steamed down High Bridge, putting the windows in and looting the shops in the chaos.

High Bridge Street isn't a big street; it is essentially a fairly narrow long nick through between the Bigg Market and Grey Street starting from the Victorian scrolled tiles of the Beehive pub on the corner and the black cobbles then rising steadily uphill after crossing Grey Street up to Pilgrim Street. But High Bridge was buzzing with activity in the late 80s/early 90s with the best music and clothes shops as you walked three-abreast down past torn rave flyers flapping on doorways along with the odd graffiti tag, a thin strip of blue sky high above between the lofty darkness of the buildings. A fusion of music and fashion with different techno tunes coming from the shop doorways as you wandered past looking admiringly at the gear in the windows.

John Richmond launched his Destroy range in 1987. It was aimed at the younger club and street culture at more affordable prices than the Manchester-born designer's main line, and consisted at first of jeans and packs of T-shirts. He's in Milan these days and attempts to contact him for comment failed. But who didn't want a Destroy denim jacket with black leather sleeves and *Johnny* stitched on the pocket or a T-shirt with rubber panels? Other designers whose clothes were popular on High Bridge included the likes of Armand Basi, Caio, Gio-Goi, Stone Island, CP Company, Valentino and Armani...and a multitude of other tops featuring futuristic space-age graphics, atomic symbols and NASA-style imagery. The shop Corridor produced their own line with distinctive flames coming out of the back of the C on their logo. Levis were still quite popular but a preference came in for the soft comfort of the French C-17 jeans, rejecting somewhat the dated Rock n Roll image of the American brand. Daniel Poole also launched a range of street clothing in London in 1987 that would become a go-to brand for ravers, clubbers, DJs and technoheads in the North East with the bright designs and cool casual wear proving popular in sweaty nightclubs and warehouses. The Shamen were high profile wearers of the dp brand in the early 1990s and Daniel himself embraced the smiley, loved-up vibe of the time.

"The most important thing was that there was a great sense of fun - it was an antidote to the Lady Di/Thatcher, prim and proper Yuppie stuffiness of the time," he said.

"It is difficult to describe that to today's generation when the main objective in life was to 'get pissed have a laugh.' Of course, if that could be chemically assisted, even better. Cheap speed that meant you could drink gallons and stay up for days, then that got replaced by water and E."

"There was non-conformity in dancing, dressing and attitude and the 'all are welcome' ethos ...that was the vibe as long as you were caring and polite and brought good energy. That was a million miles from the Top Rank Dance Hall where the wrong look at the wrong person could result in a trip to hospital," said the innovative fashion designer, who worked a lot with the mega-club Manumission that had started off in Manchester before going out to Ibiza.

"We used to love walking down High Bridge," said Mike.

"Going into shops like Strand, Milan and Marcus Price, which was not too far away.I saved a bomb to buy an Armand Basi jumper from Strand, and I also bought a pair of Valentino trousers, cut to fit, practically spent a month's wages. Trainers as well. Loved the Adidas Gazelles."

It wasn't just fashion that was changing in the North East, as the music that was coming in was also becoming really influential on the street and club culture in Newcastle. Exciting rap bands like NWA, Ice T, Run DMC and Public Enemy were bringing innovative sounds such as the scratching of records and the pounding of drum machines, as well as the attitude. The arrival of The Beastie Boys led to a craze for tearing VW badges from cars that escalated quickly into tearing badges from any cars. No-one could afford the thick gold rope chains to hang them from, mind, and Adie considered using a bog chain at least once. Leather necklace discs bearing the colours of the African flag, Mexican panchos, Kangol hats, Soul2Soul hoodies, and black scooter jackets all became must-have accessories. Black Wrangler jeans and Adidas trainers with the laces pulled out if you were into Run DMC.

"There didn't seem to be any energy or identity with music or fashion, nothing I could relate to before then," said Mike.

"I remember getting my first Walkman in around 1987, playing one of the NOW albums crammed full of mind-numbing Stock, Aitken and Waterman dribble; Rick Astley, Sinita, Mel and Kim, even Roland Rat managed a hit, urrrrggg, music needed a new spark, certainly something different."

Hot on the heels of the Hip Hop crossing the Atlantic from the United States came the sound of Detroit techno that made the chart music of people like Phil Collins in his double-breasted power suit, or Bon Jovi in their leather get-up, sound like fucking dinosaurs. The likes of Derrick May, Juan Atkins, Kevin Saunderson, and Jeff Mills coming out of the Motor City with imported sounds like Model 500 *No UFOs*, Cybotron *Alleys of your Mind* - quite stark and stripped back robotic tunes with a Kraftwerk-type feel - while Underground Resistance *The Punisher* had a tougher edge and more grinding sound. We'd all seen videos of the Frenchman Jean-Michele Jarre on his laser organ with massive light shows as kids and had also been intrigued by the seemingly cold and metallic Kraftwerk sound. They conjured up images of the cyborgs from our comic books as they stood at their keyboards in suits and ties, an electronic and computerised sound that felt contemporary to the ZX Spectrums that we'd been playing on as the dawn of the digital age rose. But listen back now and you'll hear a lot more texture and warmth to *Autobahn* than you remember from the time. When you consider that the album was released in 1974, it was a visionary and groundbreaking record for synthesised sounds; a strange synergy of man and machine.

Fellow German hardcore legend Marc Acardipane told the RedBull Music Academy how he was in Majorca in the late 80s and a girl had given him a Belgian record called *Front 242*. Although he thought the electro body music had some really nice sounds he preferred the more groovy Detroit techno stuff, but admitted: "It was not hard enough for me."

The quest for ever harder sounds wasn't restricted to mainland Europe and Mike and Adie searched out the maddest heavy tunes on their weekend trips into the city centre.

"I found a Dutch record with a nightmare vision of apocalyptic machines and flames on the cover, and I thought it's got to be hard," said Adie. "Mind, I got it home and it wasn't," he grinned.

People exchanged pirated tapes brought back from DJ sets in Ibiza or the Sheffield Technodrome that brought some more of that feeling of underground exclusivity, that you were part of something new and exciting. Even the mainstream radio stations were starting to play the likes of De La Soul, Massive Attack's *Unfinished Symphony*, the groove and soul of Inner City's *Big Fun*, the sexy strains of Donna Summer *I feel love* or Womack & Womack's *Teardrops* – 'footsteps on the dance-floor remind me baby of you... HEAVY SHOE' stomp, stomp.

Newcastle had its own pioneers on the dance music scene who were bringing out 12" promos and demo EPs on vinyl. The spooky, emotional strains of electro techno from GFX, formed by Geoff Waterston, who would later become an analogue synth manufacturer based in Whitley Bay called Orgon Systems where he designed and built the Orgon Enigiser unit. GFX released three EPs – *CXU* and *Eternal* on Radge Records in 1990 and *The Revolution will not be Televised* on A GE records in 1991.

Mick Routledge's Twelvetone had a haunted sample of something like a child's choir singing a Gregorian chant over acid house squelches on *How About That,* from Devotion Records in 1990, the B side featuring *Kinky Boots* and *Understanding*. 'Serious noise, rotate often' – the almost chemical smell of the record as you removed it to drop on the player, seeing the light shift across the grooves illuminated like a crow's wing. Mick also released *Bang* on Hardware Records in 1991, along with the trancey, spacey house of *Third Stone from the Sun (Ooh Baby)*.

Shaun Allan was a member of the band Neo-Teknik and the boss of Hardware Records, who also put out records such as his own *Maas*, SR2's *Compulsion*, P.S.I. Division's *Mindfuck 2000*, Ecstasy Club *Jesus loves the Acid* and Sub Bass *Disintegrate/Asylum* in '91. The following year saw releases such as SR2 *The Crunch* and PSI's *T.W.O.C.* EP, while '93 saw Alicante's *D'addario* and Static Experience *Baby Right/Viva!* The final record released by the label was P.S.I. Division's *Pentium* EP in 1994, the same year that the band put out *Hosaka Sondek* on Millennium Records. The North East's early rave music history was summed up very succinctly by Alex Martin of The PSI Division when he said: "There was GFX, Zero B, Hooligan X, Neo-Teknik, MIC and then there was The PSI Division."

Shaun Allan's sister Drum 'n Bass label SDI (Strategic Dance Initiative) formed around 1992 and put out vinyl from DJ Massive C *The Neuromancer*, Two Bad Boys *Carry on Up the Junglism* and *More Carry on Up the Junglism*, Count Zero *Inner Fury* and DJ Smokey Joe's *The Crimewatch Project*. Zero B's *Module* EP was first released by Great Asset in 1991, while Dave Phillips was M.I.C and the bleep and techno audio of his *OOBE1/OOBE2*, and the *Oobe 3* remix, came out in 1990.The *Gorgon/Sponge* was put out by Slippy Gimbo Records the following year.

Adie loved getting home and playing the records on the turntable of his dad's hefty music centre, a big wooden sided thing with a glass front that he span his own classic vinyl on a Sunday afternoon with the large headphones squishing down his curly brown hair after the 3 o'clock pub kick-out and a bit feed before they opened up again at 7. Farting and singing along to the likes of Pink Floyd, The Who, The Rolling Stones, Queen, Paul McCartney and Wings, Mike Oldfield. He'd been at the legendary Isle of Wight festival in 1970 and seen Jimi Hendrix and The Doors. Best of all those big old Sharp systems had a twin tape deck so you could knock out copies of tapes covered in the old TDK stickers with handwritten headers in blue biro.

The previous generation were all quite cool in their own way and had been through the festival scene in the late '60s, so they knew their music and had been there to watch some legendary acts playing at the likes of the City Hall back in the day. The first Summer of Love in '69 had introduced them to recreational chemicals, so when Tom Morgan hid a small block of hash in a pot on the mantelpiece at his parent's house he was surprised when he went back to collect it some weeks later and the stash had doubled, maybe trebled.

"About two months later me and my dad are pissed and get on about smoking dope. It turns out he keeps his stash in the same pot on the mantelpiece and I've picked up his rather than mine," he laughed.

Visits to the buzzing record shops also exposed you to the wonder of flyers for rave events all around the country. They started out as simple A5 coloured paper with block printed black ink but soon morphed into glossy colour sheets with a multitude of graphics and shapes; space rockets, the famous Spectrum eyeball, strange Dali-esque pictures, Pop art, futuristic spiralling magic eye designs, the falling men in blue dungarees on the Underground Promotions Pulse flyers, flowers, space suit helmets; faces, laser grids and planets on Fantazia. Bright, colourful and exciting – the rave scene was creating its own media and buzz somewhat like the fanzine culture from the terraces.

The final day of that 1988/89 season was a trip to Manchester and Mike and Adie were down at Old Trafford on the terrace behind the goal in flared jeans and flowery patterned shirts as the Mags lost 2-0 to repeated choruses of 'We'll meet again.' The referee ended the game with a whistle and their fans filed out waving.The police kept the Newcastle fans back with the usual PA announcement thanking them for travelling then they began to filter off up the terrace and through into a dingy, darkened tunnel beneath the seating above. United! United! The start of a rousing chorus, a thousand-plus men going back to something like an ancient tribal chant that echoes around acoustically in the confines of the space and makes the hairs stand up on the back of your neck. West Ham and 'Boro were relegated that day as well. As the buses pull away you look out around the unfamiliar streets and think what you're missing out on that night; passing groups of people in their Joe Bloggs gear heading into town for a rave, a couple of fit girls, a blonde and a brunette in their baggy dungarees and floppy hats whose eyes you try to catch from the coach window as they walk by on the pavement, off to dance in those old red brick industrial warehouses or clubs in the city. Manchester was the epitome of northern cool as the music boom and 'Madchester' scene of Afflecks Palace and mad multi-coloured designs of Central Station that adorned the Happy Monday's album covers got into the nation's collective psyche.

"I went to Havana in Middlesbrough on my own one night – it was amazing - and I also went to the Hacienda with my mate who had moved to Manchester. He was working at Dry bar, which was owned by the Hacienda, and he used to get us in," recalled Jimmy E. Rick Shepherd was another who moved from the

North East to Manchester and was soon heavily involved in the club culture and working at the legendary Hacienda. He had got slightly better A Level results than he'd anticipated as a slightly mature student at Ashington Tech in 1992, so instead of decamping to Hull Poly he found himself Manchester-bound one sunny September Saturday.

"Rock, folk, and blues music had filled my life in upland rural Northumberland during my teen years, and it was beautifully symbolic that one of the great Northumbrian poets carted me over the Pennines and delivered me to the city where the Happy Mondays and 808 State lived," he said.

"I'm not proud to recall having a fight with my brother over his continuous playing of 808 State's Cubik Olympic first thing in the morning - years later I DJ'd on the same roster as Graeme Massey at a mate's 50th and told him this shameful tale. Working on sheep farms on the Military Ranges in my summer holidays, I'd enjoyed wild nights at the isolated farming pubs; descending the west side of the M62 that afternoon I was at the edge of a world where craziness could not be gauged, where outlaws, desperados, dealers, and dancers filled the endless nightworld from Stretford to Levenshulme, from Salford to Wythenshawe. I had been warned. By several people," he continued.

"I hooked up with like-minded souls in no time and embarked on a relentless quest for whatever lay at the end of all things sensible, which in 1992 in South Manchester happened to be LSD/Acid. It was very cheap, very strong, and very easy to get. The crusty techno scene was getting going with the WARP Records Tour; the Megadogs happening at the Rocket in London, and numerous spin-off nights put on in old pubs and social clubs across the city. My own drugs experiences up to then had been hash and poppers. New buddies from Grimsby were well-versed in the ancient ways of acid and arranged a get together at a spacious flat in West Didsbury where we would take some 'trips'.Double-dip Test Tubes they were called, and changed everything forever for me. I had a healthy dose and got very lost in the music which was called Blue Room and which we played on a loop for about twelve hours. It was by something called The Orb, and was etched onto my synapses like silver nitrate from Venus. I'd never listened to 'dance music' before that night, and I didn't listen to rock music again for over a decade."

"Late to the party I was, with the Hacienda glory days of 88/89 now history, the party world I was drawn into was the hippie-techno underground, particularly the Herbal Tea Party at the New Ardri in Hulme," an area which Rick Shepherd describes as 'being pretty much lawless squatland where free parties ran each weekend without a whiff of any sort of convention' in the 90s.

"Incidentally, I did work at the 'Hac' as a pot (glass!) collector in 1996 and found it a terrifying place inundated with shark-eyed baseball-capped gangstor (sic) types from over the river.I gave the job the heave-ho after a dealer's lovely girlfriend tried to pick a fight with me. Shame really. I did have a couple of good nights there, but wrong time, I guess. Though, I did once meet Derrick May in the downstairs bar and found him to be a super-friendly bloke not at all aloof as he may have been in another life," continued Rick.

"I first saw Andrew Weatherall DJ at the Herbal Tea Party, and was bewitched for life, dancing to his sets over the years until his untimely death in February 2020. I was back in my home village when I heard, strangely.Devastated. His beguiling DJing style, devoid of predictable on-cue bass drops and gratuitous breakdowns were for me everything a mix should be: interesting and nuance-laden. Proper trance music. Not the horrific psy option. I went to his festival Convenanza in Carcassone in 2018 and 2019, I'm happy to say, and am even happier to say that I had the time of my life both times. RIP Andy."

"Through lack of money for tickets, and a natural bent for getting to know the people doing interesting things, I ended up riding around Manchester with a bucket of paste in a bag on one handlebar of a borrowed mountain bike and a bag of posters on the other, pasting them to lampposts advertising Herbal Tea Parties for the promoter who remains a good friend. Line-ups included: Weatherall, David Holmes, Slam, The Drum Club, The Psychic Warriors of Gaia, CJ Bolland, and Ege Bam Yasi, and would over the years also include Richie Hawtin, Joey Beltram, and Sven Vath. The job of fly posting was not without risk from the official men who ran tings (sic), and I was indeed threatened on a couple of occasions. One guy was shot for the same thing round about that time. A long way from the sheep on the hills...."

Rick Shepherd was about to be transported even further from the quiet seclusion of the rural idyll, in his mind at first and then physically, when he was introduced to MDMA and then flew out to the United States.

"I took my first ecstacy tablet at an Orb gig at Manchester Academy in November 1993 and danced with total abandon for the first time in my life, an experience which I would chase again and again for the next two decades and counting. The first track I ever danced to? Two Full Moons and a trout by Union Jack. The DJ was Craig Walsh. Thanks Craig.I became lost in a world of highly intriguing women and blokes who were prepared to risk their lives – it seemed – to have a good time and never go to bed. I've never witnessed hedonism quite on that scale anywhere else. The world seemed awash with super-strong pills, speed from squat bathtubs that would keep you up for weeks or until you'd wanked yourself to death, and the ever-present trips. Somehow, I managed to do what was required to stay on my American Studies degree at Manchester University, but – as part of my course – had to up sticks to go and live in Columbia, Missouri in the summer of 1994."

"Upset as I was, things continued in similar fashion Stateside. Taking no time at all (a couple of days), my compadre from Manchester and I met the local techno people and commenced a life with them putting on parties each weekend, helping them run an online record store, and going to warehouse parties in St Louis to see Plastikman, Robert Armani, Mixmaster Morris, and Hardkiss Sound System, among others. Not to mention the Grateful Dead two nights running in the glass pyramid in Memphis during Easter 1995."

The rave scene in the USA had really taken off with a massive event for 20,000 people at Knotts Berry theme park in California in December 1992, on New Year's Eve. By the following summer the raves in America were getting even bigger and the Shamen and Utah Saints headlined another huge event. Jez Willis, of the Utah Saints, was born in Carlisle and said: "When I was a kid, Newcastle was my cultural reference point and I must be one of the first musicians to actually make it out of Carlisle, but I'm still proud of where I come from."

Rick Shepherd returned to Manchester and took up residency – invariably shirtless - next to the right-hand speaker stack at Sankey's Soap which had opened during his sojourn across the Atlantic.

"The line-ups were incredible: Claude Young, Boo Williams and Glenn Underground, Jeff Mills, Alex Knight, Weatherall, David Holmes, Bandulu, Derrick May, Stacey Pullen, and on and on.If you enjoyed the delights of Chicago House and Detroit Techno you were in the right place. It probably nearly killed me but I couldn't stop myself," he continued.

"This takes us to 1997/98 when I fell in love and kind of calmed down. To this farmboy who felt he didn't belong in market town Northumbria, Manchester was magic, and scary, and magic. I'm still there. Still chasing."

'Madchester' came to the North East when Happy Mondays played New-castle Poly in 1989; Shaun Ryder in a black leather bomber jacket with white furry collar, Bez with a mop of hair and a sweaty, baggy grey T-shirt and his yellow maracas, wide eyes and huge dark pupils. They belted out their funky early classics such as 24-hour Party People, Lazyitis, and Wrote for Luck in the second gig of the 'Rave On' tour that is legendary for Shaun initially turning up at the wrong spot. The singer was running late and he'd come up on the train with the band's manager Anthony Murray. They'd flagged down a taxi to get them to the gig at the Central Station, telling the driver to take them to 'the local gig venue.' After they'd blagged their way past the doormen, Shaun spotted a saxophone as he jumped up on the stage and he started to think something was up. When he saw Simply Red's Mick Hucknall stood there, he suddenly realised they were at the wrong venue and had to do one sharpish to get to the Poly. There was another North East connection with the Little Hulton band. The WFL (Vince Clark mix) video was produced by the Bailey Brothers, Philip Shotton and Keith Jobling, who were originally from Newcastle. It was shot in the Legend nightclub in Manchester, all strobe lights, freaky dancing and trippy time lapses, and was intended as a short documentary rather than a music video. It captured the early rave scene perfectly. 12tone's Mick Routledge was another who made his way south-west across the Pennine hills from Tyneside to Manchester to further his career as a musician, sound-recordist and mixer and has gone to work successfully with such diverse artists as Jah Wobble, Ron Sexsmith, Alice Russell, A Certain Ratio, Scritti Politti, Blue Orchids, Inspiral Carpets and Spaceheads, to name just a few.

There was no real separation between the techno dance crowd and the Indie music that was being produced at the time as it all seemed to melt and blend into one long, happy party scene that was blasted out in disused warehouses, the back of a van in a field or from a ghetto blaster in a pub beer garden as much as in a club. The Charlatans *The Only One I Know*, the cheesy organ sounds of The Inspiral Carpets with the cow on their must-have 'cool as fuck' t-shirt, the psychedelic vibe of Northside's *Shall we take a Trip* or Candy Flip's remake of *Strawberry Fields*.

"Mike was dead keen to go to and see the Stone Roses and said we should get tickets for Spike Island. I remember thinking 'where the fuck's that?' – I thought it was an island like the Isle of Man or something, not an industrial estate in Widnes!" laughed Adie. The sight of thousands of people bouncing in unison at the Roses legendary gig in May 1990 as the rumbling bass and jangly guitars in *Fool's Gold* and *Elephant Stone* drifted off away from the stage into the soft evening air as the sun started descending into an orange glow was definitely something special.

"1988 was the year I was introduced to the Stone Roses. I loved the Roses, the clothes, the attitude, loved Ian Brown and wanted to be him, the first album remains one of my favourites," Mike recalled.

"There were a lot of bands coming out of Manchester and the scene was vibrant. 808 State emerged as one of the early techno bands from Manchester, and I bought their first album at Trax records in Newcastle. We would travel into Newcastle most weekends - the Techno scene was really taking off and Trax was the coolest spot for vinyl. We would hang around in there, listening to the latest tunes, and would usually have to ask the assistant, who was also playing the tunes, who we were listening to. I can remember seeing the first Butterloggie flyers up on wall and knowing then we had to make the event. GFX were featuring - local lads, early trance-like sound, I've still got one of their tracks on vinyl called *Eternal*."

A jangly, anthemic electronic tune with a dreamy vibe and sexy whispered vocals '*You make me feel*' span at high volume in the shop as they leafed through the releases. Mike asked which track was playing and the lad replied:

'It's the B-Sides, mate.' Frank De Wulf. Early Belgian techno. "Aye, what's on the A side?" said Mike. Face palm. Laughter. The discovery of the new music wasn't just exciting, but fun. Sassenach behind the wheel driving at high velocity around Northumberland's hedgerow-lined country roads scattering chaffinches in a gold Vauxhall Cavalier SRI ahead of a night in the Toon with your torso out of the sunroof and your arms stretched wide, the wind blasting you as *Stakker Humanoid* and *Everything starts with a E* pump out at high volume with a mounting sense of adventure, expectation and sheer young wild joy.

"Acid house had emerged in 87/88, Smiley T-shirts everywhere. Sassenach played crazy early tracks while we bombed around in the car. He was working through in Newcastle at the time and managed to get associated with the Gremlins; some of the lads he was knocking about with were full on lunatics," laughed Mike.

"I remember meeting them for the first time and going on a very interesting shopping trip. I came home with some decent clobber though, as well as a double dip acid tab. I halved it with my mate. It was my first real drug experience at 16-years-old and it completely blew me away - a total detachment from myself, my skin didn't feel like my own, everything was heightened, touch, taste, smell, hallucinations, colours and the feeling of learning 'the answer,' but not being able to put it into words. Something definitely shifted inside of me that day - it's safe to say I would never be the same again."

For a bunch of kids raised on time travel movies like Back to the Future or even Highlander – *I'm Conan MacLeod of the Clan MacLeod!* - hopefully this book can feel a bit naughty now, daft as the thrill of skiving from school, as it takes you back to a different age. Maybe it can capture something like the excitement of getting back together with your old friends at a wedding or escaping with the gang for a weekend break at Kielder and breathing in the heady smell of the pine forest as you settle into a lodge. Emptying a worn Head bag that clinks with bottles of booze on the bed and pulling out a plastic bag full of a weird assortment of chemicals that would make even Hunter S. Thompson pull in a sharp intake of breath. Faces glowing red and laughing at a red squirrel that scampers across the decking and clumsily spilling a plastic bottle of cheap Red Rooster on the machine controls then feeling yourselves spinning in the warm bubbly water, being sucked down a tube. Are you going to say it, or am I? Is this some kind of hot tub time machine?

2

Butterloggie

The dying summer sun receding on the confused faces of grey-suited com-
muters scurrying past the lofty Victorian elegance of Newcastle Central
Station, with grey streets, grey buildings charred and blackened by some
long-lost industrial age and pigeons flapping in the rafters then a mad splash
of pastel colours – lilac hooded tops and the faded denim of 24" flares with
white frayed bottoms from trailing on the tarmac, white cricket hats, whistles,
ice pops and happy faces.

The throng of idle chatter and a buzz of excitement as the buses begin filling
up and pulling away through the high narrow streets, over the green iron web
of the Tyne Bridge, up the sloping streets of Gateshead and on towards the
setting sun with the fast-fading rays flashing on the windscreen, on towards
the smoking chemical stacks of Teesside, then eventually pulling up outside
a large warehouse in Eston with a heaving, dancing crowd outside and a
large handmade flowered banner proclaiming: 'The Second Summer of Love'.
Hands reaching for the sky and the tinny rhythm of blasting whistles drifting
through the air. Striding with mounting excitement through large doors and
into the blackness with a piercing solitary neon green laser spinning in the
dark and an ice cream van enveloped in the dense fog of a smoke machine.
The heavy, steady throb of the boom of the bass. Orbital's *Chime* sounded
like something the huge SETI listening devices would pick up from outer
space. Almost 30 years later at The Sage in Gateshead and Orbital are up on

an elevated scaffolding platform with their light glasses on, punching the air in time with the tunes. Those famous opening chords fire up and hazy, distant memories rush in. You're transported back to the Herlingshaw Centre, which felt something like a big aircraft hanger inside, with the music literally bouncing a stack of speakers and it's like experiencing it for the first time as it was meant to be heard. 30k sound system pounding so loud that you feel it, can't help but move and groove your body. People hugging, hugging, squeezing tight in big bear embraces as the chemical euphoria brings on so much love. Big American rappers in baseball caps and black bomber jackets down off the stage and mingling in the crowd soaking up the atmosphere. Flight simulators, bouncy castles, sat up in a chill-out space of seats above the warehouse-cum-BMX arena putting a cooling can of Fanta to your sweating head. Butterloggie 5. Sun Spirit. DJ Huey and MC Lee, Trevor Fung, Collin Patterson from Bananas in Tenerife, John J from Sequins in Blackburn. PAs from Chubb Rock and Howie T, X-Plosion, Sav and Zero B. Saturday 7th July 1990, 8-4am, 3,000 people up on multi-level dance platforms and feet pounding the concrete floor to an eclectic mix of music; A Guy Called Gerald *Voodoo Ray*, pumping acid wobble from the likes of Diva *Get Up*, the house of Maurice *Get into the Dance* and techno, techno, techno - the hiss of a hi-hat, the sounds of bleep and bass in Tricky Disco's *Tricky Disco*, Unique 3 *The Theme* and Bizz Nizz *Don't Miss The Party Line*. Are you ready? This is it. Oh man, this is it.

Zero B's *Lock Up* was just one of those tunes that made the hairs stand up on the back of your arms and neck. *Module, Spinning Wheel, Eclipse*...every one a classic, melodic and soulful yet hard and groovy at the same time. Total techno - and the sound was home grown in the North-East, not imported from mainland Europe.

"It was a very hedonistic time and a good time for music technology and the evolution of instruments, but the rave scene was just something I got caught up in," said Bill Borez, the producer and artist behind Zero B, in an interview with Food Music.

"It was the '90s and I was in a Northern ex-mining town where lots of people were on the dole and I just started going out and doing these big raves, going out and playing my keyboards and making this music. It was very hedonistic, there were a lot of drugs involved, I won't say there wasn't. There was lots of different influences coming in and it was just taking all that and putting it into this kind of warehouse style. I was just making stuff in my bedroom, coming back from these big raves and spending Sunday making these tunes, to the detriment of my neighbours, I would have thought, at the time," laughed Bill, who is still making tunes today and is a prominent and successful live sound engineer, producer, artist, writer, guitarist, keyboard player, film soundtrack composer and tutor at the Institute of Contemporary Music Performance.

"*Lock Up* was made in my bedroom at my parent's house. I had a little set-up in the corner with a Roland W-30 and there was just hours and hours of playing around trying to get the presets that you wanted. The hands in the air bit, I was going around to warehouse parties like the Butterloggie and it was just trying to find the sounds that would sound amazing in that space and make you go 'whoah, what's that?' when you heard it."

The Butterloggies were the brainchild of DJ Huey (Carr) and MC Lee (Harrison), no doubt backed up by the encouragement of Club Havana boss Brian Andrews. The pair had their own show on Wear FM since its conception, had made the Havana one of the best and most respected nightclubs in the North and in the Butterloggies had brought the first legal raves to the region. When Huey and Lee got back together to start up their 'Back to Rhythm' nights at Middlesbrough's Arena nightclub in the summer of '92, Huey stated that: "Back to Rhythm is me and Lee. We are basically claiming back our roots as the inciters of the modern dance movement in the North-East and have been very active members of club society for as long as I can remember and bouncing onto each other in different parts of the world, which ultimately brought us together for the Club Havana project. That was, I wouldn't say, our most successful project but it was in terms that it was there at the right time to bring the House wave into the NE area backed up by the Butterloggie things."

The local club legends also planned to release tracks of their own to add to MC Lee and Collin Patterson's *Front Without A Capital* 12" which was released in 1991.

"I've been involved with various bands and Lee has worked on Hooligan X who've had a couple of records out already. I'm also involved with other aspects of the music industry and we are going to draw on all those factors to create our own sounds," said Huey.

"Back to Rhythm is very much a tribal thing but we are not in Africa, we are not in Jamaica, we are in the North-East and it's a North-East tribe that we are involved with. Fair enough, clubs have progressed in their different dimensions. Hacienda, Zap in Brighton and even the Riverside which are at totally different ends of the music spectrum. Those clubs deal with underground music of one form or another and there are clubs like the Tuxedo Royale which don't, but they are still clubs. We don't come from that background but at some point in time we've all been in those sort of clubs or been involved with them, but it's not where our heart lies. It lies in a progressive state. I see a lot of clubs in the NE selling out. They've made their investment in House music and now they need to get their money back," he told the *Evening Chronicle.*

"Alright, we all need to make money but Back to Rhythm intends to land in different clubs and give that club the progressive angle. Not on a regular basis, perhaps, only on a periodical one, but at least associate that club to the progressive attitude."

The Back to Rhythm project was almost an attempt to recapture some of the freshness from the Butterloggie days and Huey himself said that the links to the past were 'by way of doorway, by way of a relation there is probably going to be two or three different dimensions.'

"If you've never been to one of our nights before and you've heard about one of our nights then Back to Rhythm represents what we used to represent or what we represent to the modern person who hasn't been to one of our events before. To the people who were around it's a chance to get back to what we were doing at the time, whether it is because you are older now or because the whole House thing has become really commercial. We try to offer an alternative atmosphere. Alright, it's still going to have four walls and a sound system but it's going to have a different atmosphere just in the very way we build up the night makes it a Back to Rhythm night. Just the tension towards the night, the hype and the energy we build up in the people and the people who come carry with them."

That tension and anticipation were very much evident in the lead up to Butterloggie *The Evolution Part 2* which took place on Bank Holiday Monday, 16th April 1990, and featured Paul Oakenfold, Ricky Da Force, Colin Faver, DJ Huey and MC Lee, with PAs from Raze and E-Zee Posse. The third Butterloggie was on Saturday 5th May, being billed as The Land of Oz UK tour 1990. Guru Josh appeared at Butterloggie 4 on Bank Holiday Monday, May 28th 1990, running onto the stage with a huge grin shouting: 'Here comes the Guru!' with Lenny Dee, Carl Cox, and the Brothers of Islam while Butterloggie 6 was a bumper all-dayer at Eston in the August.

The Butterloggie started putting on raves at the Mayfair in Newcastle and one called 'The Concert' on the 10th September featured L.F.O. and K-Klass, with the DJs Mr. C, The Brothers of Islam and John J. There were certainly others, but people's memories tend to blur over time. When someone says they saw Joey Beltram play a Butterloggie at the Mayfair in 1990, are they sure it wasn't a Rezerection in '91? The then 19-year-old New Yorker did, however, play at a Butterloggie in the Mayfair on Tuesday 16th October 1990 alongside Sheffield trio Forgemasters, Ital Rockers and Brothers of Islam. He had been in Belgium recording at R&S Records, went back energised to the States and produced ten tracks – one of those being *Mentasm*, which was lost when a thunderstorm cut the power to the studio. The original *Mentasm* was much, much better than the second saving effort, explained Joey. How mad must that one have sounded? After a week he came back to Europe for a couple of months and that's when he appeared in Newcastle for the first time.

When you're told there was a legal rave at Wallsend Sports Centre called *Thrust* in '89, making it one of the earliest in the North East, but you weren't there and can't find a flyer, it makes it a bit difficult to pin it all down. *Thrust* was, in fact, an illegal rave that was broken up by the police on Saturday 14th October 1989. Although the party had initially been planned to go ahead at the Wallsend Sports Centre, a licence was refused and it was switched at the last moment to a semi-derelict warehouse in Bill Quay, Gateshead, and then back again. Police stopped and turned back two coach loads from Glasgow from going to the rave and manned Metro stations at Pelaw and Heworth with uniformed officers to turn away enthusiastic locals. When the authorities entered the warehouse, they discovered sound systems and lighting equipment. The fire officer said that there was sheeting fixed on the doors and the electrical system was not up to standard.

The earliest known illegal 'acid house party' in the region had taken place on Saturday 29th July 1989 inside an old whisky warehouse at Lime Street in Byker. Around 300 people were locked inside the building for the 5-hour event which ran until 4.30am. 40 policemen acting on a tip-off tried to break up the event but were sprayed with fire extinguishers through cracks in the main door. Tickets cost £10 and ravers were told to meet at pubs and other places in Newcastle before being given directions to the warehouse. Police were on high alert again the following weekend as coach loads of ravers from Tyneside went across to an illegal 'acid house party' in an old country house in the Brampton area of Cumbria. The coaches were monitored and arrived back in the West Denton area early on the Sunday morning without the party being raided.

By February 1990 an illegal party at Birtley was broken up by police and there were complaints that another acid house party had been held in the refuse room of the Princes Building on the Newcastle Quayside. It was front page news the following month when an illegal outdoor party in Jesmond Dene was busted. The rave was just getting into full swing when the revellers were dispersed by Gosforth police acting on concerns raised by local residents. The electronic sounds were pulsing into the cool evening sky near a waterfall in the Devil's Canyon with around 70 revellers already dancing and 130 others, who were turning up in taxis and minibuses, getting turned away. Three people were arrested by the drug squad – two in connection with organising the party and another for possession of and intent to supply LSD.

"We used to knock around with GFX all the time - we would go along to Holywell Dene with trips walking from Whitley or Tynemouth, wherever we were, a big group of us all tripping and wandering around, clambering over the huge pipes that run though the Dene, talking about everything and nothing, enjoying the acid kicking in and the feelings you got, which were only made better by being out in the dark, in the 'country' with all your mates until the sun came up then heading back often to mine to get stoned and mercilessly abused - fake tan, shave cream, pennies stuck to foreheads and so on -whoever passed out first and came down again. Delaval Hell Hole was named on one of those nights - imagine tripping and coming up to that on the dark horizon!" said Shirley, an early exponent of the 'first to sleep, first to suffer' rule.

"We used to go to Tynemouth Plaza and Geoff would DJ there along with Temperly (RIP). Boing was a Temperly classic that there must be a copy of on tape somewhere, it just cannot be found - I would love to find that! I thought I had it in amongst the stash of cassettes at home, the likes of Wear FM and my special mix tapes, but, sadly, no," she said.

Northumbria Police were so concerned by the rise in the number of 'acid house parties' in the region by March 1990 that they were getting local councils to draw up new guidelines in response to them. It was stated in an official report that 'acid house parties take place in the open air or in empty buildings and require a public entertainments licence,' and was seeking the councillors to take out injunctions to prevent raves going ahead, while the fire brigade were also being engaged to serve prohibition notices on illegal events; notably stopping a party at a farm in Houghton-le-Spring on New Year's Eve 1989 as a 'fire-risk with no emergency lighting, no toilets and no unsuitable access arrangements.' They also slapped an injunction on an illegal rave planned on land at a garage and scrapyard at Seaham in 1991.

While health and safety and bureaucracy were being used in an attempt to strangle the exciting unlicensed techno scene, the authorities were powerless to prevent the music growing in the clubs and licensed venues in the North-East and A Guy Called Gerald appeared at the Riverside that month on the final date of his *Manchester Magical Mystery Tour*, featuring the Ruthless Rap Assassins and Kiss AMC.

"I just want people to come along and dance," said Gerald Simpson, the guy himself, who was heavily influenced by the Chicago-based electronic sounds.

"We try to recreate a club/warehouse party atmosphere and hopefully people will enjoy it for the music and the dancing rather than our stage presence," he told a local reporter before the electrifying gig, as the scene was beginning to flourish in the city.

On Monday 18th June 1990 the seminal 808 State played at Newcastle Mayfair in an 8-2am show featuring MC Tunes, K-Klass and the Hacienda DJs Steve Williams and Sasha, while on the 1st November The Shamen were at Newcastle University to play an over 4-hour set with psychedelic wall hangings and a blinding light show. Two nights later The Shamen were at 'Boro Town Hall for what was basically a Butterloggie as MC Lee, Huey, Collin Patterson, Rhyme & Reason, Irresistible Force and DJ Stika joined them to put on 'an indie/dance fusion for alternative ravers.'

There was also an event called Fantasia put on by *Meteorite Promotions* in 1990 at the 3,500 capacity Northumbria Centre in Washington that featured Oceanic, Ital Rockers and the M.O.D. live on stage. The DJs were Steve Bicknell, Orde & Stu from Glasgow, Butterloggie and Wear FM's Huey and Master Reece, Neil Trix from the Eclipse in Coventry and W.A.S.K. from New York with 8-colour lasers, a ghost train and a juice bar.

"I went to a Butterloggie at the Mayfair on an obscure night – I can't remember if it was a Tuesday, a Wednesday or a Thursday, but I got into Newcastle really early with two lads I knew and we went into the old Legends downstairs beforehand. It was packed full of lads with flares on, Kicker boots, cricket hats, and I spotted something that night that was to change a whole era - instead of drinking beer they were drinking halves of Coke, juice, things like that," said Ian.

"We all made our way up towards the Mayfair to get in and I'd ever seen anything like it. The Mayfair had a bouncy castle in, the music was pulsing and the smell of poppers was heavy in the air."

Ian recalled how he used to buy poppers (amyl nitrate) on the door at Walker's every Friday and Saturday night a couple of years earlier when acid jazz was the prevalent sound and all the lads wore spats and were brilliant dancers, and how the small bottles were labelled names such as Liquid Gold, Gold Rush, or Liquid Dynamite.

"You got a three second rush then a stotting bad head... the lads started passing my bottle around and when I wanted them back, they told me calm down. No, I want my poppers back! Sod your peace, love, unity!" he laughed.

"There was people in there who if you were on the piss in the Bigg Market on a Saturday night, you would keep away from them - but these lads suddenly became your mates, they were talking to you, and hugging you, and we were all dancing and pointing to the main man, the DJ, and it was all new, a different style."

"I'll never forget the MC saying: 'Should we keep on moving all night, keep on bouncing over the Tyne Bridge, man!' and it was new style, it was unbelievable. The cheering, the air-horns and whistles, it was packed... hand in hand from Butterloggie you would go to Rockshots and everyone was talking about the Butterloggie on the Thursday night, so things were gathering momentum and picking up in the North-East fast."

Ian clambered over the top of the balcony, paused for a second to soak up the techno sounds, then jumped, freefalling for a couple of seconds before landing on the springy softness of a bouncy castle. It was more than just a leap of faith; it was like falling headfirst into the 1990s.

DJ Kidda, from Middlesbrough, is now a major music producer and DJ down in Brighton and he recalled in an interview with *DMCworld* that in 1988 his home town was 'still about football and violence and football-violence.' No-one was going to argue the score on that, and one of the Sunderland lads noted that 'if you went through to Middlesbrough just the year before you'd have the Frontline chasing you through Linthorpe Road with Stanley knives.'

Boro's Frontline had a mean reputation and received national headlines in 1986 when they trashed Darlington. Running battles throughout the town, smashed windows, and further fighting inside the ground with pool balls being lobbed and 103 being arrested and a fair number taken to the local hospital. Pick axe handles, Stanley knives and even antique swords were displayed to the press by the Police in the days following the carnage. The Frontline's notoriety on the hooligan scene made them one of the top firms in Britain.

"Having said that, there was always an underground, from the kids that attended the massive Breakdance comps that soon after got into jazz-funk, then house slowly trickled in," said Kidda. It was a similar story in Newcastle with the likes of legendary House DJs and Trax owners Scott and Scooby getting started out at in the scene by breakdancing in Tiffanys on Saturday afternoons from 12-3pm. The club hosted breakdance competitions called The Sidewalk with groups like the Electro Breakers, Broken Glass, Rocky City, and the London All Stars putting in appearances around 1984-86.

"They opened the Havana on Linthorpe Road in 1989, Ecstasy arrived and there was a version of the 'Summer of Love'. I couldn't afford the drugs and the clubs at the weekend and, by all accounts, 'Boro wasn't quite ready to put down its broken bottles in the name of love, so I avoided it, saving my pennies for a weekend in London at a Saturday night out at The Wag," said Kidda.

"The club ran a few organised raves which were OK, but spending £40 to watch dock workers gurn to Guru Josh miming '*Infinity*' with his fucking saxomophone was a lifetime away from Andy Weatherall playing Shoom," he continued.

"It was a scene of itself and people would travel from all over the country to come to the Havana and Philmores in neighbouring Saltburn for the vibe but then like everywhere else it got monetized and violent again. Undeniably, the drugs made people nicer and less likely to fight and probably saved a few faces in the process, but creatively 'Boro was just about ravers. Nobody from that scene really made tunes, which is a big shame – but big up MC Lee and Collin Patterson the resident MC/DJ Havana crew who made a bit of an impact in the early '90s as Hooligan X."

Another one of the Sunderland lads who travelled down to the Teesside raves on coaches said: "We would go down 'Boro and have lads shaking our hands and making us welcome then, sure enough, after one Butterloggie too many it kicked off outside with some older 'Boro lads and you could tell then it was all changing, as shady 'gangsters' were taking over to cash in on the drugs scene."

Glenn Petersen would go on to become one of Tyneside's leading lights on the Gabba scene as DJ Smurf and his rave journey also started out at the Butterloggie. He said in an interview with *Scottish Hardcore*: "I used to listen to Hip Hop on Jeff Young's Big Beat radio show on Radio 1 on Friday nights.

Then he started playing 'House' music, and these weird twisty records known as 'Acid house'. Wongle, I thought, this is mental this is. I was saving my newspaper round & pocket money up and would buy two or three hip hop or acid house 12"s every week."

"Then one day I got a flyer for an 'acid house party' called Butterloggie in Middlesbrough, Easter 1990. E-zee Posse, Raze, Ricky Da Force from the KLF and Evil Eddie Richards of *Jolly Roger* and *Acid Man* fame, headlined the event. None of my mates would come with me, so I went all alone. I was crapping myself on the coach on the way down, all these people asking me if I wanted to by whizz, acid and Es, waaah. I was on a bus full on junkies," he laughed.

"Eventually got in the place, a huge warehouse. I stood inside for a while, looking around, amazed at what was going on, two huge bouncy castles, everyone dancing mad, hugging and that, MC on a huge stage, it was amazing. I stood in the same spot for about two hours, until I plucked up the courage to dance. Incredible it was. These 'acid parties' were on every Bank Holiday in 1990, with people such as Guru Josh, The Shamen, Nightmares on Wax, and even Lenny Dee, back in 1990! The music was so varied back then. In the space of 20 minutes you could hear a Hip Hop Record such as King Bee *Back By Dope Demand*, Belgian techno Neon *Don't Mess With This Beat* and Happy Mondays *Step On* and that - the Butterloggies were amazing."

It should have been no surprise that electronic music would prove so enticing to a generation that had been raised listening to the bleeping sound of Pong, the game that plugged into the back of the TV and bounced a square ball between two moving blocks, or the messy jangle of a ZX Spectrum game loading up from a cassette tape with the colourful strips of moving lines. The sound of early technology and the increasingly easy availability of Bontempi organs or Yamaha keyboards were bound to lead to pioneers in the genre; everyone must have sat down to set away a drum machine and play a few wonky notes on a keyboard at some time in the early 1980s, and those with more talent would move on to the more grown-up Roland 303 or 808 machines. It was the TR-808 that would provide the classic sound of House music. The 808 was only sold for three years, from 1980 to 1983, and only around 12,000 were ever manufactured, but the impact of the drum machine with its classic cow bells and drum patterns cannot be underestimated. Marvin Gaye's *Sexual Healing* is credited with being the first commercial record produced on an 808, while the machine's successor the TR-909, which contained pre-programmed samples, was also a huge influence on the music which was being produced in bedrooms all over, from Detroit to Durham, in an underground, secretive world of DAT tapes and cables and musical technology. Hell, computers were bulky boxes that still had the green text and flashing cursor on the chunky screen at the time, so for your average person on the street electronic music production was a complete mystery. When a young Bill Borez bought his first Roland W-30 his dad was the guarantor and wondered why he wasn't buying a car instead, but Bill said 'I need this, this has got to be in my life,' as he strived to capture and produce his own variant of the Chicago and Detroit techno sounds.

"When the W-30 came along I could then just lift these sounds individually from records – I could get the right kick-drums, the right snare-drums and start making tracks. It's very limited but I think that limitation is where the old rave sound comes from, definitely," he said.

The underground music would start to emerge from the bedrooms and garage studios to hit the dancefloors at places such as the Madison nightclub on Corporation Road in Middlesbrough – known to locals as the 'Madhouse' – which was putting on House nights in 1988, with the likes of the DJ from Marrs, CJ Mackintosh, doing a Live version of *Pump up the Volume*, Einstein, a live show from T-Coy, Derek B and the resident DJs Funky Nige, Georgio and Alex Lowes playing House, Soul and Hip-Hop on a Wednesday night in February at a Levi's sponsored 8-2am event that broke away from the suit and tie weekends and allowed a casual dress code – smart jeans included. It doesn't sound like much now but when the bouncer was king and your whole night depended on getting past them and actually into the venue, it was a big deal. Acid House was the cultural driver behind the ditching of ridiculously rigid door policies and the relaxation into a more casual style with trainers and T-shirts eventually being allowed into nightclubs as they attempted to keep up with the anything-goes street fashion of the unlicensed and uncontrolled warehouse scene.

The Mall in nearby Stockton was another suit and tie place that was certainly running Acid House nights by the end of '88. The flyers for the 'Acieed House Nite' parties had the famous smiley logo with a bandana and eye patch. Jolly Roger (Evil Eddie Richards) and Royal House appeared at 'Acieed 1' in November and T Cut F featured at 'Acieed 2' the following month. Kool Kat Records did a giveaway at the event, which had a cheesy 'Get it on Maties' slogan. Liberty's in Birtley was also putting on Acid House nights which were heaving with sweaty bodies in polka dot shirts, smiley T-shirts and pirate bandanas, jerking and waving their arms as the room throbbed to the hypnotic sounds. 2,000 packed into the Mall again the following December for the 'Final Massive Jam of the '80s' with Boy Wonder & Eze-E from the Warehouse in Leeds, Yogi Haughton, Funkmaster Hutchy, Alex Lowes, and Rob Boogie from MacMillans in Yarm playing out the decade.

The first of the Butterloggie raves had also taken place on the 16th December 1989 and the line-up included Mike Pickering, Little Louie Vega, who was the House DJ from Studio 54 in New York, Huey & MC Lee, Eze-E and Boy Wonder, Evil Eddie Richards, Trevor Fung, Unique 3, Forgemasters, the 'keyboard genius' Mad Phantom, and the She Rockers – Betty Boo was a member of the London hip-hop trio who went solo and enjoyed some chart success. With her short bobbed black hair and big, sultry, smoky brown eyes, she was also a massive early crush. Swoon. Betty (Alison Clarkson) also provided vocals on the Beatmasters *Hey DJ*. The sheer energy and euphoria not only generated within the former roller rink in Eston but in the days building-up and journey to get down to Teesside were captured by Shirley, who recalled her first proper rave outside of the illegal scene that she'd been a big part of.

"We drove down, I think, in Fred's Volvo, beat-up and eventually missing a front seat. We hung around outside waiting for the rest of our friends to get there. Loads of people waiting to get in, people we knew from the town, lads from Shields that my friends knew. All of us waiting outside this huge warehouse in the sunshine, the anticipation building for whatever was coming," she said.

"We scored acid from one of the town lads that I knew from Rockshots and dropped them even before we went in; it took ages to work unfortunately -or maybe not - by which time I'd already found him, told him it didn't work, and necked a second!"

"I have no idea if this was the same night but Guru Josh was on, we were all standing on the boxes facing the stage, the lads, little Shirley and me. Hats on, dancing and tripping in our own little worlds, lost in the music then you'd feel an arm around you and a big hug, so much love and friendship amongst us all...the music."

"Little Shirley and I went for a wander and found this lad who we named Guru (for his resemblance to Guru Josh) - he was Guru for all the years we saw him around, we'd see him 'hey Guru alright?' and he'd give us both big hugs and some spaced-out chat. Then wander off or maybe stay with us for a little while dancing."

"The gyroscope there was amazing - imagine having this lush trip and then the feeling of weightlessness and getting lost in that feeling like nobody else is there. My friend little Shirley was the master of disappearing, between us we spent a lot of time looking for her wherever we went, she'd be fine then it would be too much and she'd disappear off to a quiet corner or the loo. Someone would go 'hey, where's little Shirley?' and the search would begin. On one of those searches I found her in the toilets, needing to pee we went in to one of the empty ones, locked the door and found a purse. We opened it, of course. There was nothing in but a bottle of body shop dewberry perfume, 20 quid and a bat cap! Naturally we split the trip and came out smelling of dewberry. That smell takes me back to then and those days in a heartbeat."

"Driving home again, passing the Penshaw monument as the sun's coming up, magical. Of course we stopped and went up to it, still off our faces but coming down.

Getting home was half the fun. I remember coming back up from the Hacienda one time and we were so lost, we went around the roundabout two or three times until the police spotted us and pulled us over... Fred's driving of course, then there's four in the seats and little Shirley and I jammed in the boot... the policemen was like 'are you alright?' and has a look around the car, Fred goes 'um yeah, we're a bit lost trying to get back to Newcastle,' - the policeman gives us directions and sends us on our way! We were dying!"

laughed Shirley.

Mike also had a huge grin as he remembered the night that one of the bouncy castles got half deflated during the night at a Butterloggie and three lads got trapped in it.

"One of the towers had been going down for what seemed like ages and eventually it sagged down. The lads were trapped with their heads sticking out as someone sat on the end to stop it going back up. People were running along the top and jumping down on them then bouncing off at mad angles. We were creased up laughing watching them, man."

"We'd picked up our tickets at Trax, and one of the Gremlins sorted us out seats on the coach down and back. There was a raffle on the coach down for a Havana punch – a brown gloop of E, speed and LSD, mixed into a toffee-like blob," continued Mike.

"When we arrived there was someone zipping about on roller skates to the sound of Ancodia by 808 State, mental, it was just that type of night. The atmosphere was really good back in those days, a lot of Newcastle, 'Boro and Sunderland lads all in the same venue, but really good vibe, a lot of smiling and hugging. You could feel the white doves working their magic and it was so refreshing to go for a night out and not anticipate any violence - it definitely felt exclusive, a new culture, being there at the start, everybody in sync...."

"There was also a decent vibe at the Mayfair Butterloggies - I remember the chill-out area being covered in camouflage netting, heaps of it on the floor, people crawling around in it with GFX's mystical melody *Eternal* playing in the background - strange days," he smiled.

The huge success of those first legal raves led to the Butterloggie promoters *Metomorphic Productions* to take The Soundclash UK Tour on the road in December 1990 which played a home-town gig in Middlesbrough, then visited the Mayfair in Newcastle, the Blue Monkey in Sunderland and other clubs at Ayr in Scotland, and Blackburn, Bradford, Sheffield, Nottingham and London. It featured a top line-up of DJs including Fabio, Grooverider, Carl Cox, Ricky Da Force, Jonn-J, Eze-Groove, DJ Sy, Andy Weatherall, Huey, Collin Patterson and Craig Walsh with PAs from Beloved, Hooligan X, Zero B, Nightmares on Wax, Ital Rockers, X-Plosion, Black Raddical MK2 and Forgemasters.

GFX had recorded their tracks at 'The Chill on the Hill' with John Ogle being the sound engineer along with Geoff Waterston, and Bass Generator being the distributor. Local legend has it that Geoff built a little talk box to create the robotic, futuristic vocals on the records and used to play his live PAs with it gripped between his teeth, until he broke one. GFX also pioneered a home-made pirate radio station which brought the sounds to many bedrooms across North Tyneside, people just sitting chilling on the edge of a bed or on the floor listening to the new sounds. Pirate radio was a big part of developing the rave scene and getting the music out there. It was obviously bigger down in London, where DJ Jumpin' Jack Frost got started out. He had grown up in the same tight community as the Ragga Twins in Brixton Hill listening to Funk and Reggae, and he was a 'box boy' who carried the speakers for sound systems to get into venues around the late '70s and early '80s. The renowned DJ, producer and record label boss looks back on those days fondly as he went around the city in vans with the Reggae boys wearing burgundy Farahs, diamond jumpers and beret with a coat hanger in to make it like a Frisbee. He admitted he was a 'little scallywag' in his youth, which you can read all about in his brilliant autobiography *Big, Bad and Heavy*. Frost was DJing at a pirate station called Lightning, playing Acid House, when he received a call from a guy called Tony Colston-Hayter who was running the massive Sunrise parties.

"He said I really like what you're doing, and would you like to come and play at one of my parties?" recalled Frost in an interview with the Allcity TaxiTalk show.

"He must have been listening to me on the radio and he's paged me, so I rang him back and it went from there. First of all I played at Heaven, and then at the next big Sunrise event. After that I went on to play at Energy with Grooverider, Fabio and Carl Cox and that's how I got into it. I was really lucky because I got spotted by really big promoters early, you know what I mean, and that's what kick-started me into doing what I do and where I am today."

"The first Acid House tune I bought was *Land of Confusion* by Armando, which was a fucking insane record! I played it and was just like 'what a tune.' Without pirate stations, there probably wouldn't be the scene that there is today. Pirate stations gave birth to rave on a mass scale," he said.

"It brought it to your front room, it brought it into your house. Look at tunes like L.F.O. – that tune was banned by the BBC and it went to number one in the national charts. How does it do that? Pirate stations, mate."

There was a pirate station running in Newcastle on weekends from the summer of 1988 called STS with DJs going by the names of Evil C, The Spoiler, Brother T, Shady Lady and Bob Stone, who played a mix of indie, reggae, soul, jazz, hip-hop and funk from secret locations on 94.6FM. Brother T told the local press in a rare interview that: "There's nothing glamorous about it. We have to climb roofs in all weathers to fix up the aerial, and have had to scamper out of the back of a house and clamber down a fire escape clutching our equipment while Government inspectors were at the front. If we suspect they are on to us, we just pick up our equipment and run for it." With a maximum fine of £25,000 for broadcasting without a license, which was made a criminal offence in 1989, hitting the airwaves wasn't without its risks. Another pirate station, called NBC radio, had been operating in Jesmond with DJ 'Colonel Blimp' and another putting out a sketchy reception to a three-mile radius in the student area, but they shutdown the operation just as DTI investigators were closing in on them. The North-East's availability for receiving techno sounds on the radio were boosted in November 1990 when the community-based station Wear FM was granted a four-year licence to broadcast and a number of the region's DJs were putting out shows – notably *Crimewatch* with Smokey Joe and the *Blackout Sessions* with Howie, as well as DJ Huey, MC Lee and Zero B. The signal on 103.4FM could be picked up as far afield as Morpeth, Durham and North Yorkshire and both Tall Blonde Phil and Tom recalled that it was 'a class station back in the day.' Lads from Hexham would drive up to the town's racecourse on a Friday night and sit in their cars to pick up the signal.

Wear FM was based at the University of Sunderland's Foster Building on Chester Road and a former employee recalled that 'the dance shows were very unique in their time and the studios often stank of smoky substances.' The mixing was done live on vinyl and the DJs gave a lot of shout-outs on air to various crews, which, along with the revolutionary techno sounds that you just wouldn't hear on commercial radio, gave the station a very 'pirate' feel. Eris used to travel down with her mates and sit in on recording sessions with the DJs, though her memories of the time are now a little faded and fuzzy.

"To be fair, the psychedelics and amphetamines that were involved in the majority of the situations have quite probably added to the almost ethereal, dreamlike quality these flashes of the past now have for me; what I'm left with is a set of windows in time, almost forgotten sensations and a recollection of some of the best times of my life," she said.

"In my early teenage years, I was shy. Although I seemed outgoing, the class joker, I was very self-conscious. One situation I always dreaded was having to dance in front of people at parties and 'discos'. I'll be the first to admit, I am a horrific dancer. Two left feet doesn't even begin to describe my uncoordinated efforts. I was always very aware that, whilst my friends developed the skill of 'looking good whilst moving in time to music', my own efforts usually looked more like I was trying to escape a swarm of angry bees," she laughed.

"That all changed for me when I discovered the rave scene. Suddenly, I was caught up in the bigger picture; focused on the feeling, the 'vibe' of the time rather than my own inhibitions. I remember discovering the tune by Stakker Humanoid. It was like nothing I'd ever heard before, both shocking and exciting. The fast, brutal acid sound track and beats spoke to me. On a skiing holiday to Austria when I was 14, I recall myself and my best friend dancing like lunatics to this tune on our hotel balcony – much to the amusement, or horror, of other hotel guests."

The station was run on a budget of £190,000 and reached a potential audience of 300,000 Wearsiders. It won a prestigious Sony Gold Award in 1992 as the top UK station of the year. The Wear FM project had began in 1985 when the Sunderland Community Radio Association applied for an experimental licence with the Home Office, which was knocked back by the pinstripe suits in London. That set back didn't deter them and they were successful when the chance was offered again by the IBA in 1989.

"We differ from commercial radio because at certain times of day we aim at different listeners. We have a mainstream format from 6am to 6pm, whereas we go for a 16-25 audience in the evening with high energy dance music and a chart-based schools programme," said then boss, Australian Pieta O'Shaunessy, in February 1993. The police launched an investigation into financial irregularities at the station just before the licence was up in 1994.

While the radio was increasing the availability of the sounds, the legal events in Newcastle were also on the rise and on the 30th January 1991, a Wednesday night, M.I.C. headlined a 'Psychofix' Solenoid at the Newcastle Uni Student Union which ran from 8-4am. Flying Saucer Cult, Emperors Nu Clothes, and A Cup of Sunshine were also on the bill along with guest DJs. The Riverside in Newcastle played host to a 'Not the Rave Festival' on a Wednesday in February, which featured M.I.C, GFX, Lucid Dream, Bedlum and Hooligan X.

The multi-layered rhythms and sounds in Dave Phillips' *Oobe* records were being heard in warehouses and clubs everywhere, a wonderfully iconic soundtrack of classic, timeless North-East techno. Dave Phillips was the writer, producer and programmer behind M.I.C. from 1989 to 1998.

"M.I.C never actually played Butterloggie... there was some confusion about that at the time – it's a long story," said Dave.

M.I.C. did play a live PA at the One Love Sound System *Blast Off* rave at Hayton Castle near Brampton on Saturday 18th May 1991, which ran from 11pm to 8am and featured DJs Yogi from Manchester, Toni Adams and Bri from Glasgow, and Andy Baxter from Newcastle, under the guise of it being a birthday party for one of the lads from up the West End.

Butterloggie was a pioneer ahead of smaller raves such as the *Convulsion* in June '91 which featured the Wear FM DJs Maitre D, Binni, Lowsa, 4 Star, Crocksta and Lant E at the Parkview Sports Complex in North Kenton, as well as monsters such as the big *Galactica* raves in North Yorkshire which saw 3,000 packed into the Spa Complex in Scarborough in December that year. By the 3rd of July of '92 around 7,500 were at York racecourse for a massive Galactica 8 'til 8 all-nighter in a huge marquee that was promoted as 'Yorkshire's biggest ever party' by organisers Pan Galactic Enterprises. The 'greatest ever line-up to be assembled in a big top' starred N-Joi, Bassheads, Elevation, S.L.2, Terrorize and DJs Carl Cox, 'Evil' Eddie Richards, D.J. SY,

Nipper, D.J. Lime, Face, Mikey B, Big Beat, MC Steve, D.F.A, Lisa C and the Triple X Dancers.

The was some concern among the establishment in August 1992 that New Age travellers with sound systems would descend on the rural North-West after flyers for two raves in Cumbria were spotted by the police in Suffolk and it led to injunctions being taken out at several farms and beauty spots in the southern Lake District. The flyers were promoting raves followed by cave parties. Cumbria Police spokesman Mike Head said: "They are said to have been put out by a man who calls himself Billy Badger and suggest that the travellers might also like to visit the Great Fair in Carlisle."

A disused quarry in Coniston was being used to hold cave raves where the organisers had to haul generators and sound systems out to the isolated locations to capture the amazing acoustics, and it was reputed that an irate Cumbrian farmer who was sick of the throbbing bass-lines once blasted some speakers with his double-barrelled shotgun. Applications were also made to blow up the entrance to the caves to prevent the events from going ahead, while further out West in February 1992 Whitehaven police had called for extra powers to deal with illegal rave parties being held in isolated barns and warehouses. The crusty techno scene of dreadlocks and dogs and camper vans with their fusion of electronic music was terrifying to the authorities and there were worries that new age travellers would descend on land near Haltwhistle the following summer.

The world inhabited by the crusties with their travelling sound systems was a different scene to that inhabited by the casuals in the ranks of the hardcore ravers, however, and in October Galactica was back at Ripon racecourse where 8,000 listened and danced frenetically to the sounds of Joey Beltram, Jumpin' Jack Frost, Micky Finn, Colin Faver, Trevor Fung, Rob Tissera, Shades of Rhythm, Dream Frequency, Awesome 3 and Hyper. MC G-Force said it was 'massive' to be up on the stage with Joey Beltram that night as he sweated under the tarpaulin and looked out with his microphone in hand across the green laser illuminated crowd as it bounced to the sounds. "He played a load of Paul Elstak's Dutch stuff that night and it had just come out, it was literally just released so no-one had heard it before. It was a mad night," said the *After*

Dark man.

'Boro also visited Newcastle in a mid-week League Cup tie that month. The Frontline attacked the Three Bulls Heads in Percy Street sending terrified drinkers ducking for cover as they caved in the windows with rocks.

"We got there early and parked the car at the back, up near the Trent House, at about 5.30, so all the city traffic had mostly died off and it was pretty quiet, but there was that kind of buzz that something going to be going on," said Ian.

"As we walked out of the car park, there was about five 'Boro lads with red shirts on hanging about the Trent House. We told them to fuck off and all that, and they just started laughing. We thought nothing more of it and went down into the Three Bulls Heads, which was one of the main bars at the time. About quarter to seven, I've never heard anything like it – there was two doors into the Three Bulls and they burst open, and every single window between those two doors were put in, closely followed by a load of 'Boro who smashed anybody and anything that came in their way."

"They then headed up to the ground, to the Leazes End, where I think they met a load of lads from Darlington Top Bank, their crew, and the Hartlepool boys, all the Teesside lot - I know from knocking about in those days, you don't mess about with anyone from Teesside, like. They were nutters - still are," he laughed.

The legend is that Ecstasy stopped the hooligans fighting and ended the 'English Disease' that had been rife around the grounds since the 1970s. Maybe it did – for a while – but it seemed a long way from MC Lee's shout-outs calling for unity over the microphone. Newcastle posse! Sunderland posse! all together on those dance-floors with wide grins, shaking hands and hugging, lit up by strobes, the sweat pouring off steaming bodies with long hair wet and limp. The boom of the bass.

3

Rezerection

A stunning dark-haired dancer in lycra cycling shorts stands at the lectern like a sexy preacher as the Prodigy's *Everybody in the Place* booms around the tightly packed darkness of the Mayfair club. She's gorgeous. Her hands in the air, a buzz of expectancy heavy in the hot air. Now that's how to open a rave. Lights up. Reaching for the sky. Speed cruising around the body functioning so slick, loose. The soft texture of black trousers with silver zip up pockets so fucking comfortable against your skin. Big grin, nodding and winking at the people around. Stomping as the crushing polyrhythms roll around the darkness, jaw grinding and eyes rolling back in your head in sheer pleasure. Sweat pouring off your hot skin. You feel like Darth Vader at the top of the stairs with multi-coloured lights flashing in your face, a frantic strobe chopping up the mass of moving people below, an important Hardcore tune building up to a mad level. Something big is going to happen. *I am your father, Luke.*

The music is so innovative, acid bleeps and tweaks, it's like being in the future. The future is now. History, the past, all time has evaporated all that matters in right now. The tune seems to have been running forever. You don't ever want this moment to end. Neon green clock faces and space invaders float around beautifully smoothly in the blackness when you close your eyes, slipping together with a neat and definite precision. An alarm is going off somewhere, and you're not sure if it's in the track or in your head. You float down the stairs feeling increasingly unreal as faces swim up towards you and zip past. Your vision is tunnelled and twisted. You're unfazed when a girl in tight silver hot-pants that you recognise as having starred in a children's TV series smiles and gently squeezes your wrist, chewing hard on some gum.

"What you on?" she asks.

"E and a wrap."

"Me too," she grins. You stand around nodding to the tunes, hands lightly touching and stroking each other's goose-bumped skin. This is pure hedonism. Total pleasure. Smiler bounces past with his shirt off, spots you and pulls you tight into a bear hug.

"Alright, man! You've got to try this!" he shouts over the booming basslines. He hangs a vibrating back massager around your neck and rush after rush race down your spine, circling the top of your scalp and coursing down your neck.

You take it off and run it up the actress's back and slip it over her long hair. "Fucking hell," she gasps in ecstasy, her eyes rolling, breathing heavy and warm as she slumps into your arms and grinds her firm body into you. Your cock is hard as a brick.

"Thank you – that was amazing," she whispers in your ear as you hold each other tightly. You don't know where your body ends and hers begins anymore. It feels like you've melted together. You break free and give her the thumbs up as you wander off. Places to go, things to do, cranked up on the manic energy of the speed. We are part of something special here. Worshipping the ancient thump of the drum. You want to get out there. Off your face. Cabbaged.

Stevie wandered into the chill-out room by mistake. Calm House tracks and people lounging around on luxurious, soft sofas. A big cool guy was signing autographs and chatting to a group of girls.

'Bloody Hell,' thought Stevie, 'it's only Carl Cox, the three deck DJ maestro!' He bounded over and pulled the only thing out of his wallet that he thought he could get signed by the legend. A Sunderland FC travel card.

"Can I get your autograph, mate?" he asked, standing face to face with the Hardcore hero, holding out his card.

"It's a red pen, mate," said Carl.

"Aye, can you sign it please?" said Stevie. "The pen's red," explained Carl, grinning. Stevie's card was also red. It wouldn't show. He shook his head, messed up, pulled at his receding dark hair and retreated back to the throb of the dancefloor.

Later that morning, coming down at Stevie's house, there was a knock at the door.

"Who the hell's that?" said Mike. "It'll be the milkman," said Adie with certainty. Five in the morning: who's out and about apart from hardcore ravers– milkmen. Seemed pretty logical. No one thought anything more of it. Stevie went to the door and was stunned as two uniformed coppers faced him. It's like stepping outside the bubble into a different reality.

"We've had reports from the neighbours that the house was being burgled," one of the policemen tells Stevie, who's standing there in his slippers. "Can we see some ID?" says the big copper. Stevie reaches into his pocket and saves the day - producing the bloody red Sunderland travel card. Carl Cox may not remember the red pen incident, but the internationally renowned DJ and producer has some fantastic recollections of the Rezerection.

"My memories of back in the day when I was playing at the Mayfair in Newcastle... I absolutely loved the crowd there. It was something very special," he said.

"Of course it was always in the week, on a Thursday night, and the people that wanted to be there, were there. I was always very happy to make the journey from South London to get myself there and to play to some of the most up-for-it, noisy crowds that did not leave until we finished, so this was amazing."

"Of course it then moved to Edinburgh, up into Scotland, and this was where Rezerection was really on fire. So many great DJs played there – Lenny Dee, DJ Scott, Richie Hawtin, the blonde guy – they had the best of the best DJs and the people really followed the DJs, the music and the crowds. They were really enthusiastic and the noise was so deafening sometimes we couldn't even hear our first record when we were playing them through the whistles and the noise and the atmosphere. This was something that I just loved."

"I was always there as much as I could be and felt like a bit of a resident if there was a Rezerection event," continued Carl. "I did my first Live Show there in Scotland at Rezerection and I remember being in the middle of the dancefloor – it was like a circular, round set up – and it was just great, just wonderful that I was able to do my Live Show and to be appreciated for what we had done and what we had created. That is something I'll obviously never forget."

Carl Cox was just 15 when he bought his first set of turntables. When he returned to the UK from Ibiza in 1987, he played the very first night at Danny Rampling's legendary Shoom and was spinning tunes at illegal warehouse parties around the capital. He went on to own the Intec Digital label and has performed around the globe as one of the biggest names in dance music.

The Rezerection nights at the Mayfair started on the 2nd May of 1991. They were generally on the first Thursday of the month and initially ran from 8-2am, before shifting to a 7pm start, in the 1,500 capacity venue. Tickets for that very first Rez cost just £6.50 and N-Joi were the headliners along with The Scientist, Neo-Teknik, 12-Tone, SR2 and local hardcore techno punksters P.S.I Division, who were Alex Martin, Alan Clark and Steve Ramshaw, with Mark Gales and Richard Henderson joining later.

"We got started in Alan's bedroom in Jesmond," said Alex. "Three lads in a bedroom in a block of flats in the centre of town, a tall structure poking out from above the library - Fairy Towers as they were affectionately known to the locals."

"Our first gig was in Sunderland as Northern Electric. It was a Wear FM do, and we didn't have a name then so we called ourselves Northern Electric. We tried out our bedroom tunes on a bunch of ravers in that hall in Sunderland and decided it was way too much fun not to do it again. I think we played about six tunes - *Mindfuck 2000* was one of them and that became our first single."

"We launched that as the PSI Division because we still didn't really have a name for the first Rezerection. The name reflects a mutual interest that runs through all members of the PSI. And it can also mean many things, as there are many divisions in life and Psi is but one of them. Rez was a Shaun (Allan, Hardware Records) thing and we didn't really have a name until a week or so before the gig. The PSI Division we nicked outta Judge Dredd. It was mental up there on the stage. Loved every minute of it," continued Alex. Judge Dredd was a moody, square-jawed and unshaven, hard-hitting and quick-on-the-trigger futuristic cop in a helmet and uniform with eagle shoulder pads from the 2000 AD comics of our youth. The PSI Division was 'the branch of Mega-City One's Justice Department that deals in supernatural phenomena, using Judges with psychic abilities,' according to the website Fandom.

"Rezerection 1 saw the birth then, of the PSI Division and their long association with Hardware Records and the Rezerection production team and crew. It also launched the PSI, as we became known, all over the north of England and as far south as Plymouth, and north to Edinburgh and Aberdeen. Memorable gigs, amazing people, parties, outdoor and in. Gigs that never were. Police station cells with a travelling party mob well known for spectacular outdoor parties. Signing records for the coppers."

Howie and Huey from Wear FM and Bass Generator were the DJs at Rez 1 and they would appear regularly throughout the existence of the event. On the Thursday 13th June, Rez 2 featured Shades of Rhythm, Forgemasters, M.I.C, and 12 Tone live on the stage while the DJs were Sasha from Manchester, Winston from Sheffield, Huey, Howie and Bass Generator. Later that month, on Wednesday 26th, a Solenoid night at the Mayfair took the Rez's lead and saw Bizarre Inc., M.I.C, Destroy, G.F.X. and P.S.I. Division performing alongside Bass Generator, the Wear FM lads and Ants, from Blackburn and Blackpool.

Tom Morgan, his dark hair cut in curtains and his skin suntanned and brown, recalled being stood in the queue outside Rez 2 and a lad he knew walking up and down the line, openly saying: "E's, Whizz, Coke," with a poncho on and a bum-bag underneath.

"It was that fucking open, because no-one had a clue back then. I took two microdot acids that night. Started freaking out after a couple of hours thinking the people on E were trying to suck my soul out. Needless to say that was the last time I took trips at a rave!" he said.

The third Rezerection on July 11th saw Ragga Twins, Friends of Matthew, Neo-Teknik and Zero B take to the stage while the DJs were Face, Howie, S.L.P.

and Bass Generator. MC Hardcore General came up from Raindance in London to reel off his rapid rhymes on the microphone. The Rez had an unofficial resident MC, too. You'd find him sat on the formica or in the sinks under the bright glare of the lights in the restroom as people queued for the cubicles. MC Toilet, with his white gloves, walking stick and nutty raps, just loving his own groove as the music throbbed and pulsed at a diminished level through the walls, reduced to a vibration; a legend in his own right. Newcastle, make some noise!

"In the Mayfair you went downstairs when you wanted to dance, feeling the atmosphere, the heat and sweat, whistles, Vicks, masks, the local dance crew all synchronized and cheesy-as off to the right of the stage, or upstairs when you wanted to take it a bit easy, wander, have your own space to dance," said Shirley, her head getting lost in the packed moving crowd in the darkness, squeezing through the bodies to find her own spot and then getting her feet moving, hips swaying, her arms loose and fluid in the groove.

"I remember dancing and Nirvana's *Smells Like Teen Spirit* coming on in amongst all the dance tracks. Stopping and thinking *What???* then loving it and looking at my friend Teagan, and both of us were like - lush!" Special little moments like that which brought big gleaming eyes and warm connections, to embrace and share the love with wide smiles. The Rez was an event that you looked forward to all month and the small thrill in the pit of your stomach began even as you were setting out your clothes in your bedroom, perhaps with a tape playing low in the background, peering into a mirror to put on some dark eyeliner.

"The ritual of getting ready - hot pants and a tight top were the usual outfits," said Shirley. "Making sure you had whatever you needed for the night, either getting sorted on the way to the town, or knowing who you needed to see would be at the Rez, then standing in the queue waiting for the bouncers to let us in.Meeting up with friends on the way up to the town or in the queue, excited and talking about whoever was on that night, hyping each other up."

"Looking forward to seeing friends we made at other raves - you might never see them any other times but when you bumped into each other or found them where they normally danced, there was big hugs all round and nattering like nobody's business - usually complete shite but nobody cared," she laughed.

Howie and Bass Generator were spinning again alongside Face and Andy Baxter at Rez 4 on the 1st of August with MC Hardcore General again on the mic. The Leeds group L.F.O., Altern8 and the P.S.I. Division were the Live PAs. Builder's dust masks and white paper suits, heavy reverberating bass and ghostly melodies. Pure techno sounds straight out of the earlier warehouse raves that had been so popular across in Blackburn and the Ribble Valley. Wear FM DJ Smokey Joe described the illegal acid house scene from a couple of years earlier down South in a BBC North documentary, saying: "It was excellent when it was illegal. It was absolutely wicked. There was a buzz to it, and there was the buzz of getting busted as well. The police used to come along and turf everyone out – there was one party I went to in London in 1988 and the police wanted to clear the place so they thought they would just set the siren on the vans off. Unfortunately, one of the top tunes at that time had this siren going through it – *Can you feel it? Blaaa, blaaa.*"

Later that month, the Rez was about to go supersonic. Joey Beltram stood behind the decks at the split-level Mayfair, which had a balcony around the top floor, overlooking the pulsing, stomping crowd in the darkness below illuminated by a flash of purple lights, a golden sweep, the rapid flicker of a strobe light chopping movement as whistles blasted out. It was the 22nd August 1991. Rez 5. The New Yorker, from Queens, cranked up the volume as his sounds pulsed around the enclosed sweaty elevation of the underground blackened room. *Mentasm...* fierce rave stabs twisting and throbbing as the dancer's faces contorted into a smiling grimace, pumping their clenched fists as crippling rush after rush swept over the crowd. People had heard nothing like it...the low throb of *Energy Flash*, the blast of an air horn, the arms of people on elevated dance platforms reaching down to drag people up from the seething mass. These are the nights that leave ghosts behind; an imprint on a collective psyche, the weird, heavy vibrations rumbling under the very pavements of a city. Sets from Carl Cox, Howie and Bass Generator ensured that the energy levels were maintained, while live performances from Outlander, from Belgium, who had started out playing around with a cheap keyboard in his bedroom, and Badman, kept the atmosphere at a manic peak. Mental! Mental! Mental! chants the MC as the weird, warped, twisted electronic sounds emanate at high volume.

"Tracks just happen and that's it. I never go back and do something over. If things don't fall into place within a few hours, I'll abandon it, and I'll start over from scratch," Joey told Generator magazine.

"I don't try and go for a minimal sound; I work on a track until I feel that it's done, and that's it. Some tracks are fuller than others, but I just work on something until I think that it's finished. Everything has to have a name right now. Things just can't be."

Beltram's fellow New York DJ Frankie Bones, who would also appear at the Rez, wrote on a message board: "I know for fact that the sound generates from a JUNO-2 Roland Keyboard preset which I am pretty sure is #86 on one of the banks, entitled 'What's That!!!' - it is right there on the keyboard itself. Mundo first used it in *Enemy Missile*, but Joey was the one to make it into what people call the 'Hoover' sound."

That sound would soon feature on hundreds of records as Hardcore was cranked up into an aggressively euphoric mangle of synthesised audio – *Terapia* and *Orgasmico* by Ramirez, *Run Science* by The Effect, *Chemical Reaction* by Toxic Two, *Brain Refresh* by Metal Hammer, *Hiroshima* by B29, to name just a few.

PCP star, techno innovator and ace producer Marc Acardipane, aka Mescalinum United, The Mover, Pilldriver, Marshall Masters and Resident E, discussed the sound during a RedBull music academy lecture and said that: "Joey was the first one. When I heard the track, I said, "He's an alien. Where did he get that sound from?" This is maybe a thing that you guys don't have anymore today, there are coming sounds you heard them somewhere all the time. But with us, we heard sounds that you never heard before in the beginning. I remember when I heard *Mentasm* in the club, it was unbelievable when it hits. The second track was *Dominator* from Human Resource and then we came with the street version, *9mm Is A Classic*."

The Prodigy would also use the sound on their classic *Charly,* which they were performing live at Rez 6 on Thursday 5th September. Ticket prices were up to just £10. DJs Rap (from Raindance), Nipper, Stu Allen, and Howie appeared alongside on the decks. *Like a mighty wind, like a mighty wind, spirit come down come rushing in...* looking on intently down the swirling, smoky circle of a green neon laser tunnel that breaks, fires off two straight lines then reforms into another circle above the seething mass of the dancing crowd. Standing and blowing out heavily at the top of some stairs on white doves with the walls literally wet with condensation, glistening and gleaming and dripping so the venue almost felt like an organic, living thing. Mike, his long straight hair swept back wet and tied in a pony tail, surveyed the carnage as every nerve ending in his body crackled to life with a tingling charge.

"People that you wouldn't expect to were getting swept up in the rave scene," he said. "I'd been sitting on a bus with a lad I vaguely knew called Jock and he asked 'have you seen the light?' with a glint in his eye. I had seen the light. I loved the Rez events, people bobbing up and down in the queue which snaked away down the street; dressed for the event in Valentino jeans, Travelfox trainers and a Nigel Cabourn top, excited with the anticipation of what lay ahead. I still remember the Rez tickets, square, sparkling, *Carl Cox* or whoever in big italics, the big turnouts; heading down those carpeted stairs through the entrance into the arena, which would usually be pretty full up already. There was no mistaking the Vicks, that strong smell of eucalyptus oil wafting through the venue."

Just four nights after Rez 6, the infamous Meadow Well riots broke out in North Shields after two young joyriders were killed when they crashed the stolen car they were in while being chased by the police. The distant wail of sirens rousing people from weird half-sleeping dreams and a strange chopping noise outside that comes in waves from a Police helicopter with a beam of white light searching in the distance. The tiles gleaming on roof tops as the beam arches and out past the cranes at Wallsend, the dark sky is strangely orange. The blue police lights revolving and flashing up roads at speed miles away. It also kicked off up the West End in Benwell, Elswick and Scotswood with the derelict Dodds Arms pub getting torched. The PSI Division's TWOC EP was released around six months later. Taking Without

Owners Consent was a charge from the car thefts, joyriding and ram-raids that were notorious in Newcastle at the time, but the PSI's Alex Martin, who had a penchant for Jamaroqui-style hats, told the *Evening Chronicle* that the problem was not just restricted to the area.

"Twocing, nicking cars, the phrase twocing has been around for years. People think that it's a total Newcastle thing but it's not. People just want to hype the North-East as the biggest car theft area in the country," he said.

"I can't see how they can say that, when somewhere like Manchester is about three times the size of Newcastle, with three times as many cars and probably three times as many thefts. We're deeply affected by what happens in the North-East because we get a bum deal. The riots in the North-East, albeit small ones, have more effect because they're small. They're sporadic and because it doesn't go on for too long, no-one really gets hurt. It starts because someone gets hurt, it's not to hurt anybody. It's the resentment against people getting hurt. That's the difference. Newcastle people are great, but mess around with them and they can be your worst enemy."

While the mood in the city was apprehensive, there was a throng as you descended the staircase down into the Mayfair venue, a low buzz of chatter, an anticipation building like electricity before a thunderstorm, or a static tension as weird as the silence and strange light before a heavy snow fall. You could feel it. 26th September 1991. Rez 7. Utah Saints doing a live PA. Colin Dale, Top Buzz, Face, Howie and DJ SS on the decks. The explosion in your head as the music kicks in.

"I remember getting in and the opening song came on - it was the Old Spice one (*O Fortuna*) and the sound system had the whole place shaking," said Smiler.

"It was fantastic, and if you were coming up on a cowie you would have to hold onto something. I'm sure at the end of the night they played the Flintstones. It didn't help if you were on white lightnings - you could feel it go through your whole body. The vibration was like an earthquake. I used to lie on my back on the dance floor and do bicycles with my legs and feet," he laughed, down in the darkness surrounded by a forest of legs, aural shockwaves and bass booms, illuminated by the intermittent flash of lights. The Mayfair's burgundy carpet with semi-circular blue swirls that appeared to breathe was strewn with empty plastic water bottles and bent Pepsi cans as people sat back against wooden panelling to take a breather from the sonic warfare and total auditory assault that rumbled from the speaker stacks. It sometimes felt as if you were in an old cinema or theatre in the venue. But with even the Escape Room promising 'sheer hardcore' from Bass Generator, there was no place to hide at Rez 8 as Carl Cox, Grooverider, Stu Allen, Howie and Fabio shook the underground venue again on the 23rd October 1991. Hardcore General commanding his troops with the microphone; climbing scales of off-key synthesised tunes, simple as nursery rhymes, increasing in tempo and repetition that leave you wondering just how long you've been dancing to them – sometimes seemingly forever, drifting off into a trance, at others feeling it grind and pulse as the music and chemicals synergised to snap you back into the very moment, the sweat dripping off the ceiling and landing on your head like rain.

Rez 9. Thursday 14th November 1991. Moby *Go*. The strange strains of the Twin Peaks sample that runs throughout the tune rising to a beautifully melancholic high as a multitude of heads bob under the purple of lights in front of you. Dancing in a human train around the top floor, thumbs up and grins. Sub Bass also did a PA while the DJs were Frankie Valentine from the Technodrome and Eclipse, Carl Cox, Top Buzz, and Howie while the MCing was done by Man Parris. Have you watched the new movie *The Doors*? Jim Morrison, man. Cool as. Need to get a pair of black leather pants and a white Indian top and grow a beard - or at least a black *Lizard King* snake-skin Destroy shirt. Wear some shades and nod along knowingly to the tunes from the balcony. Morrison famously predicted the future of music in a 1969 interview when he said that: "It might rely heavily on electronics, tapes. I can kind of envision one person with a lot of machines, tapes and electronics set up singing or speaking and using machines." E-rection sampled one of Morrison's spoken-word poems on their 1992 track *Suck my Dang-A-Long*.

"The Rezerection was a scene in itself and being held every few weeks, it was the highlight of the month," Eris recalled.

"My first 'Rez' was number 3. I went on acid. I was walking around the balcony and got talking to some bloke. He asked what I was on and I told him it was acid. 'Why aren't you on a Dove?' he asked. The truth was, I tried ecstasy a couple of weeks before but it hadn't done anything. I told him this and he laughed, pulled a bag of pills out of his pocket and gave me one for free. Talk about the night of my life!"

"I danced like I'd never danced before, I talked to everyone I encountered but most of all I was so amazed by the feeling of elation, the sense of 'oneness' with the Universe and everything in it. I felt incredible and I recognised the beauty and brilliance of everyone there. I heard things in the music that I'd never heard before. To say I had an epiphany just about sums it up. Later that night I bumped into the bloke who had given me the free pill and he was so happy to see the result of his generosity! But not quite as happy as me! After giving him a massive hug, I danced off into the distance and never saw him again."

"The Rez was so busy. The queue outside used to be massive. We'd be standing in the crush, nervous about being searched by the bouncers, hypnotised by the sounds of the bass from inside, desperate to get in and begin the night. Every Rez was different. Every one had a new atmosphere," she said.

"Standing in this crush once, I was wearing long boots. The crowd were so tightly packed together I couldn't move. Then a girl standing behind me accidentally dropped a lit cigarette down the back on one of my boots. I wasn't able to bend down to take my boot off due to the crowd so had to stand there and let it burn through the back of my ankle. I'm sure I still have the scar. Did I care? Absolutely not. I just wanted to get inside and drop my pill!"

"At one Rez, I had a broken leg. I went on crutches with a cast on. This was a great idea as I got to the front of the queue straight away. Once in, I danced and waved my crutches in the air, God knows how I didn't knock someone out. At the end of the night, no one was ready to finish. Ever. We would rush off to get to house parties and some of them would stretch into the day after and beyond. I was never ready to finish, I'd never have enough, always felt like I was the last man standing!"

The Rez went hard into 1992 as the first massive all-nighters in the Edinburgh Exhibition & Trade Centre at Ingliston over the border in Scotland started up. There was no expense spared on the huge productions which ran from 8 at night until 8 in the morning with flyers boasting 96k sound systems, vari lights, terrastrobes, Xenon projections, two Argon laser systems and laser projections, smoke machines, strobe flowers, golden scans, amusement fairgrounds and inflatables – as well as the usual line-up of top DJs and live PAs. Saffron from N-Joi up on the stage with her short dark bobbed hair and a tight sliver jumpsuit as her melodic voice belted out 'I'm in love with you... want you to love me too,' from the haunting *Anthem*. Piano breaks and wide grins, pure joy, over 10,000 people reaching for the sky in unity.

The Ragga Twins also played a Live PA. When they had first played the Rez at the Mayfair the year before, Flinty Badman and Deman Rockers had just started to hang around after their set, which then comprised of the tracks *Hooligan 69*, *Spliffhead*, *Ragga Trip* and *Illegal Gunshot*. The lads were from the Reggae scene and originally did the PAs, then went home. It wasn't until they performed at an open air show at Essex County Showground alongside the Prodigy two months before appearing at Newcastle that the Ragga Twins started staying back and enjoying the whole rave experience as they stepped out into something completely new

"It was like, wow, what have we been missing? Why have we been going home all the time?" said Flinty in an interview with FACT magazine.

"We stayed there and the music was just pumping out and we were in the tent and it just took us, serious. On the Wednesday we were in the Astoria; we weren't even billed or anything, we were just *there!*" continued Deman, as the likeable Brixton duo brought the house down at Ingliston alongside DJs Grooverider, Fabio, Nipper, Top Buzz, Face, Micky Finn, Howie and Bass Generator with MC Man Parris on the microphone on Saturday 8th February 1992 in an epic game-changing event.

A fleet of coaches lined up down St. Thomas Street, just around the corner from the Hotspur and across the road from the Haymarket bus station, in the city centre on a Saturday afternoon that begin filling up with people in their party gear; wide-brimmed hats, black waistcoats, striped loon pants, almost like the crowd embarking in *Further,* Ken Kesey's legendary psychedelic bus in the 1960s. It was a similar story all around the region with coach loads from Sunderland, Middlesbrough, Carlisle and even as far afield as Birmingham making their way up the A1 to that first Ingliston Rez.

Getting to hold the huge events at the venue just outside the Scottish capital wasn't without its problems and bureaucratic red-tape. Paul Ludford recalled that: "We had a hell of a lot of meetings up in Scotland. The people who owned the centre took a lot of persuading, but that was only the first hurdle. We still had local authorities to get round. They are very big on noise control in Scotland - if you fart outside the noise limit, they'll be up your arse with the sound meter."

Sound issues were always a problem and in May 1992 plans for a Rezerection at Hexham's Wentworth Leisure Centre were abandoned after the organisers could not guarantee keeping the noise levels inside below 100 decibels. An application to hold six raves for up to 6,500 at the former JP Bell factory in Felling, Gateshead were turned down by the local council and the promoter, David Wright, of Talisman Promotions, pulled the plug himself on an application for a massive all-nighter dubbed 'Britain's Biggest Rave' in two marquee tents in a field Birkland Lane, Marley Hill, after a flood of complaints from local residents. An event for 2,000 at the council-owned Louisa Centre in Stanley had the application turned down while plans to hold an all-night rave for 3,000 at Berrington Lough speedway track south-west of Berwick-upon-Tweed in the September of 1992 also fell foul of getting an entertainments licence granted and the allowing of the crumbling stadium to be used for anything other than the motorsport. A 5,000 capacity rave planned for Paradise Field at Ludworth near Durham City was also outlawed by the police and council that month.

Back in Newcastle, Stevie, Mike and Adie could literally see into the foyer. As you queued to get into the Rez at the Mayfair, you shuffled up the narrow pavement three deep. Past the industrial waste skips across the street. Past the dated brickwork and occasional metal-shuttered shop front, edging your way forward. Up the cobbles to the corner, chatting excitedly, then on past the sharp ninety-degree turn just six feet under the square canopy to the glass doors and into the venue. Rez 11. Thursday 2nd January 1992. Shades of Rhythm as the Live PA. Nipper, Face, Top Buzz and Bass Generator on the decks. They watched as official-looking people came out of the doors and said: "That's it, we're full. Sorry, nobody else can get in." Confusion. We've got tickets? A quick look back around the corner at the huge line still stood there. What's going on? You don't get it, it just won't sink in. Three people from the door...you've got to be kidding. What the fuck? The rumours were that a gang of lads had kicked the back doors of the fire exit in, busloads down from Scotland. Total deflation. Some disappeared off to Rockshots where DJs Scott and Scooby attempted to lift the mood by dropping a few harder techno tracks into their usual mellower House sets, while others just drifted away into the night. Standing in the light cast by the windows of Burgoynes wine bar across the road hoping that you might miraculously still somehow get inside as police with dogs clear the last of the stragglers, but you don't.

At the end of the month, however, on the 30th January, Dave Angel, DJ Sy, Evil Eddie Richards, Slipmatt, Howie and MC E-Mix were back to play the Rez. Then a couple of weeks after Valentine's and the MDMA has got you sexy, dark, sensual, as if Lil' Louis' *French Kiss*, Frankie Knuckles' *Your Love* or even Donna Summer's *I Feel Love* is running on repeat in your head, eyes lit up like a pinball machine, the stars spinning, the seven sisters fixing a twinkling point in the cosmos where a girl is getting oxygen from St. John's Ambulance in the darkness, or dancing in jeans at dawn in the mist among the cars parked on a field, a mad splice up of intense images reminiscent of the scenes on the big projection screens. Frankie Bones, DJ Rap, Trevor Fung, Simon 'Bassline' Smith, Howie and MC Man Parris providing the audio soundtrack to any amount of chemical-fuelled romances that were began on the dance floor with tactile sensations on goose-bumped skin, arm-hairs raised with a static charge and pupils so big and black that the colours of the iris were as thin a sliver as an old moon; bloodstreams flooded with endorphins and breathing so heavily it felt like you were coming up on another E.

Carl Cox headlined the following Rez on Wednesday 18th March alongside Grooverider, Stu Allen, Julz and Screech, Bass Generator, and MC Man Parris while on Thursday the 16th April Moby returned to play his second Rez. He recalled in a later interview with *Rolling Stone* magazine how the music and scene at the time was 'just about naive, genuine, uninhibited expression... people would just raise their hands in the air and blow whistles and dance like crazy for seven hours.' With Carl Cox, Andy Carroll, C-Smooth, and Bass Generator also on the bill, it was another night of sensational, hedonistic audio delight.

But by Rez 16 on the night of Thursday 7th May, you wouldn't have been surprised to have seen someone stood in the corner with their face to the wall like in the *Blair Witch Project*. The sound was getting darker and moody with nightmare horror clips and shrieks sampled into the music. The drugs were getting heavier, too. Snowballs and Flatliners. Stu Allen, Mickey Finn, Mickey B, Evil Eddie Richards, Bass Generator, MC Magika ... Spencer C, Guy and Mickey Roots in the Escape Room. No hugs or big love, no dancing in a conga line. The tortured screams in the P.S.I. Division's *Total Control* reflected perfectly the atmosphere at the time.

"The Techno scene up here has kind of died a wee bit because GFX aren't about anymore, which is a shame because they were the first basically. And I don't know what they've done or where they've gone but they're not gigging anymore, they're not doing anything. The two records that they had out didn't really do what they should have," Alex Martin told the local press. The P.S.I. Division were held in really high regard by legendary New York DJ Frankie Bones, who included them in his top 10 that year, and were still going from strength to strength.

"So we are the only real Techno band in Newcastle, probably always will be because nobody else wants to really look at it as a band thing. We set out as a band and we're still a band. We've lost a couple of members along the way who didn't want the band thing as much as I wanted it, so we've got new members in who are into the way we are."

"Being from Newcastle is an added bonus because we're not really influenced by anything that is going on anywhere else. We're kind of isolated up here. When we do get something we tend to shake the death out of it, then get rid of it and then move onto something else. I think that Techno will be around much longer. It could be Newcastle's own thing - the Techno that comes out of Newcastle is already totally different to the Techno that comes out of anywhere else. It's a lot harder," said Alex.

The first Tenogen took place at the Riverside on Melbourne Street in Newcastle two nights later. The 7-2am event had Colin Faver, Doc Scott, Keith Suckling, Binni and Smokey Joe behind the decks in the DJ booth. The flyers stated 'no vicks, no pricks, no drugs, no thugs' and although it looked very much like a usual hardcore line-up, the Tenogen mission statement read: 'this is not a rave, not a club. We emanate from the underground, funky beats, friendly people.' With a 25k bass driver sound system, bubble machines, virtual reality machines, dance platforms, and a live PA from Pill Head, who was performing his new release *ROM 1*, it was difficult to see what the difference really was to a Rezerection. Pill Head was Steve Ramshaw, formerly of MIC, who had left the PSI Division to go solo. Tenogen was a Hardware Records event and the promoter James Todd from the label said that they wanted to open a club night 'purely because of the fact that we've had the label and the bands.'

"We've either been at, gone to, spent money on or supported just about any reasonable dance venue in the UK. The biggest decision we had to make was whether we should do a few one-nighters or establish a regular club. We decided to have a club and more importantly an Underground-type venue," he told the *Evening Chronicle* about the Riverside venture, a club where GFX, SR2 and Bass Generator had played the previous August.

"Riverside was always our first choice purely because of the fact that the amount of people who have always said that it's an architectural warehouse venue, it's just like a warehouse, a shell you can do more or less with it as you want. Riverside has got a sort-of underground, decaying atmosphere."

Solenoid also ran a night at Madisons nightclub in Newcastle a few nights later with Bizarre Inc. and M.I.C. supported by Evil Eddie Richards, Howie and Mista Ben. While the Tenogen club experiment unfortunately ended after only the second night, which featured the PSI Division and a strong DJ line-up including Dave Angel, Jon e Bloc and Simon 'Bassline' Smith – problems with the venue being the main reason cited for the disastrously short-lived run – there seemed to be no stopping the Rezerection juggernaut in the city and on

Thursday, 4th June, Joey Beltram was back across from the United States to build up a journey in sound to a furious crescendo on the decks in the Mayfair with Face, Nipper, Peshay, Bass Generator and MC E-Mix. The escape room featured Spencer C, Guy and Urban Sound System, while on Thursday 25th June more big names were back in the Toon with Carl Cox, Jumpin' Jack Frost, DJ Rap, Screech and Julz, Bass Generator and MC Magika at Rez 18.

The face of the girl sat on the leather settee beside Stevie appeared very bright and clear as he tried to focus on her eyes, her face softly dark with smeared mascara, while unreal hallucinations tipped and tilted the room into funhouse angles as they talked at an after party in Jesmond following the next Rez on Thursday 6th August. He was aware in the back of his mind that he had to go to work in just a few short hours with no sleep and the black microdots still working their magic. Any hopes Stevie harboured of getting some sort of chill-out before he left were shattered as the front door of the flat burst open and what he thought were around 20 men in urban camo gear and baseball caps bounded in, loud and excited. He had no idea what was going on, but later sussed out that it was Rat Pack and their entourage still all hyper and buzzing from their live PA at the rave alongside DJs Micky Finn, Carl Cox, Bass Generator and MC Lennie. More tunes, more laughter, more madness... as he left and caught an early morning bus back to his flat, he felt as though he was sliding off his seat and had to constantly readjust his position to stop his body slipping like jelly onto the floor, the engine of the bus sounding like hardcore as it changed up through the gears. M.I.C. also appeared live that night.

On Thursday 3rd September Lenny Dee made his first appearance at the Rezerection. The hard acid and industrial techno sounds such as *The Motherfuckin' Beast, Microdot,* and *Bug Spray* in his frantic set punched into the minds of the disorientated ravers, blinking and feeling as if they were drifting in and out of consciousness in the darkness; an electronic elevation of unreality after placing the small square paper blotter of a Flying Key on your tongue. The sounds were perpetuated by Carl Cox, Ratty, and Bass Generator with a PA from New Atlantic, while on Wednesday 30th September it was Grooverider, Pilgrim, Stu Allen, Bass Generator and a PA from Suburban

Delay that brought the noise and insanity to the Mayfair.

The Wednesday night of the 4th November saw Rezerection host The Prodigy Experience, supported by Sy-Kick and the DJs Devious D, Phisics, and Richie in a show that ran from 8-12 midnight at the Mayfair. Two weeks later, on Thursday 19th November, the 22nd and penultimate Rezerection at the Newcastle Mayfair took place and featured Carl Cox, Beat Creator (Micky B), Seduction and Bass Generator with a Live PA from Felix. For an event that had initially been just envisaged as a one off, then extended to six events, and on, it had been a fantastic rollercoaster run. Local MC Sneaky Eye - *Enter the Sneaky Eye* – made his debut at the rave.

The bigger events up at Edinburgh had been running alongside all year and at Ingliston on Saturday 4th April 1992 Dave Angel, Grooverider, Carl Cox, DJ Sy, Face and Screech & Julz appeared, with live PAs from Dream Frequency and Shades of Rhythm. Going up into Scotland had the added edge of casuals from the Hibs Capital City Service 'taxing' people of their money and drugs in the toilets. The Hibs boys had previous. When Newcastle's Bigbird crew brought a highly successful Saturday night version of their Thursday night Rockshots set over the border to Wilkie House on Cowgate in 1989, they were greeted one night by the shocking and disturbing vision of the CCS throwing Sieg Heil salutes in time with *We Are Family* by Sister Sledge on a heaving dance floor before it all kicked off big time.

Tom recalled having a couple of hairy experiences at the Rez in Scotland, and said: "I got cracking on to this bird, canny fit. Then her mentalist Jock boyfriend shows up. He starts talking to me. Well, actually he was telling me he was going to inject an HIV infected needle into me. I shit bricks, man!"

"Another time one of the lads got caught selling what he thought were pills for a lass we knew. The security take him in the back. He's fucked. Bang to rights. However, in typical jammy bastard style, the pills are snides. Fuck knows what was in them but he's off the hook and the rozzers let him walk!"

The quality and safety of the ecstasy was certainly diminishing as professional criminal gangs looked to profit further from the drug trade. If you had the presence of mind to crack open a capsule sold as ecstasy for £15, in many cases you'd find half a trip and a thimble-full of speed inside.

The speed itself was being increasingly chopped and cut with body-building supplements, glucose, or worse, losing its crystal element and becoming more of a powder. The Es themselves occasionally took on a seemingly more metallic, manufactured buzz or were even sometimes just straight ketamine, the horse tranquiliser. The strange carnival-like atmosphere was enhanced by the flashing lights and revolving colours on fairground rides down at one end of the massive venue, teacups and dodgems spinning in the darkness. The low vibrations and high pitches in the music and the introduction of the bouncy 'rockcore' sound that would eventually transform into Happy Hardcore over time. Mike and Adie were going absolutely mental down at the front by the stage, their wild dancing clearing a small semi-circle around them as a strobe light went off right in their faces, hanging onto the metal railing for grim life as vivid, crazy hallucinations flooded their vision.

One of the stage dancers was sat across the way on the bus back to Tyneside. "I saw you inside," she said warmly, shaking her head and grinning at the recollection of the sight of them flipping out on the powerful LSD that over-rode the MDMA and amphetamines already coursing through their bloodstreams.

Other events up at Ingliston with huge, spectacular production values and themes that year included 'The Castle' on the 23rd May which featured Bizarre Inc, Love Decade, Opus III, Carl Cox, Andy Carroll, Evil Eddie Richards, Jumpin' Jack Frost, Bass Generator and MC Man Parris, along with a host of dancers, huge puppeteers, and fire eaters. BMX stunt riders, skateboarders, robots and pipe bands would all feature up on the stage with the scaffolding and lighting rigs at Ingliston, the dry ice hanging high like fog in the kaleidoscope flashing around the metal girders of the high space that weird art objects hung from. Coming out of the sets of glass doors in droves at the end with ears ringing, some whistles still blowing, blinking into the daylight with lank hair and damp clothes, chewing hard on gum; unforgettable all-nighters. And as you're swept along in the crowd outside you're handed flyers but it's strangely subdued and quiet as the enormity of the night just really starts to sink in.

'The Pyramids' took place on Saturday 4th July with SL2, Bassheads,

Mysticism, Face, Simon 'Bassline' Smith, Mikey B, Keith Suckling, Kenny Ken, Julz & Screech, Bass Generator and MC Magika, while 'The Luminaire' on Saturday 15th August featured N-Joi, The Prodigy and Suburban Delay; Grooverider, Micky Finn, Derrick May, Tom Wilson, Andy Carroll, Terry and Jason. In October 'The Millennium' event starred Grooverider, Tom Wilson, Rap, Mikey B, Face, DE-V8, Jumpin' Jack Frost and MC Lennie. GTO and Dream Frequency were live up on the stage.

The Rez should have gone ballistic at another massive event called 'The Castle' at Donnington Exhibition Centre near Derby on the 19th December 1992 with another top line-up booked including The Prodigy, Proper Talent featuring DJ Rap (Divine Rhythm), Grooverider, Carl Cox, Face, Doc Scott, Ratty and Bass Generator with MCs Man Parris and Sneaky Eye, but the 8pm-7amwas cancelled. Fantasia had held a massive outdoor all-dayer for over 25,000 people in the July of that year at Castle Donnington and the Rez were obviously hoping to take their production down South to be as big a success.

"When I think of all we did and how many people we met it just makes me want to cry. I think I speak for everyone when I say if we could have just one more night, I personally would not waste one minute of it," said one girl who was there at the Fantazia. The P.S.I. Division played a live PA at the monster rave which is remembered as a high point for the entire scene and the biggest ever in the UK.

Frost was crystallising and gleaming under the sodium streetlights on a dark evening as the crowds lined up down the narrow alley-like Low Friar Street to get into the Rezerection 'Au Revoir,' which took place at the Mayfair on the 29th December 1992 and featured a familiar line-up as Carl Cox, Nipper, Face and Bass Generator took to the decks with Shades of Rhythm as the PA and Man Parris and Sneaky Eye MCing. It was the final time that lads and lasses in a mix of Day-Glo kit, hi-vis waistcoats, designer gear and floppy hats would descend the dark staircase to hear the deafening boom and frantic rhythm of the likes of Defcon1, DJPC, Terrorize, The Time Frequency and Force Mass Motion that gave the Tyneside Rez its trademark Hardcore breakbeat sound. Mike Wells, the man behind Force Mass Motion, began his journey into electronic music by playing around with his Commodore Amiga 500 as a kid. He'd been impressed and fascinated with the demo of sampled sounds and graphics that the early computer provided and when he'd found out the software that was used to write the music, he was able to run it back through a sampler that his older brother had made at school to get that 8-bit digital crunch sound. The tune that had so fascinated Mike was the acid squelch and robotic drift of *Stakker Humanoid*, and he also recalls how he'd been fishing on a riverbank and he'd heard that same tune drifting over in the air from an illegal rave taking place a couple of fields away.

He began taping Kiss-FM through his VHS player and taking samples off that to run through the back of his computer and make tracks that he played to his mates. He was working at Waitrose as a 17-year-old when he handed a cassette tape of his tunes over to Colin Faver who was DJing at *The Event* in Brighton one Saturday night and was stunned when he received a call at his parent's home on the Monday morning where Faver told him: I played your tape to the guy who runs Rabbit City – and do you want a record deal? "How mad is that?" said Mike. "I got the goosebumps. It was proper crazy." Even more amazingly, Mike's first live gigs in 1991 were massive affairs across in Germany in Frankfurt and the massive 14,000 capacity Mayday event in Berlin, while he was still studying Aerospace Engineering at University in Kingston.

The track '*I need your lovin'*' by N.R.G. was Mike's abiding memory of his first Mayday. "I MC'd for him!" he laughs. "I'd MC'd for myself - there was nobody there doing it - and his manager came up to me and said 'Mike, you were just superb' and I replied 'I've never done a gig in my life!'"

"He asked if I could MC for N.R.G and I replied 'if I can keep one of his T-shirts,' so I've got a long-sleeved white top at home with N.R.G. on it."

"It all kicked off for me in Germany," said Mike. "Two gigs a weekend, Energy rave in Switzerland, and on the circuit with all the English DJs. England for me was shit for gigs though – I never got many gigs here at all."

Mike hails from a small town in East Sussex and his classic rave anthem *Panic* was created when he sampled a riff from the Prodigy's *Fire* and put it into his S-950 sampler. "They were an expensive piece of kit at the time – living the dream!" he laughed. His success led to tours in Australia and around the world but Mike is a grounded fella and he described the loneliness of experiencing the weekend madness from the DJ booth on your own.

"It's a bit depressing when you're being bigged-up by people all weekend and then you get home, you get off the plane and all of your mates are at work all week. So what are you going to do – sit in a studio all week and try and write the next thing? It's not an easy thing to do." But the techno/trance producer offers a valuable life lesson when he says: "When the shit's down, you've just got to be able to turn your hand to stuff."

DJ Smurf was a regular at the Mayfair before he took to the decks professionally himself and he said: "When the Butterloggies eventually died off, and after going to a Raindance, Amnesia House and an event called 'Time' in Birmingham, Newcastle came alive with the Rezerection. I went to them every month, and got well into them, rubbing Vicks vaporub on my face and on my balls."

"Then the big Rez all-nighters started up in Scotland. The music was mainly breakbeat with the likes of DJ SS, DJ Sy, DJ Face, N-Joi, Prodigy, and Shades of Rhythm. I wasn't keen on the happy piano and breakbeat sounds, and preferred DJs like CJ Bolland, Dave Angel and Joey Beltram who at the time were playing all noisy head-fuck techno. It was hard to get hold of the records they were playing, so I was still buying breakbeat records, but more of the harder, hoovery stuff."

Rezerection promoter Paul Ludford said that 'the dance thing started purely by fluke' when a friend wanted to do a show at the Mayfair and asked him to help because of his background in production. Paul was the co-owner and founder of Kitchenware Records in Newcastle, and had put on the Soul Kitchen nights at the Casablanca and Tiffanys in the early '80s. He was also the manager of Prefab Sprout and The Kane Gang.

"It was the first time since the punk scene in about 1977 that I'd seen that attitude of the people that came. It completely knocked me out. I was so used to that stand-offish attitude of the pop music scene. The atmosphere at Rez was electric – everyone was there purely to enjoy themselves. I never thought

I'd see that again; it was like a breath of fresh air," he told the Fantasia Rave Archive.

Partner John Fairs said in the local press: "We went to a couple of other raves to check them out and we really enjoyed the atmosphere. It was something I'd never experienced before. Having gone to them we realised that there wasn't anything at all in the North-East of England like it at the time. Absolutely nothing. So we approached the Mayfair to do that one show and from that one show it just snowballed."

The underground Mayfair ballroom was gone by 1999 and was replaced by the ultra modern Gate complex, all glass front and exposed steel girders with pubs and restaurants as Newcastle rebranded itself as a fun hedonistic modern city for revelling stag-dos and hen parties centred on the Quayside and regenerated City centre. Rezerection had left Newcastle, but the party continued in Scotland with the events just getting bigger and bigger in 1993. DJ SS, from Leicester, appeared at a number of the Rezerection events up at Ingliston that year and he admitted that the scene was changing and evolving rapidly at that time.

"Rave was getting cheesier and I had that hip-hop perspective. I wanted the breaks, the basslines, not white gloves and big pianos. I wanted to connect back with my peeps. Not just ravers wasted out on Es. I wanted to connect with regular people who wanted the music I wanted," he recalled in a later interview with UKF.

SS played at the event 'The Diamond' in May '93 with Joey Beltram N-Joi, SL2, DJ Rap, Bass Generator, Grooverider, Marc Smith and MCs Lennie and Sneaky Eye.

That August also saw another significant change as Rezerection staged their first huge outdoor all-night rave at the Royal Highland Showground. The Event 1 featured live PAs from The Prodigy, Terrorize, Rat Pack, Dream Frequency, Suburban Delay, Q-Tex, Sons of a Loop de Loop Era and Ultrasonic. The DJ line-up was Grooverider, Rap, Bass Generator, Easygroove, SS, Scott, Seduction, Trixter, Tom Wilson, DJ Dell, Terry & Jason and Marc Smith. Lennie, Sneaky Eye and Man Parris MC'd.

The intensity was back indoors at Ingliston on the 23rd October with PAs from Shades of Rhythm, GTO, Rhythmic State, DJs Carl Cox, Grooverider, Ratty, Marc Smith, Bass Generator, Mikey B, KMC and MCs Ribbs and Sneaky Eye, but the whole vibe was changing as some of the original faces burned out and fell away or just moved on to different things. Others became casualties as the pill intake went up to four, five, six a night, and went for days without sleep or food as they pushed the boundaries to the very limits. Ecstasy was becoming less of a love drug and more of an endurance feat as nutty new starters in ski hats and white gloves bounced and got in your face in their enthusiasm to embrace the bass. The path of excess doesn't always lead to the palace of wisdom and the energy-sapping pursuit of the everlasting weekend was taking its toll. Dark circles under heavy eyes, skinny bodies and comedowns that lasted for days. Something had to give.

The Rez in Scotland on New Year's Eve 1993 is widely regarded as the turning point in the direction of the North-East and Scottish rave scene as the breakbeat sound peaked with PAs from N-Joi, Carl Cox, Concept, QFX and Suburban Delay. Carl Cox also took to the decks to do a DJ set that night, with Seduction, Bass Generator, SS, Marc Smith, Dell, Technotrance and Tom Wilson alongside him on the line up. The MCs were Sneaky Eye, Magika and Warren G. While the sound in London and the South would start to head away down the more stark and stripped-back drum and bass Jungle path, the North-East and Scotland's preference was for more of a Euro-influenced hard techno that would see the rave scene becoming increasingly fractured and split over the next couple of years. But for those who were there, at that time, it felt like the music would never end.

Ants crawl up the spine. Frantic rave stabs pulsating from a stack of black P.A. speakers, the bass-line low and rumbling, an earthquake about to blow or a heavy truck thundering past to shake the pavements, the walls, to shake you back among the sweaty bodies, the heat, the condensation dripping from the ceilings. Do you recall the euphoria of being up on an elevated dance platform in the darkness, waving a green neon glow stick? Thumping techno and lasers spinning in green and blue smoke-filled tunnels then clicking into a grid of squares descending over the silhouetted hands reaching for the sky, your trainers sticking to a floor tacky with gum with ears still buzzing and vibrating so hard from the noise that you feel shaky. Wraps of speed cut out of a pornographic magazine with white powder in them, peeled open in the bad yellow light of the toilet cubicles to catch a glimpse of half a leg in suspenders, a pink tit with a perky nipple, a big, black hairy muff, and dab at bitter crystals that twist your face like lemon juice. We danced in fields, in tents, in leisure centres, we danced in clubs, in motorway service stations. We danced and the dull throb in the darkness disturbed the foxes and badgers on their nocturnal jaunts in the woods, the lights fading into the stars from a fairground ride like a fallen UFO and they felt it was the apocalypse. A girl with dilated black pupils held hot and sweaty in elated embrace as the music hits a frantic peak. Hardcore. We are hardcore; double-dipped test tubes, strawberries, flying keys, white lightning and dollars. The tracers, the disjointed thoughts, your jaw grinding, face contorted, stomping with clenched fists and the rolling whites of your eyes, dancing 12 hours straight, 8 'til 8, this is our *Saturday Night Fever*, our *Quadrophenia*, a robot on the stage with a girl in high black boots and fishnets, clusters of flashing lights, the mayhem, hoover of the music, the smell of Vicks and sweat, and the rush as she runs her fingers through your hair. Close your eyes and see the green geometry spinning in a tunnel through your optic nerves, the hallucinations diminishing in size as they revolve. Feel the weird force that pushes your hands apart, that threatens to whirl your head clean off, the tactile sensations of smooth skin, of firm tits pushed tight against your chest, of words whispered lightly on your neck. And it's all Love and Unity and everyone is one and we're all tanned and grinning, big blue UV smiles that last so long they feel like a grimace. Jaw hurting, lip curled like Elvis, chewing on your cheeks as each wave hits you until a piano break puts the lights up and the hands in the sky; air horns, whistles, humidity. Ecstasy. Get on one. Sorted. You're off your nut, completely stoned. You're fucked up in the back of a Sierra, in a dodgy flat playing low menacing Acid House, against a back rail away from the crowd, in the cool white tile of the toilets with the tunes reduced to one dull repetitive thump as the world awakes outside and the paranoia starts kicking in. Daylight brings the downfall. We're coming down on buses home when someone slaps Simon & Garfunkel on the tape deck and the emptiness lasts a lifetime. *Hello darkness my old friend.*

4

Nocturnal

Mike's first motor was a beat-up two-tone chocolate brown 1970s Marina and he and Adie had to stuff the headlights with loft insulation as they splayed out at weird angles so the road ahead wasn't lit too well, but you could see what was in the hedgerows alongside just fine. So they pull up outside a rave on a cold, fresh moonlit night with frost on the road in south east Northumberland, December 1991, the slag heaps and pit wheels gone and replaced with Japanese electrical components factories, when a lass in silver hot pants and roller boots and glitter eye shadow dishing out flyers taps on the passenger window to hand Adie one and he has to shrug and hold out his hands as he can't roll the window down as they've had wedge it up in place with old clothes pegs jammed in the bottom. They certainly knew how to travel in style wearing black leather coats and jeans and designer T-shirts with rubber sleeves and black pants with silver pocket zips and boots for stomping twelve hours straight with sweat pouring, the dull throb of the bass-lines vibrating through the car above the purring engine, face flushing red, coming up on E and the anticipation that this could be the greatest night of your life.

Adie feels a dull excitement swell in his stomach as they stand among the large queue of talking people outside the rave kitted out in the latest John Richmond *Destroy* gear. He's pressing his face against the cold metal caging where he can see the huge tarpaulin sheets in the fields 500 yards away and watches with childlike fascination the rainbow of colours flashing against the material. Whistles, air horns and heavy bass-lines carry up on the gentle breeze, through the moonlight darkness of a crisp winter evening. Just beyond the tent is a highly luminous yellow and red fairground to add to the surreal dark-carnival atmosphere.

Coming to the end of the queue, he reaches into his pocket and passes his ticket to the large security guard who wears a luminous yellow jacket with an 'Event Security' badge - and there it is; the tent looms in front of him like a vision.The music inside is at a fever pitch, and the kaleidoscope lighting crashes across the canvass in mad waves.Several people standing around the outside grin and nod their heads in acknowledgement as they pass through the small entrance and into the rave.

Adie is immediately struck by the intense heat inside; several people in the huge crowd leaping and dancing frenetically in front of them are topless; the sweat rolling off their backs and down their bug-eyed foreheads. This whole event feels like a huge shamanic healing of our injured souls. A man with a luminous yellow dust mask with a large black letter E on the front bounces past waving two thin fluorescent tubes above his head. A girl with eyes rolling chewing hard on a kid's dummy winks as she jerkily throws her arms out.

The hardcore techno music is grinding like a mad electric machine with a forever-speeding drumbeat that sends the whole place into a crazy delirium. A girl leads him as she makes her way through the lines of smiling, twisted faces and the crowded dance platforms towards the stage, squeezing his wrist and grinning. Green laser lights arch and spin creating huge smoke-filled tunnels. A strobe light flashes incessantly, illuminating the huge octopus that hangs strangely static in the blackness over the crowd. The MC is screaming: "C'mon, make some fucking noise!" which is greeted with cheers, whistles and the occasional blast of an air-horn.

A massive film projection behind the DJ's and erotic lycra-clad dancers on the elevated stage swirls in a thousand inconceivable colours that seem to draw Adie's spirit from his body. He feels more and more unreal as he stares with huge, black pupils at the insane, constantly changing screen. Images of childhood, snippets of marching pipe-bands, cartoons, all flashing before his eyes - and they are all connected.Everything is connected in a blissfully beautiful moment of obscure knowledge - but in an instant it is gone. He feels a twinge of frustration. He had it, just for a second, and then it was gone. The girl has long straight black hair, beautiful big brown eyes and as she dances a golden light behind shining behind her gives her black outline a clear quality, the acid making her arms appear spliced into four sections as they move to the tunes, the white teeth of her wide smile blue in the UV light that makes her skin look like Shiva the destroyer. Her old self shattered and rebuilt and shattered again, an infinitesimally small occurrence in a galaxy of spinning stars that doesn't even matter. "I can see your pain. I feel it too," she whispers in his ear beside a tall stack of black speakers. "When you are hurting, I am hurting."

Smoke begins filling up the dance floor, the whistles and air-horns blasting out again.

He sees bats out of the corner of his eyes flapping in the top of the tent, sections of roof collapsing - but when he looks straight on everything is kind of normal. He gazes intently at the flashing lights and can't count them.

"There are snakes on the floor," a clear voice says and he turns quickly and says "What?" to the man dancing behind him. The lad's topless, sweating, wearing a red bandana on his head and chewing on his cheeks. "What, mate?" he shouts, grinning, trying to be heard over the music. Is he trying to fuck me up? Adie ponders.

His mind can't think straight, very heavy images, noises echoing and metallic as his head spins and he's not walking but drifting through the crowd as if underwater. Feeling like when you're drifting asleep in a hot car as a child and don't know if something's really been said or not or it is all part of a mad dream. He's losing his grip on reality and it feels like hours since he spoke to that bloke or did he imagine it?

Adie finds he can't even look at the girl, casting quick glances but never catching her eyes with a full gaze as if it would betray his feelings, the dull ache that seemed to be sucking his stomach slowly down a tube. And suddenly she is there in front of him and she's smiling and pulling him close to her, dancing, and he feels her hot skin wet with sweat as he puts his hands on her warm waist. Her breath is hot on his neck, her pert, firm breasts pressed against his pounding chest, her eyes so seductive with huge black pupils.

It feels like they've melted together and his muscles are so relaxed that his shoulders unwind like an uncoiling serpent. He feels so high and so happy to be there dancing with her with the hardcore techno grinding on, the bass lines rumbling up through his feet. She lightly kisses his neck and her lips are so soft that it sends crippling rushes around his body, electric sparks shooting out of his fingertips as they caress the base of her spine. Her soft hair is on his skin as she dips her head onto his shoulder, feeling so close like they've connected on some higher spiritual plane. A strange deep connection that only acid can bring on.

But his lips are dry and cracked and it feels like he's got sand in his throat. He needs to drink. Next thing he knows, Adie is standing by a booth with horrible blinding white light and he's got two bottles of water, one in his hand and the other tucked under his arm and he doesn't know how he's got there. He fumbles in his pockets for cash and peels out a note, too messed up to deal with change. No, I don't want change. I need water, he thinks. Adie twists the top off one of the bottles and the cold liquid feels fantastic as he gulps it down, feeling it freezing all the way into his stomach.

He floats back through the crowd looking for the girl. He needs to get back to her - it is a good mission to focus on and he wants to slide into her embrace again, just to be with her, to talk to her. Am I walking uphill or downhill? I'm not really sure - why have they put sloping floors in? Surely they can't have put sloping floors in? His vision tunnels sharply and the tent zooms out to look like a massive aircraft hanger but the girl is very clear and is kissing a fucking DJ from a pub in town passionately. The DJ has a stunning blonde girl with him and is locked in an embrace with her, stroking her arms and they're laughing and joking. Adie's brain seems so disconnected but soon catches up with his pixilated eyes and he feels sick.

A sudden surging wave of hollow sweeping depression thumps into the pit of his guts. He goes to hand her a bottle of water and she's not speaking to him. Not even looking at him; she's jabbering excitedly with the blonde girl and the DJ has turned and said "Cheers, mate," and taken the bottle of water off him. Before he knows it he's saying: "No problem, man," and walking away giving the DJ the thumps up as he winks at him. Beside a dance platform, skin-headed Ian is panicked, edgy and completely paranoid.

"Them lads over there are going to stab me," he says, rubbing his nose.

"They started dancing in front of me and quickly flashing their hands up and that. They're trying to fuck me up."

"Who?" says Mike, laughing.

"Them bastards. Fucking Mackems."

Ian had spent over an hour sitting staring at his Adidas Samba trainers and trying to avoid eye contact. He wasn't the only one whose mind was flipping out. Pac man's mate from Ashington started crying on a bad trip as he thought he was covered in cobwebs and they wouldn't come off no matter how many times he brushed himself down with his hands, and he thought everyone was after him. The faces of devils and flames flash in the strobe lights like a vision from hell. We call it Hardcore. The smoke swirling thickly around the tent, flashing multi-coloured lights and neon green laser tunnels. Always the booming bass. Adie's head is buzzing like a burnt-out circuit board. A police helicopter whirs low overhead, or maybe it's just the tune.

The first Nocturnal big outdoor event 'The Beast' took place in Ashington at the Lakeside Hotel in QE2 Park on Friday 13th of September 1991. The Northumbrian town was formerly known as 'Britain's largest mining village' and the rave was held on the site of the former Woodhorn Colliery which had been converted into a museum and pleasant green woody leisure space near the tracks of a old shunter line on the outskirts of the lined terrace rows. A safety boat was placed on the inky blackness of the central man-made lake behind the massive marquee with a buzz of generators constant along with the rumble of the bass which drifted off into the orange and purple of the cooling evening sky as the sun went down, and ran from 10pm-8am.

"*Take Me Away* hits the sound system and the whole atmosphere erupted - people blowing whistles, chewing hard on baby dummies dressed in hot pants, body suits, brightly coloured puffer jackets, jeans and T-shirts stuffed into their belt loops. Designer labels from Moschino, Destroy and McKitterick," said the stylish Ashton Martin, with a cool air of sophistication as she appeared through the madness of the moving bodies, her stoned blue eyes half closed in the chop of the strobe.

"Walking around the tents in a heady daze watching people either immaculately made up and perfectly styled with the top brands from High Bridge Street – where Barbarella was the girls' shop - to sweaty messes with perspiration spraying from their hair as they danced and stomped. Some danced a kind of tribal dance, some danced as if it was their last-ever dance, hands up to the heavens, and some waved on a chilled trance state unaware and oblivious to the chaos around them," smiled Ashton.

"Drinking bottles of over-priced water or energy drinks, desperately trying to stay hydrated, then the lad I was there with drops to the floor with leg cramp; everyone moving from dance rooms to chill-out rooms with bean bags on the floor. There were dark corners to hide into, to take your next drug to bring up your high again and poppers to keeping you going in the interim, while mingling with all kinds of new friends that love you as much as they love the music. It was addictive."

Dark-haired Di with her big brown eyes and wide smile recalled Nocturnal 1 as: "Bouncy castles, inflatable tunnels, Prodigy '*Charly*' and wandering around Ashington completely spaced at 8am wondering how to get home." Those first few meows sampled from the '70s public information film raising a huge roar of recognition from the crowd as the mad, heavy hoover sound kicked in.

"It's all about dancing really. If you go out to a rave you want something you can get your teeth into, something hard, and people like hard music," a then 19-year-old Liam Howlett told the Channel 4 TV show Rapido.

"Something soft would just mellow the atmosphere right out and it has to be an intense atmosphere in a rave. That's the reason that the hard stuff is played so much."

Hard and intense was certainly a good description of the event.

"Nocturnal was on the edge of a riot all night - a brilliant night," recalled Alex Martin from P.S.I Division, who were up there on the stage with 4-Hero, Zero B and Eze-Ozo. "It was rebellious. Punky. The Police were in the wrong, they knew it, and we egged them on. The Nocturnal posse showed defiant restraint. There was too much love in the place," he smiled.

"We played all over the country - Manchester, Oldham, Liverpool, Coventry, Middlesbrough, Edinburgh, Leeds, Bolton. We tried London once, took our Northern sound into a House club. They freaked out and pulled the plug on us. We didn't care. They looked scared, man. I could see our 'agent' and publisher at the back laughing their tits off. Was mad that."

"But that kind of sums up what it was like, and about. We had fun on the stage and others had fun on the floor. It was loud, there was shouting, and beats, widdly synths and fat bass. And stabs, lots of stabs... no pianos mind. Not in the P.S.I."

Jimmy E and four of his mates were dancing on the stage when it collapsed. "We just carried on dancing," he said. "A mate told me to rub Deep Heat that he had in to my balls because it gives you a great rush - prick, I had to go to the St. John's ambulance and they gave me loads of water to tip on them. God knows what they thought of me!" he laughed. Altern8's Mark Archer recalled doing a gig up at Newcastle in the early 1990s – it was possibly Rez 4 with L.F.O and P.S.I. Division - and said in a later interview that: 'our eyes were watering because of the smell of Vicks and Olbas Oil. I had no idea why it purely stank of Vicks, but it was from the people that had taken Ecstasy and then rubbed Vicks on their chest so that when they breathe in they get a rush.'

"The mate that gave me the Deep Heat took a different E to me that night and it was trippy. He had a bad night, and said when he got home a poster of Blondie on his wall came to life and they jumped onto his bed and did a concert for him," said Jimmy E.

Imagine that; Debbie Harry with her sultry, smoky eyes moving her hips seductively right there on the duvet for you in a shimmering short silver dress. Class.

Meanwhile Shirley was dancing, dancing, always dancing and feeling the music moving her body with each tingling sensation rising along with the pitch in the rhythm, lost in sound under the canvass of the huge tent, twirling her fingers above her tousled short brown hair with tracers coming off them under the flash of a golden strobe. Being whipped around and around on a circus gyroscope, the weird dizzying sensations and strange isolation of being at an event without her usual group of friends that made the noise and madness something less of a joyous celebration. But then feeling that euphoria of recognition, bumping into a couple of friends from Uni as she wandered around the less packed outside of the space, hugging tight with others she didn't expect to see like Stevie, and Adie, and smiling wide in spotting other friends she knew from around about.

"Nocturnal was one of my least favourite raves, perhaps. It was more mainstream and maybe less loved-up than Rez or Butterlogie – that makes me sound like a rave snob - but going from those or a rave in Jesmond Dene to Nocturnal - no comparison!" said Shirley. Tasting the chemical tang of speed in the back of her throat and placing a blotter of acid on her tongue, not into taking much E so she could avoid being stuck sat with a lolling head monged against a back wall in the black; having the hassle of losing a purse and looking about for it on the floor while off her face – then the relief of finding it that released another wave of chemical pleasure. Shirley was aware of eyes on her at times throughout the night; sweating, topless, gurning bodybuilder blokes in bandanas sizing her up with strange looks that she couldn't quite get.

"I was a bit like hmmm? Then found out later I had a black long waistcoat on with a pink top that you couldn't really see under the lights. That explained it!" she said. Tom found himself slumped in the darkness lit by a purple light with his head in his hands. While Shirley had avoided the Es to escape the heavy, dilapidating initial surge that could leave you spaced-out, immobile and dizzy as it began to kick in, he had necked and was riding out the storm as it came on really strong, the relentless peaks and surges in the music twisting his face into contorted expressions.

"Just before Nocturnal a lad we knew decided to go into business making his own pills. Big fucking white capsules. They had who knows what inside, but they kicked like a mule," he said. "That was my second pill of the night after a fairly run-of-the-mill first one. I was wasted for at least an hour. Totally cabbaged. Then, I started coming up. I felt fucking indestructible and danced my tits off for hours. I never found out what he put in them!"

Evil Eddie Richards, Smokey Joe, Slipmatt, Binni, Stu Allen, Andy Baxter, The Drop and Keith Suckling were the DJs at Nocturnal One, the daylight then breaking and going through Morpeth bus station in a gang decked out in leather waistcoats and boots and thin black jumpers with futuristic designer graphics on at 8 in the morning singing *Dominator* to the bemused looks of the locals as they went by, dancing and chanting on their way to an after party. There had been an earlier 6pm-12 midnight event held at the High Pit entertainment complex in Cramlington on the 7th January 1991 called *Konspiracy* which featured the Wear FM DJs Binni, Andy Baxter, Craig E Mac and Smokey Joe with a 15k sound system, 3d lasers, UVs, roboscans, a lighting system, strobes and projections which paved the way for the big outdoor all-nighters.

The Nocturnals were Northumberland's very own raves and an event dubbed 'The Beast Returns' took place at Bassington Fields near an industrial estate on the edge of Cramlington on Friday 13th December 1991. The flyers for the event were a demon face mask and a few people were milling around outside the tent dancing with them on secured with elastic. It set the tone for a night of powerful hardcore. Rez 10 had taken place at the Mayfair on the Monday night before it with Frankie Bones flying in from Brooklyn NYC to do a fierce set. Micky Finn, MC Screech & DJ Julz, Carl Cox, Howie and Bass Generator were also on the decks in an amazing evening.

"I don't think you'll ever recapture that brand-new crazy vibe that we had in the late '80s and early '90s. There's something about that piano era that just slipped by the wayside a little. We got it, on the underground club circuit, but some of those tunes, for me, need to get robbed – not in a horrible way," laughed Micky Finn as he discussed his music projects with DirtyFreqsTV.

Colin Faver, Grooverider, Binni, Jumpin' Jack Frost, Devious D, Micky Parks, Micky Wilson, Smokey Joe and DJ Rap brought along their records in their metal cases to rumble the speakers with annihilating audio at 'The Beast Returns.' Charissa Saverio (DJ Rap) was a leading female DJ and producer on the hardcore scene and she has gone on to own two labels of her own – Propa Talent and Impropa Talent – and is also a successful model and actress. "I like the rush of a big tent...you put on a record and everyone just goes fucking mental," she told *The List* in 1996.

SL2 were the Live PA up alongside the metallic gleam and jerky movements of the eight-foot tall Promobots robots and MCs in urban camouflage pants, baseball caps and black scooter jackets on the stage. *DJ's Take Control* and *On A Ragga Tip* both brought chart success for Slipmatt (Matt Nelson) and Lime (John Fernandez) with the former reaching number 11 and the latter number 2 as rave music started to move out of the underground. SL2 were on the same XL Recordings label as the Prodigy.

"The original rave sound from the late eighties and early nineties has so much character. It was a new, fresh and fast-evolving sound at the time which made it very special, if not magical. The memories it conjures up for a wide generation of people are, for some, including me, the best and most exciting times of their lives," Slipmatt later told Skiddle.

While the music and the atmosphere was undoubtedly exciting, being so heavily engaged around the dangerous street stimulants that were being traded illicitly in dark corners also led to an increasing number of people who wouldn't ever consider themselves as criminals being swept up into the possession and selling of ecstasy.

"At the second Nocturnal in Cramlington I had found a clear zip lock bag on the floor with four white pills in. As I had already bought my drugs, I decided to sell these ones. It was my first time in selling... I didn't want to sell to anyone I knew as I had no idea what they really were or the origin of them, but it was a quick £80. That's how it starts," admitted Ashton. By the time the Rezerections had moved up to Edinburgh, she and a gang of friends had travelled up on the train carrying gear on them to shift on among the huge crowds.

"We all went to a friend's house the weekend before where a dealer was to bring us the drugs to sell up there. We sampled them all that night and got totally off our heads," she recalled.

"I had to then do a split shift at work the following morning still off my nut. My then-boyfriend and I decided that to make more cash from the drugs we'd cut them with Superdrug's own brand cold care capsules. Once at the Rez we split up into small groups to sell our heavily cut stash... we heard my boyfriend had been caught by the security/ police, so we all split up and girls and guys swapped clothes in the toilets so we wouldn't get recognised by anyone or get taxed!"

"Then about two or three hours later he re-emerged and said they had tested the drugs but could not prove they were Class A - so cutting them saved our bacon. We made money that weekend and paid for our holiday and a silver locket for me."

Nocturnal moved indoors on Valentine's night in 1992 to the Arena in Middlesbrough for 'Beauty and the Beast' which featured Slipmatt, Binni, Stu Allen, Dave Angel, Smokey Joe and B-Jam, while the fourth and final Nocturnal was called 'The Circus comes to Town' and was back in the outdoor tent in Bassington Fields on Saturday March 14th 1992. The local BBC filmed a documentary called 'Rave' at the event, which you can now see on YouTube. Nocturnal 4's flyer was now a clown mask and it ran from 9pm-8am with the respected Graham Auld being the organiser and promoter as 3,750 people descended on the field. With the event under increasing scrutiny from the authorities and the media, Mr. Auld, a property developer by trade, was at pains to stress that he had done all he could to keep the event as clean possible and pointed the finger at unscrupulous club owners for the dark perception that hardcore was attracting.

"It is difficult because drug use is connected to the whole dance culture, but it's something that if you freely allow through the doors will attract the wrong kind of people and trouble," he told the local press.

"The main problem which has given raves a bad image are some of the clubs which clicked on to raves and started playing dance music and calling them rave nights. They were getting the crowds in but weren't doing anything to tighten up the security on the door. No one was searched properly, so there were loads of drugs getting in, as well as the dealers and then the weapons. That's when the real trouble happens, stabbings and that. But the problem is not so much the people that genuinely go to raves for the music, and all right a proportion of them do take drugs, but the people who run them. They're spoiling it for everyone."

'Circus' had two arenas, with the main stage hosting Hype, CJ Bolland, Krome, Binni, Doc Scott, Kenny Ken, Smokey Joe, Colin Dale and DJ Rocky. There was a Live PA from Fierce Ruling Diva (*Floorfiller/ Rub it in*), while a second tent had, for 'the first time in the North East,' a Garage and Up-Front

House Arena with Havana resident Colin Patterson flying in from Tenerife, along with Darren Price, Craig Walsh and Sarah J.

Northumbria Police's then Chief Inspector Stuart Christison was left somewhat perplexed by the event and told the documentary makers that it was: "Something utterly unique in my 20 years service. I've been to one or two events, but nothing of this type at all. I think it is best described as being surreal."

"I spoke to quite a number of the young people attending before the event and in general they seemed perfectly nice young people who, in some cases, had travelled a very long way to be here. When the event started and the music, the strobes and the lights and all the rest of it came on, the situation changed. They still remained nice people, but all of a sudden they would start dancing frenetically as if beyond their control. They would just carry on and bop off into the distance...there was no communication among them, they were in a world of their own."

Smiler clambered up out of the crowd onto the stage. Stepped up onto a stack of throbbing, pulsating black speakers and started throwing shapes with a huge beaming grin on his face, flicking his long, straight hair back off his sweating brow. Felt like a God up there as he looked out over the sea of arms under the canopy with a multitude of flashing lights sweeping over the skin. Then he got a wobble on and felt a flash of panic as he thought he was going to fall and sent the speakers crashing down with him. Giving it the big Hawaii-Five-Oh as he struggled to keep his balance then jumping back down blowing with relief. Later on he kissed a lad he thought he was a woman, he was so blissfully gone.

"What about the bird I pulled?" he later recalled. "She had six toes on each foot - I thought I was just seeing things, so I waited till the morning and counted again. She had two little toes hanging out of her sandals on each foot. I couldn't get over it," he laughed. Smiler and his pink back massager. It used to pull all the birds, he said. The euphoric rush as it sent little electric pulses soaring around their bodies, eyes rolling back in pleasure. The heat, the sweat and noise, the party atmosphere with a slight edge and undercurrent of menace as faces from the local crime families, or the Gremlins and the

Seaburn Casuals, eyed each other through the darkness. As daylight begins breaking through the canvass Smokey Joe drops a Jungle mix of '*Here comes the Sun,*' with the generators humming and that strange feeling of emerging blinking from a tent into dew. "I ended up in Consett for two days after a Nocturnal and had to go back for my car. When I got back all that was in the field was my car and nowt else. Happy times," recalled Pac man.

Although Nocturnal Promotions had an application to hold a fifth event with a 900 capacity at the Concordia Leisure Centre in Cramlington approved in July 1992, the rave never went ahead. Plans from another promoter, Mavis Renwick, to hold an all-nighter for 4,000 at a warehouse in the middle of the Transbrittania Enterprise Park in Blaydon in May '92 were refused after objections from police and council inspectors.

"It just seems they think people are going to spend £25 for a rave only to stay for an hour then go out on the rampage in Blaydon," said Mrs. Renwick, who also cited the Nocturnal success as she hoped to apply to put another event on.

"There were 8,000 people at the rave in Cramlington recently, and that went without a hitch. I'll just have to find a warehouse in the middle of a field."

Other raves, however, were happening all over the region as the hardcore scene hit a peak. MK Promotions put on an event called 'The Ice Gathering' at the 4,500 capacity Whitley Bay Ice Rink in October 1991 with Shades of Rhythm, Messiah and Geneside II as the live acts and Asterix & Space, Bass Generator, Andy Baxter, Smokey Joe and DJ Blaster appearing on the decks. Rezerection travelled the length of Hadrian's Wall to put on a rave in Carlisle at the Sands Centre in April 1992 with Grooverider, Fabio and Bass Generator appearing at the large council-owned venue by the river Eden, where the Cumbrians were also running a rave called Phobia at the time. Rez were back in the December with Terrorize doing a live PA alongside Grooverider, Mikey B, DJ Face and Bass Generator. Pink Panther records in the city was the place for picking up vinyl as well as tickets for raves and the coach travel to get there. Phil C went on to become a DJ himself at the likes of the rave clubs Annabels and the Pagoda in the city and also spent some time working at the

Pink Panther store.

"I can remember getting a white label of *Oblivion (head in the clouds)* by Manix in Pink Panther on the day of a Phobia at the Sands and Carl Cox played it that night. The place went mental and nobody that I was with believed I had it sat at home," he said. It was a dark and cold Friday evening on the 31st January 1992 when the crowd began arriving up from the underpass under the City's largest roundabout into the car park of the leisure centre and standing around in excited groups to line up and get into the cavernous sports hall, where they were totally bombarded by acoustics and the mad flash of lights and lasers.

"The Prodigy turned up that night - it was meant to be Altern8. The place stank of Vicks and everyone was drinking bottles of Purdey's that were in dustbins filled with ice," he recalled. Almost a mist in the air, that strange grey cloud that lingers around the edges of the range of a smoke machine, the coolness and sanctuary of opening a door and taking a breather on a staircase while the manic tunes inside are reduced to a pounding bass.

"I was chuffed to bits getting an import of *Dominator* by Human Resource. I'd first heard it on Pete Tong and kept asking for it for what seemed like months. *Euphoria* by Dream Frequency was also one I heard on Pete Tong that turned out to be the B side of *Feel So Real*. I've still got that one and wouldn't part with it," continued Phil.

"It was hard to get the tunes unless they got signed to a major label - most of the tracks seemed to be sold to shops in London out of the backs of cars as white labels. I remember going to Newcastle for records in the early 90s and going to Trax on High Bridge, which later turned into Flying Records."

"I went up to Glasgow one afternoon to go to 23rd Precinct with some of the lads in a red Fiesta with tunes belting out of it - it would be a tape with either Ratty or Seduction on it!" he laughed.

"I didn't have much money that day but came home with a copy of *I Trance You* by Gipsy. The Prodigy went into Pink Panther on the day of one of the Phobia's before I worked there - there was a big display going up the stairs for the Experience album and they all signed it when they visited the shop. Everybody that came into the shop wanted it, including myself, but he wouldn't part with it."

The madness at the Phobia continued throughout 1992 and on Saturday March 7th Rozalla and Inner City were the live PAs as the Sands boasting fire eaters, dancers, multi-coloured lasers, 20k of sound, inflatables and human gyroscopes on the flyer. The DJ line-up that night was Mike Pickering from the Hacienda, Techno Titan, Colin Faver, and local DJs Oliphant & Thompson and Rod. Undercover police swooped to search more than 80 people among the 1,600 waiting to get in to the rave and charged 18 with possession of drugs including Ecstasy, LSD, cannabis and, strangely, heroin.

Phobia were also running massive events in Leeds and across Yorkshire, and also appeared on home turf in Newcastle at the Poly Student Union on Friday 12th June across three floors with SL2 and Rhythmatic starring along with Nipper, DJ Seduction, Evil Eddie Richards and Bill E Wizz. Local lads Andy Baxter, Simon Gibb, DJ Rod and MC Jason Bushby also appeared at the 8-2am event. A couple of weeks earlier, on Friday 22nd May 1992, Phobia were at the Sands Centre in Carlisle where Dave Angel, Slipmatt, Nipper, DJ Rod, Oliphant & Thompson, New Atlantic (*I Know*) and Urban Hype produced the sounds. Slipmatt later uploaded his set from a cassette tape onto the music site *Soundcloud* and recalled that 1992 was 'the golden year of Rave.'

"I had forgotten all about this party but after listening I do remember it, especially the long journey there and back," he laughed. "Phobia was a big player in the North back in the day and will always have a major identity in the history of rave."

There had been social unrest and riots on the Raffles in the city around the same time as the trouble on the Meadow Well in 1991, and there were further outbreaks of public disorder on the estate late in July 1992 when 11 people were arrested after a stolen car was burnt out in front of a community centre. Just a couple of weeks later

Phobia was going from strength to strength and on Saturday 1 August DJ Sy, Trevor Fung, Bass Generator, DJ Rod and MCs Jucki G and Memo lined up along with Bass Heads and the face painters, stilt walkers, jugglers, and the Phobia dancers to once again rock the Sands.

As well as the legal raves that were taking place in Carlisle, an illegal event had been held in a disused brick building at the old power station in the city in August 1990. Pigeons flapping and cooing in the rafters as the sound system was rigged up in a cold concrete space near the buzz and vibrations of the pylons and big grey electrical industrial power equipment. The police blocked off the Willowholme industrial estate and during the ensuing riot the windows of nearby Chivers Sports were put in and the shop looted of Sergio Tacchini tracksuits. A police spokesman said that they'd been 'confronted by a mob of around 200 who hurled stones, sticks, bottles and breeze blocks at them.' Carlisle City Council had issued High Court injunctions against five organisers to try and stop the illegal warehouse parties that were taking place in the city five months earlier. A police spokesman claimed that a number of parties had been held in 'unsuitable premises, that known criminals had attended them, and there had been some drug use.' Around 200 had been at a party at a disused warehouse on Port Road in Carlisle that March, while 16 people were arrested at an illegal 'acid party' at the Old Tannery at Ulverston in Cumbria in January 1990.

The police had also put a stop to other illegal raves around the region. Four lads were arrested for possession of amphetamines when the police raided a building in East Hartford, Cramlington, where a rave was planned in 1994. The event did not go ahead, police stated, because 'the caretaker did not turn up.' They also broke up a woodland rave near Ladycross Quarry in Slaley Forest, near Hexham, in June 1995 and surrounded a former working man's club in Choppington, Northumberland in March 1996 to stop an event going ahead. Later that year an all-nighter in Darlington was also handed an injunction to prevent it from happening. The 1994 Criminal Justice and Public Order Act introduced by the Government prevented the 'gathering on land in the open air of 20 or more persons (whether or not trespassers) at which amplified music is played during the night (with or without intermissions) and is such as, by reason of its loudness and duration and the time at which it is played, is likely to cause serious distress to the inhabitants of the locality,' with the music definition including 'sounds wholly or predominantly characterised by the emission of a succession of repetitive beats.' The establishment were so terrified by the boom of the dance scene that they were making it a criminal offence to have a party and gave the police the power to 'remove people attending or preparing for a rave.' At another unlicensed rave in Tranwell woods in Northumberland in 1997 the police seized cannabis, amphetamines and magic mushrooms when they descended to break it up after the muffled bass emanating through the trees had alerted nearby residents. Northumbria police's then Det. Con. Steve Truby told the local press that the rave was 'a sophisticated set-up attended by people from as far away as Leeds. They had their own DJs and generators to support the sound and lighting equipment.'

Over the border, the Scottish hardcore dance scene saw Rez also putting on an event at Glasgow Barrowlands with Dave Angel and Shades of Rhythm, as well as their regular Edinburgh all-nighters. In the September of 1991 STREETrave had put on a Nuclear event at the Loreburn Hall in Dumfries on a Sunday night with Club Havana's Hooligan X, Andy Carroll, Bass Generator, James Barton, Jon Mancini and Binnie on the decks. Moby and Two Unlimited provided the PAs.

"Really, that was their crowd. We were coming in on Mancini 'the Genie's' crowd. That's what I used to call him - I named him Mancini the Genie," grinned MC Lee in an interview for 'The story of STREETrave' documentary in 2009.

"You also had Boney (Iain Clark), but I'd say at the time Mancini's crowd were more into their tunes − Boney's crowd were a bit younger...that was my interpretation on it, you know," he said, smiling and relaxed in a peaked cap and white T-shirt.

"Me and Collin (Patterson) actually coming to Scotland to play was a big thing. I don't think he realised how much of a big thing it was, because me and Huey actually opened the door to it. He came in, really, when we'd already opened the door to it. The Scottish people were more passionate about it. In England it was more of a, you know how the English are, 'we've started this, we're cool,' where the Scottish people embraced it and it was close to their heart."

STREETrave had Utah Saints and Bassheads at the same venue that November, while in the March of 1993 Q-Tex were at a Cyberzone rave in the Victoria Hall in Selkirk.

In August the pounding sound of Terrorize *'It's just a feeling'* rumbled around Hawick Leisure Centre from their Live PA. Both towns are set deep in the Borders, the surrounding dark hills that couldn't be seen against the blackness of the night sky but could almost be sensed as a looming, ominous presence as the rave scene hit warp factor 10. QFX were also on the stage that evening at Solaris in the former textiles town in an 8-2am show that also featured DJ Tosh – billed as Northumberland's number one - with DJ Destroy from Rockshots and the Blue Monkey, DJ Diane, DJ ZBD, MCs Shimmy and Shady and the mercurial Scottish DJ legend Tom Wilson as the headliner.

Tom had also played at a small rave in Hawick Town Hall that year, the wooden floor hard on the feet as the dancers pounded away to metallic, robotic, grinding tracks in a repetitive hypnotic beat that lifted them unto another level of consciousness, lost in a world of their own for hours on end. Some sat around on chairs at the edges; smart young girls with long blonde hair in tight black lycra tops with white shirts tied at the waist and long baggy sleeves grooving and skinny lads with white gloves punching out the tunes illuminated by the spinning lights and flashing colours.

Tom Wilson was a regular around the bigger clubs and Scottish events including Awesome 101, Fantazia, Rezerection and Fubar. He had worked with acts as diverse as N-Trance, The Time Frequency, Belinda Carlisle, Ice MC, Scooter, Mary Kiani and DJ Dado and had a long-running dance music radio show called Steppin' Out, while his Bonus Beats show on Forth FM gave local up-and-coming DJs the chance to air one-hour mixes. He also produced records of his own including *Technocat* and *Let your body go*. Tom died following a heart attack in 2004 aged 52.

STREETrave had been putting on events as early as September 1989 at the legendary Ayr Pavilion. They also ran nights at the Irvine Pleasuredome, but the main spot was at the Pavilion on the seafront where Hacienda DJs Graeme Park and Mike Pickering brought the Manchester sound up for the first all-dayer called 'West Coast Jam.'

They also put on huge Eurodance all-nighters at the Prestwick airport terminal from 1991 that featured some of the biggest performers and DJs around. The Eurodance in May 1993 featured The Prodigy, Shades of Rhythm,

Love Decade, Q-Tex, Ultra Sonic, Slipmatt and Lime (SL2), Dave Angel Mark Hadden, Jon Mancini, Boney and MC Lee, all appearing in front of a huge and enthusiastic crowd. An 'underground' event ran concurrently that night with Nightmares on Wax & Havanna, Eze & the Boy Wonder, Bob Jeffries, Colin Patterson, Yogi Haughton and Kevin Wilson playing a separate arena. There was another huge Eurodance at Prestwick that December with the Prodigy, Shades of Rhythm and Dream Frequency headlining it.

"The Eurodances' were unbelievable," recalled MC Lee.

"I couldn't imagine pulling up at an airport and someone closing the airport for the night. I don't think anyone could. It's like going to Heathrow airport and telling them to close it for the night. I don't know how they got around the air tower, customs...how can you have customs at a dance party, right? There's a rave going on and Her Majesty's Customs officers are around the corner! How they got around that I don't know to this day, because I couldn't do it."

The earlier Scottish illegal 'acid house party' scene was initially centred in and around Edinburgh and Glasgow but had also seen an outdoor rave in September 1989 in Dronley Woods near Dundee. Police were alerted by a local farmer who'd been woken around 4am by 'loud, rhythmic music, which was so loud he thought it was actually in his house,' thus proceeding what was billed on flyers as 'Scotland's First Acid Party' in Aberdeenshire by a couple of months. Andrew Chevis organised the £10-a-head rave at a secret venue 'within 20 miles of Aberdeen' which was called off after being rumbled by Grampian Police. The organiser of the Dronley Woods rave, which ran from midnight to 5.30am, was charged with a breach of the peace and fined £100. Across the water in Ireland, the first 'acid house party' to get raided by the gardai took place in a disused Dublin warehouse at Hanover Street in October 1989 where 800 were packed in. By April 1990 the Dubliners were raving at a night called Orbit at the Olympic Ballroom.

Dodger was one of young up-and-coming guys involved in and around the notorious Aberdeen Soccer Casuals in the late '80s before getting into the rave scene. The ASC had a long had the reputation as the hardest crew in Scotland until the arrival of E and electronic tunes somewhat decimated their squad as the NE of Scotland took to raving with some gusto.

"I was still a bit young to get into the rave scene in '88 but I can remember the Summer of Love being splashed about the papers. I was aware of House music though as it was played in a Boogaloos which was an under-18 night on a Monday in Aberdeen," he said.

"I was still more into the football - but in early '88 there were a heap of us from the fitba who went to Flicks for a night out. We ended up fighting with a load of Dundee lads; we got to know them quite well. I actually missed out a big part of the summer after breaking my nose at a Punk gig and getting blood poisoning which put me in hospital for three weeks."

Dodger was smoking a bit of hash and drinking beers and in early '89 he first heard the Stone Roses on a trip to Edinburgh. It was another one of those magical moments where everything just seemed to slot into place as the jangling guitars and thunderous bass sound-tracked a generation.

"We had heard about this club in Aberdeen called Fever. A bunch of lassies we hung about with had drifted away from us lads and started going, but our faces never seem to fit," laughed Dodger.

"We used to go out to a club just outside Aberdeen called the Craigmile. It was a hit or a miss - one day you could have the night of yer life, the following week it could be a kicking outside. But house music was starting to be played a lot more and in May 1990, four of us got tickets to see the Stone Roses at Spike Island on the banks of the Mersey. That's when we first came across Es. We were all too scared to try them, but we were taken aback how open and friendly people were. It's not called the love drug for no reason," he grinned.

"1990 was about going into town and catching the house groves in places like the Cotton Club, Bensons and a Bar called Styx. I had still never necked a mythical E by then though. At the tail-end of the year I had started hanging about with other lads and lassies from other parts of Aberdeen and in early February I ventured to an event called The Weekend of Love at the Beach Ballroom in Aberdeen. I took about 3 grams of speed and I felt on top of this world. It felt like the whole of Aberdeen and the Northeast of Scotland was bouncing on the suspended floor. It was crazy, I had caught the bug."

5

Judgement Day

Bass Generator slipped the gleaming black vinyl from its sleeve and set it on the turntable, placing the needle down and holding his headphones up to one ear as it crackled to life and then began to rumble powerfully out of the speaker stack.

Charly Lownoise & Mental Theo's *Ultimate Sextrack*. You know the one – *jack, jack, jack the penis* - a bit daft, a bit nutty, but loud, pounding and euphoric. It's amazing how grooves on what is essentially a disc of plastic can produce such a sonic shockwave as the repetitive thump of the cacola hits you in the chest.

Records are made of PVC, the same black material that fitted tightly to the curves of the lesbians that writhed sexily on the metal beds and swings and tied each other up at the later monthly Fetish Parties in a small bar in Newcastle hosted by Bassy G and his fellow Geordie DJ Smurf, who was always up for a laugh and donned his girlfriend's nightie, pink rubber gloves, big brown Caterpillar boots and pink socks to spin dark PCP-style gabba and Old Skool techno and acid house to a crowd of Goths and transvestites. "They really got into the hard beats and dark sounds," Smurf grinned.

Bass Generator had been up in the DJ booth playing tunes since 1987 and produced his first record in 1989. He launched his own label – Bass Generator Records – in 1990. One of the first releases was Bass Generator's *The EP* in 1991, a 12" that had *Is The Clonk Alright?* on the A side and *Megablast* and

Tibetan Jam on the B side. There were four records released by the label the following year: *Rhubarb & Samples* by Bass Generator/MIC, *House Is Dead/In My Mind Part 3* by Bass Generator, *Return of The Brain* by Million Dollar Brain and *Tears (In My Mind Part 2)*, which was another of Bassy G's own hits.

1993 saw the productions getting even harder as *The Event (Or Is It?)* by Bass Generator, *The Experiment* by Genetik, and *Hellbound / Go Bezerk* by Lord of Hardcore (Scott Brown) were put out there by the Geordie producer. *Exceleration* by NeuroTek, *The Technotrance EP* (Hyperact Remixes) (Volume One), *Squirt / Splash* by Water Pistol, *Recall / Intruder (Remix)* by Science Rhythm, *The EP* by DJ Excel, *1·6·8·EP* by NeuroTek Featuring DJ Excel, *Bounce, Bounce, Bounce* by M.I.C and Smokey Joe/Brother T/Dylan Dogg's *Smokin' Studio EP* all followed in 1994.

With the likes of Volume, RPM, and Trax in Newcastle, Blaze in Cramlington, and Off the Record in North Shields all dealing in techno records and selling tickets for events at the time, former Trax employee Bassy G opened his first specialist dance music record shop in Newcastle in October 1992, and another followed up in Edinburgh. The Rezerection resident DJ's basement shop was down on sloping Dean Street heading towards the swing bridge, descending a narrow steep staircase with walls covered in graffiti art and flyers, into a room full of vinyl that pounded with a warped bass drum sound. He originally called it 'Loony Toonz,' but got into bother with American cartoon giant Warner Bros., who threatened legal action, and he had to change the name to Bass Generator Records.

As rave music began to become more mainstream around the March of '92, the popular DJ told the *Evening Chronicle* that 'dance music is basically turning into pop music' as he discussed the popularity of gigs vs. clubs at that time.

"You're getting all the stuff in the charts and it's becoming regular, it's even dominating the Top 20 at the minute. You go to a club now and you see all these kids who are about 14 and 15 and the reason they are there is because it is pop music and it's on Top of the Pops and coming out of the radio all the time," he said.

"They are getting into a scene and they think 'this is the new thing and we're all going to be into this.' And that's where they are all starting to come from. They haven't been around, they aren't cultured club goers, they are kids who've been into it for a couple of months because their mates started a few months before that and so on. It's pop music and that's the problem. There's no gigs in this field though. I class it as raves and clubs. They're all going to raves because they like having lot of people there, they like being hot and sweaty. As far as clubs go, it's probably not because they don't want to go to clubs, it's that there aren't any decent ones to go at the minute. The majority of clubs won't have a rave night because of the bad reputation surrounding them - they feel that they might lose their license and that's another problem."

With the Rez firmly positioned up in Scotland after 1992, Newcastle's local rave scene was taken over by Bass Generator's Judgement Days at Whitley Bay. Scott and Scooby had been running House nights at Global, bringing the likes of David Morales and Frankie Knuckles across to play, while the first Judgement Day took place at the Park Terrace club out at the coast by the North Sea on the 12th October 1993 from 8-2am and featured Bass Generator, Easy Groove, Michael Devlin, and the MCs Sneaky Eye and Naz.

You get outside from the darkness, the noise and the lightshow onto the sodium-lit street and as the cars drive by their engines sound like hardcore with your ears still buzzing as you head back to an afters party. 3.27 a.m. and Ian and Adie sit contentedly on their sofa deckchairs sunbathing in the glorious sunlight of the sitting room bulb. Every now and then they break from their talk about roast beef and mustard sandwiches and bottles of Guinness to demand if people have tickets for this trip to the coast. Most people look bewildered; Stevie grins at them in his laid-back way, so he is allowed on the bus. Rob can feel the soft sand squeezing through his socks on the carpet, and the sea rolls gently in from behind the T.V. Seagulls arc and cry in the clear blue skies of the bare magnolia walls. The desperate feeling of an out-of-season British coastal resort can be overwhelming. Dilapidated guest houses and boarded-up amusement arcades, empty, dank pubs and tacky gift shops. The golden glow of a fish and chip shop provides some respite, but the sea crashes hard on the harbour walls sending spray high into the colourless sky. Always the sad, dull roar of the sea.

Mike and Big-chip are in the kitchen laughing at shiny tins of Spam, breathing tablecloths and wallpaper that is slowly sliding off the walls. Big-chip likes to talk about building and violence and Mike gets into this. Wendy and Miah sit cross-legged with huge gleaming black pupils in the corner of the beach giggling and smoking someone else's cigarettes. A golden packet of Bensons decimated. A crazy-looking older woman with wild dark hair asks if she can have one, then starts screaming and shrieking obscenities as she realises they are hers. She storms out of the house and into the moonlit fret but returns later and people look at each other in disgust as she apologises. It's so false. A front. *Yeah, I can see behind the mask, can see those cogs spinning in your head like a cheap Tenerife fake Tag watch.* Miah and Adie leave the after-rave party and are struck by the cool fresh air as they blink into the pale blue light of dawn. The amazingly clear architecture of an ornate sandstone bank appears far too big and unreal as they walk arm in arm through the empty, silent streets. Birds sing. Thousands of birds. Starlings. A solitary black London cab roars by with men with no faces pressed against the glass. *There was no driver, I'm telling you- it was a ghost car!* Back home to crash into bed and uneasy vivid dreams of a psychedelic, tie-dye, triplicate Hitler ranting in German.

Unemployment up the West End was running at around 25% in Benwell, Scotswood and Elswick in the terraces that ran down towards the Tyne and the huge former Armstrong Vickers tank factory that had once provided jobs for 25,000 people. Homes were famously sold for just £1 as feuds between drug gangs, arson, crime and witness intimidation gave the area notoriety on a national scale. 'West End, the best end' was the refrain in clubs as gangs from Newcastle's former shipbuilding East End - Byker, Wallsend, Walker, or from at the mouth of the Tyne at North Shields – shot daggers at each other across the dance floors. The Ragworth Estate in Stockton and the Pennywell in Sunderland also had issues with firearms and gangs. The social depravation in parts of County Durham and Teesside saw them ranked down alongside the rough end of Romania in EU tables. It was no real surprise, then, that the North-East should embrace hard tunes for tough times; post-industrial noise to annihilate reality and dance away, head down, into oblivion.

Joey Beltram flew over from NYC, over two years since his last appearance in the UK at the Rez, for Judgement Day 2 on November 25th 1993. DJ Excel and MCs G-Force and Sneaky Eye also appeared alongside Bassy G as the room reverberated to the hoover, stabs and rumbling bass of the traditional break-beat sound with the added harder influence of Dutch and German hardcore very much in evidence throughout the night. Bass Generator's big anthem 'The Event' also boomed from the speakers to a huge reception on the dance floor.

When Phobia teamed up with Judgement Day for the third event at the Whitley Bay venue on Thursday 10th Feb 1994, the sound in the North East and Scotland was very much heading down the hard, happy and bouncy road while the south of England took a more drum and bass, ragga-influenced route as the rave scene continued fragmenting into different genres. The likes of Westbam, Tanith, Dye Witness and GTO were to dominate the new sound as Bass Generator took up a residency at Fubar in Stirling and was voted the best hardcore DJ in an independent poll in both 1993 and 1994 (he'd been just edged out of the top-spot by Carl Cox in '92) and played at over 1500 events around the globe throughout the decade. He also set an unofficial world record of playing at seven different events in one night.

"I loved the freshness of it all and the camaraderie of the Scottish crowd back then," Bass Generator recalled in one interview. "Rez Events 2 and 3 stick out in my memory – I can't remember the others – Fantazia, Big Bang... my favourite nights were probably the hundreds of small venues all over Scotland that I did in 93-95. Great times!"

Joey Beltram and Bass Generator were back in action just nine days after that Judgement Day up at Ingliston at the Rezerection 'Lurrvre Special' with Dave Angel, Mrs. Woods, Blu Peter, Randal, Technotrance, Dell, and Rob Tissera. Q-Tex, Dye Witness, Bass X, and Inner Seduction provided the PAs while the MCs were Robbie Dee and XXX.

Bass Generator said he didn't remember much of his Fubar residency in 1994, as he 'drank way too much.' It was a state of intoxication that his friend DJ Smurf could very much relate to at the time.

"I got barred from DJing at Nosebleed for nearly a year once, for being completely rat-arsed one night. In the old days the promoters used to buy me a bottle of whisky every time I played there. One night I drank most of it before I played and had to get carried to the DJ box. The left deck was forked as well. Every time the arm got to a certain point on the deck, it stuck. This and being pissed led to a very bad set. I'm pleased they did ban me in a way, because it taught me a lesson. Now I just get wasted after a set!" he laughed.

Smurf was a regular visitor to the Bass Generator record shop and it was there that he discovered the harder, darker sound that he preferred and would go on to champion.

"I was in the shop one Saturday and there were loads of 'stompy' techno records in. They were mad! The likes of 'Poing,' Dye Witness, and the early hard stuff on Bonzai Records. Excellent," he said.

"I decided that day to ditch the breakbeat collection, and concentrate on this mad 'stompy' stuff. The 'stompy' term turned into 'gabber' then there were tons of records getting released on Ruffneck, Knor, Brrr, Rave and so on. I was spending 50 quid a week, most weeks, buying all these new Dutch records. I got a bank loan for some Technics, and done a few tapes, all of the new gabba stuff."

Although Smurf had made his first appearance as a DJ at Walker's nightclub in Newcastle on New Year's Eve in 1991, he got his major break and made his debut at Judgement Day 4 on Thursday 24th March 1994 playing records alongside his hero Lenny Dee. He wore a large sombrero hat with cut out pizzas hanging from it (GTO's *Wet Salami* was his favourite tune at the time – the B side *Eat Zat Pizza* also being popular then) as he pumped out a fast gabber set at 200+ beats per minute.

"I couldn't believe I was on the same night as Lenny Dee, and back in those days it was surprising how many people had never heard of the man. The odd one-off gig followed, including getting barred from the Fubar in Stirling for being too fast, and gigs in the early days at Nosebleed in Rosyth," continued Smurf.

"As the music I was buying and playing got harder and harder, Judgement Day only had one arena at the time, so I hardly ever played there, and put on small events around Newcastle called 'Dolik'ed' to keep the ever-growing hardcore gabba scene alive in the North East."

The excitable and engaging New Yorker Lenny Dee told Don Jenkins of the excellent *Milk the Cow* podcast in an interview that: "I embraced Newcastle big time. I love it up here, man. I love Scotland, the North of England, all of it. Just wow – the kids were maniacs and I was a fucking maniac with them! I was DJing but partying with the people and that whole part of my career up here was just awesome."

Don recalled kids walking around that Judgement Day in hi-vis jackets with 'Lenny Dee is God' written on the back of them, such was the high esteem in which the DJ, producer and boss of Industrial Strength records was held on Tyneside.

Bass Generator was playing again at the Rez 'Let's Wobble' in April 1994 which had PAs from Ultrasonic, the Rhythmic State, the Ascid Project, and Massive. The other DJs in the line-up were CJ Bolland, Stu Allen, DJ Jim, Colin Dale, Music Maker, Gordon Ross, Davie Murray, ZBD, DJ Scott, Matthew Murray and Easygroove.

The Belgian producer and DJ CJ Bolland was actually born in the North East, in Stockton-on-Tees in 1971, before his family moved out to Antwerp when he was three. Bolland was making hits in around 1989 with *Do That Dance* and *Pulse* on the famous label R&S. He also had *Horsepower* on the 1991 Ravesignal 111 EP.

"I started doing my own home productions in the early acid house era and then I met Dave Angel. He really introduced me to the Detroit sound and I was like 'this is amazing.' At the same time there was this really hard four to the floor beat coming from Belgium. So I would mix that sound with my love from Detroit sound and it worked really nice," CJ told Four Four mag. He was uniquely positioned within the Euro techno scene to see it originate and develop as both a sound and a scene.

"It originated everywhere, Germany is definitely hugely influential, but so are Belgium and Holland. I mean, Holland invented Gabber!" he laughed.

"So I don't know who the very first person to ever do a hard techno tune, but what I do know is that it was happening very early on in Belgium, Holland and Germany."

When CJ was signed up by the R&S label in Ghent he was sitting around in the studios and would meet some of the biggest names in what would become hardcore.

"I was just happy to be there and having fun all the time. Don't forget at the time, all these guys coming in, Dave Clarke, Richie Hawtin would drop by, Joey Beltram was there, we were all just young kids, including myself. I remember having Juan Atkins there and that was the first time I was star-struck. I was only 17 at the time and this hero of mine had just walked in. But as for everyone else, we'd just hang out. We were actually writing too many tunes," he laughed.

Bass Generator was back to spin his records again the following month at another Rezerection at Ingliston as the harder stompy sound just got bigger and bigger. PAs from Digital Boy and Dance Overdose were backed up by DJs Westbam, Tanith, Carl Cox, Tin Tin, Daz Sound, Technotrance, GT Sampler, Davey Forbes and DJ Force. MCs XXX and Sneaky Eye were up on the stage with the dancers.

That summer, the massive Rezerection 'Event 2' was the biggest rave held up in Scotland to date with around 16,000 ravers at the huge event which was held outdoors at the Royal Highland Showground on Saturday 30th July 1994. Bass-X and The Rhythmic State performed alongside a star-studded line-up of international DJs such as Carl Cox, Laurent Garnier, Richie Hawtin, Loftgroover, Dark Raver, Paul Elstak, GTO DJ Squad, Robert Leiner, and, of course, Bass Generator. "Shout out to the Newcastle Massive!" "Sound of the DJ giving it to ya!" There were further PAs from the likes of Juggernaut, Ace the Space, The Source, The Rhythmic State, and Human Resource, while Lenny Dee's set at Rez Event 2 was hailed by many as one of the greatest ever – at one of the best raves ever - with people claiming it gave them goosebumps just to think about it.

Lenny grew up in SheepsheadBay in Brooklyn and started out DJing at a local roller disco in his teens. He started making music of his own in 1985 and teamed up with Tommy Musto to produce records under the name Looney Tunes. Once he had come across to play at raves in Britain and across Europe, his style got harder and faster and he launched Industrial Strength records in

1991.

"I had to go the UK to really see what my music did to people," recalled Lenny in one interview. "Frankie Bones and I rocked the NYC underground back in the early days for sure, but it was an uphill struggle."

The prevalent sound was hard acid and techno, only for the headstrong, as the Dutch influence began to really push the tempo upwards. DJ Misjah comes from Numansdorp near Rotterdam in the Netherlands and his Dye Witness classic *Observing the Earth* had been released in 1992. Misjah had been playing about with cassettes, decks and turntables since he was a child, and when he got a simple drum-machine he began to programme drums and start making his own mixes and loops, being very much influenced by electro music and hip hop.

"I was just messing around and just recorded something on a cassette tape. A friend of mine recorded what I was making and Midtown Records heard the tape. They were like, "Yeah, yeah. We want to release it," he told Hard Data. Misjah had some great memories of playing at Hanger 13 in Ayr, and said: "For me, it was never hardcore. There were some tracks that obviously were hardcore, but it was mostly a cooperation with somebody else making some hardcore, happy hardcore. It's not like anything that came out of Rotterdam at that time because there was much harder. I never really cared for what others were making. I always did my own thing and if somebody wanted to call it hardcore, somebody wanted to call it house or whatever. Doesn't matter."

That attitude of not conforming to any particular genre or label and just doing your own thing was a vein that ran through the rave scene to keep the music fresh and innovative, and was an outlook shared by the Prodigy. The band appeared at the Mayfair on Thursday 15th September as a leg on their UK and European tour with Carl Cox, Bass Generator, Technotrance, Connas, Michael Devlin and B-Jam as the supporting DJs.

"We don't conform to any particular style - we have our own sound and people tune in to us," the band's Liam Howlett told the local press ahead of the gig. Music for the Jilted Generation - the jilted generation being 'the generation that have been brought up listening to dance music,' and jilted because 'ten years ago teenagers didn't have to dodge the police to go to parties, they didn't have the Government trying to stop them going out and enjoying themselves.'

"We are successful with a hard style of music that we have built up through a lot of live shows – we've moved on from the hard rave style to more of a hip-hop feel and we've started playing a lot of festivals," he said. Rather ironically, it had been Liam's flat experience at The Event 1 that had changed the band's direction for the album, which would go on to be regarded as an angry anti-establishment classic.

"I'd really had enough of the so-called rave scene as it were. It was so far removed from what we had first got into it for, it had become really cheesy. It had become boring. I can pinpoint the moment to when we played a gig called Rezerection in Scotland, and I remember looking out into the crowd and seeing loads of young kids with glow sticks and I remember thinking 'this just isn't me anymore.' I can't do this anymore," he told Radio 6 music.

Technotrance was the resident DJ at Fubar in Stirling from 1991 and was also involved in a number of PAs that included Suburban Delay, D-Tox, and Hyperact, playing such massive events as Awesome 101 and the Rez. He also made a number of appearances at the Judgement Days and is the boss of the Malevolent Force records label today. His friendship with Bassy G was one of the driving forces of the big connections and interactions between the Scottish and Geordie DJs as they criss-crossed the dark border roads at night playing at clubs and events that embraced the bounce and the bass kick drum.

In the October techno legends Derrick May and Frank de Wulf appeared at the Rezerection at Ingliston. Miss Djax, Dave Angel, Ralphie Dee, Blu Peter and Trevor Rockcliffe were the other DJs while the PAs featured the intensity of Terrortraxx on Tour with Neophyte featuring Body Lotion, D-Tox and Bass Reaction as the gabba sound that was bubbling just below the surface and was about to explode into the North East and Scottish scene.

That was a shame for the likes of Detroit-influenced Geordie techno duo USL, who made a rare brief appearance on a Tyne Tees TV 'yoof' show called Bad Taste in 1995. Sitting on the edge of a sofa with mugs of tea in their hands, they engaged in some nicely deliberate inane banter for the camera.

"Cheers," "You deserve that cup of tea, Chris, after that excellent mix."

"Oh, hi there, you must be the guys from the Bad Taste show." Camera nodding, in the style of *The Word* or *TFI Friday*, the whole *loaded* magazine gonzo production culture that was popular and, to be honest, groundbreaking at the time.

"Why don't we play them a song?" "What, right here, right now?" "Yes," "Yes," "Yessss," before launching into a phenomenal hard techno track in the Tyneside style with their mountains of equipment, keyboards and speakers piled by the closed curtains of a bay window. But having been unable to track down any white labels, releases or PA appearances on flyers by the band, it seems like the USL sounds were victims of bad timing and were sadly destined to remain in the bedrooms rather than rumbling the dancefloors as the bouncier Euro music took centre stage in the region's rave culture. Fellow Geordie Techno, then drum and bass, magician Mick Clarke kept putting out the releases as the noisy continental music dominated the rave scene. He continued on his own long personal journey in synthesiser music with his ambient Dub project *Too Far North* with Johnny Tate, his Techno as *Splendex*, in 1996 and his speed garage *The Nice Phenomenon* in 1998, among so many others. Mick could justifiably be dubbed the 'Godfather of Geordie Techno' and he is still producing today as Iron Blu Music and he has the Intergalactic FM radio show operating out of Den Haag.

The Dutch producers Mental Theo and Charly Lownoise first met when they'd both been DJing at a Mallorca reunion in 1993. Their first single was *Flight to Frankfurt – DJ Fuck* as they set off on their journey producing happy hardcore and gabba – but it was far from plain sailing at the start as their pounding tunes got a mixed reaction on the dance floors. Mental Theo said: "Now it's just about humour and fun for us, but when we started the trend was mainly terror, skulls, hell and thunder. Everything fucked up. Where everyone was cool, we were happy. Believe me, we got a lot of cups, tomatoes, eggs and ashtrays thrown at our heads. Especially ashtrays. We were different from others, but we were happy. And after us everyone suddenly started making that sound."

His musical partner Charly Lownoise told Vice: "I think our music is fun for young and old. I have a 20-year-old cousin who loves our music. When I ask him why, he says it makes him happy because it is energetic. There is already so much rubbish in the world, it is nice when you can find something that connects people."

The unrelenting high-volume tunes from the Netherlands, supplemented by Techno from Italy and Belgium, was like sticking two fingers up at the commercial House super-club scene. While Rotterdam had led the way, Amsterdam was the home of mega-commercial techno duo 2Unlimited who had stormed the European charts with their accessible TV and radio-friendly sound. The stunningly beautiful Anita Doth in her tight PVC gear belting out the big choruses was obviously a massive attraction but the band was actually put together by the Belgian producers Jean-Paul De Coster and Phil Wilde of Bizz Nizz fame in '91 and, like it or not, was a precursor to what would follow from Holland. "We were just having fun with the record and with the lyrics and we thought it was just going to be an album track. Next thing we knew it was released as a single and we thought oh! we'll see what happens – and it became our biggest one," Anita told MTV about 'No Limit' in '93. Amsterdam also came out with its own brand of the happy hardcore bouncy sound to rival Rotterdam by the mid-90s.

"I was out on holiday in the Canaries with Mike and we were sitting on the apartment veranda in the sunshine drinking stubby bottles of lager, listening to the small radio that we'd taken out. We tuned it in through the white noise and the first track we heard on the local station was Technohead's *I wanna be a Hippy*," said Adie.

"It was mad and it was funny, with the bouncy umpah-like pom-pom-pom-pom beat. That was first time we'd really heard of Mokum records. We were still grinning about it when we hit the clubs that night." The record sold 1.3 million CD singles.

Mokum had been around since '93 with strong connections to the Radio 100 pirate station and their *Terrordrome* and *Thunderdome* compilations and would be huge throughout '95-'97 as Dutch hardcore hit a global peak. Technohead were a British outfit, however – comprising of 'the other' Michael Wells of GTO and Tricky Disco fame and his late partner Lee Newman.

"I like to make hard, fast music, but I wouldn't say that I'm a part of the gabba or happy hardcore scene. They are movements that pigeonhole music, and I believe that you have more longevity if you aren't bracketed. In my music I work under a lot of different names and always try and be as original as possible," Michael told Hot Press in an interview around the time, as the record exploded into the charts across Europe. But with the success came that pressure to produce something similar musically and he admitted: "After *Hippy* it was really difficult for me to make other stuff as Technohead. I didn't want to be seen as some kind of performing clown, churning out the hits."

DJ Smurf had started producing his own hard Geordie Gabba records by that time when he got an Amiga 600, then upgraded to a 1200 that he got second-hand from a computer store in the Metro Centre.

"I started messing about learning to produce on a tracker program OctaMED Sound Studio, which was free with a copy of a computer magazine," he said.

"I wasn't part of the original *Geordie Gabba Mafia*, but with starting to produce tracks and lots of DJ gigs, it seemed natural for me to be a part of the GGM. Original member, DJ U.E.P. had his first release in 1997 on The Screwface Label – 'The GGM EP' - then we both had releases on DJ Freak's Hard of Hearing label, entitled 'GGM v. Extrement.' Extrement were a bunch of good lads from Leeds."

"I had two tracks on there, 'Cockrot' and 'Nobrash'; I got the names for the tracks after seeing the words wrote on a bus stop and thought they sounded amusing. Towards the end of that year, I had produced a couple of other tracks that would later be released the following year on the Killout label."

"All of my releases will have some sense of humour in them. In the old days I loved tracks by Rob Gee, Charlie Lownoise & Mental Theo, Euromasters and so on, as they were hard and had funny samples or noises in them. The gabba dance floor was full of mad people, stomping around looking fierce and a hard record with a funny sample, or a strange noise, would bring a slight smile to the hardest of gabberz, which was nice," said Smurf.

"On the music production front, by '99 I'd upgraded to a PC, but was still producing music on the PC version of OctaMED soundstudio. I had two vinyl releases that year, the most famous being the 'NewcastleAustralia (Bloody

Fist) v Newcastle England (GGM)' EP on Strike Records. This featured the 'Fuck Me Geordie' track. The track has samples from a TV series called 'Our Friends in The North'. The '*I am not mental*' shouty parts being the most recognisable. Weirdly, the first bar of the track (8 beats) was missing from the start of the pressing on the vinyl. Prior to this release coming out, all communication between me and Mark N @ Bloody Fist, was done by a fax machine," smiled Smurf.

"The second release was on a double album compiled by DJ Freak: 'Kill Out Compilation vol 2: Dirty and Sick Hardcore.' Two tracks were on here; 'Get Off Your Backside' (which also had samples from 'Our Friends in The North') and 'Smurf Holio,' which was full of Beavis & Butthead samples."

"The tracks were recorded to a D.A.T. tape direct from the Amiga, so the quality of these tracks was pretty low, as they were produced on the Amiga in 16-bits. There wasn't any VST's back then, so no EQ'ing, compression or mastering."

Such technical data was probably far from Smurf's mind just three nights before Christmas in 1994, the lights twinkling in Fenwick's window on Northumberland Street as small groups of ravers made their way through the town to the event. Judgement Day VI had moved back bang into the city centre into the Newcastle University Student's Union opposite the Haymarket.

"Judgement Day was great, playing in front of a home crowd, but there was a slight tendency to get a bit wasted there with the free alcohol backstage. But that was left to after a set, which was usually early!" said DJ Smurf.

"There were some great times at Judgement Day. One party was on a huge ship on the Tyne in Newcastle. A small room was hired for Bassy G's birthday, and Lenny Dee and myself played. A big PA system was hired and the vibrations of the music caused half the roof to come down. They won't let us have another party there!" he laughed.

"The gabba room at Judgement Day was crazy. It used to be in a tiny little room, with the only light being a strobe and a light for the DJs. From it opening its doors at 6pm, the music was a constant 250bpm+ right the way through till 1am. DJ Tron came over from the USA and he loved it. He said it was great playing such fucked-up fast music to people and seeing them really get into it. The room was ram-packed from start to finish and it eventually got moved into a bigger room."

The fierce and fast Rezerection 'Awakening of '95' all-nighter at Ingliston on the 31st December provided another platform for the dark banging hardcore to hypnotise with DJs Lenny Dee, Paul Elstak, Gizmo, Tin Tin, Tom Wilson, Scott Brown, Mikey B, Marie-Chantal and Davie Forbes all cranking up the volume and the BPM on the stabs and bass drum kicks to the delight of the stomping, stamping crowd. The PAs were provided by Q-Tex, The Rhythmic State, Bass X, NeuroTek, Danastak, and Hyper-Act while the MCs were Cyclone, Double Zero, Crime, XXX and Gavsie.

The hypersonic heavier sound was going stratospheric as the relentless rushes brought about an aggressively joyous euphoria that swept over the huge, packed, hot and sweaty space. But you had to wonder how much heavier it could go.

6

Rockshots

Nightclubs in the 1980s were pretty shit. Just look back at old episodes of the *Hitman & Her* to see glaikey blokes in ill-fitting suits that look like they've just walked out of an office pulling some wooden moves and trying to look cool. Imagine something like the cast of the *Wolf of Wall Street* on a gleaming fresh dance floor with twirling lights, only without the Quaaludes, or the fun, and you'll get the idea. Shirts and ties, braces, and populist chart music. At least Michaela Strachan was easy on the eye, bopping off from her piece to camera in her tight cycling shorts and funky hats.

That all started to change towards the end of the decade in Newcastle as the likes of Maceys, Madisons, Walker's and Manhattans began to play the sounds of Hip House, House and '70s Funk to a hipper crowd, tunes like Lord KCB *I'm Housing It*, Mike Dunn *Born This Way*, DJ Bizzy B, the hypnotic repetition and uplifting pianos in 49s *Touch Me* or even Inner City's *Good Life*.

"The back room at Balmbras was amazing and played Chicago house and acid house – Joe Smooth *Promised Land*, Candy Statten *You've got the Love*, Lidell Townsell *Get the hole, get the hole*, Maurice Joshua *I've Got A Big Dick*, Jolly Roger *Acid Man*, Marshall Jefferson... on Tuesday nights we went around Madisons, Walker's and Tux2 which was more the likes of Eric B and Rakim, Public Enemy, Housey hip hop, which is where all the jazzy dancing came in – holding a foot up and jumping through it. Wednesday nights were at Rockshots," said Sassenach.

The predominantly gay club played Hi-NRG and early Chicago House loaded with samples...Jack to the Sound of the Underground, Maurice *Get into the Dance*, the Whoo! Yeah! sound that got into so many records then, before putting on Acid House nights around the October of '88. The then club secretary told the local press that: "It's a great atmosphere, people love the music, and they all come along in their Smiley T-shirts and denim jeans, or spotty dresses and shirts – and most of them are drinking Lucozade at the moment." The management were naively adamant that no drugs were involved and said they had 'surveillance cameras in the club to watch for drug taking.' The prevailing attitude in the regional press was that Acid House and electronic dance music was 'just a craze' that they felt would be 'over by Christmas.'

As the music reverberated around the venue, Ian clambered up on the stage and started dancing wildly. Unfortunately, the dry ice machine went off around the same time and as he bopped along in his red Kickers and mustard-coloured top with a wide grin, he fell off the end and disappeared.

"All that was left on the stage was my cricket hat, which had fallen off when I fell. As I rolled around in the darkness among the legs I didn't have a clue where I was!" he laughed.

With a big square brick entrance with rails and steps leading up to the doors of the former cinema building on Waterloo Street, Rockshots had something of a glamorous feel, like going into the faded chic of one of the famous New York discos of the '70s, and was famous for its state-of-the-art light-shows and powerful sound system.

The potential for violence on a night out around Newcastle at that time was ever-present, so Sassenach was carrying a cut-throat razor tucked in his boots or strapped on his shoulder until one Wednesday night in Rockshots in late '88 when one of his friends in the Gremlins handed him a little white pill called a Fantasia. After dancing frenetically all night with the chemical stench of poppers ever present, he made his way up the sparkling streets in the still freshness and stood in a top-floor flat up the West End entranced as he looked out from the window at the lights of the city slowly swirling around and around in the dark. MDMA had landed in Newcastle.

The bother didn't disappear overnight though and in May 1989 there was a gangland-style shooting outside a packed Manhattans nightclub. Two well-known doormen were the intended victims of a ski-masked shooter with a pump-action shotgun and his two accomplices. Another club doorman at Tuxedo Junction had his face slashed with a craft knife by a 31-year-old Wallsend man also that month. He'd had been barred from Tux2 just days earlier as staff suspected he was dealing ecstasy and had kicked him out. He told the doorman that he was as good as dead, threatened to blow his legs off and launched a metal pole at him like a javelin before returning with the blade to launch his attack on the 48-year-old victim. The attacker claimed he'd taken four ecstasy tablets on the night of the assault and was jailed for four years.

One of the first big early seizures of the drug on Tyneside happened in November '89 when a courier from West Denton was lifted at the Gallowgate bus station after travelling up from London with 1,000 pills in a rucksack. The courier claimed that he owed dealers money and was told at a rave at Hayton Castle that the debt had been taken over by someone else. He was given a package of cash and told to go down to The Smoke and exchange it for another package from a passing car. The deal had gone smoothly but the police had been tipped off and were waiting when he stepped off the coach. The 24-year-old was sentenced to 2 years for possession of a Class A drug with intent to supply.

A month earlier an unemployed 25-year-old Newcastle man was jailed for 15 months after being caught with over 100 ecstasy tablets rolled up in a sports sock and £500 cash. The prosecutor claimed that 'ecstasy had only recently appeared in the Tyneside area,' however, a 24-year-old North Kenton woman, who was married into a well-known underworld family, had been caught in possession of cannabis resin and 3 ecstasy tablets on a visit to Durham jail as early as that April, and in May another 25-year-old Newcastle man was charged with intent to supply after being caught in possession of £3,000 worth of ecstasy pills.

One of the first seizures of the drug in a club in the area happened in early December '89 when drug squad officers searched Bentleys in the Cloth

Market in Newcastle just after midnight on a Friday night and discovered cannabis resin, LSD and ecstasy tablets on the premises, and five nights before Christmas a suspected ecstasy factory on Tyneside was busted. Drug squad officers searched two houses in Gosforth and Jesmond, and a flat and business premises in Newcastle. They seized lab equipment and substances which were sent off to the Home Office forensic labs for testing. Regional Crime Squad and Serious Crime Squad were also involved in the raids. Four men, all from Newcastle, were arrested. "Three are to face a charge of conspiracy to produce the controlled drug Ecstasy. One has been bailed pending further enquiries," said a Det. Insp. from Northumbria Drugs Squad.

In the following 12 months 498 people were arrested for possession of drugs including heroin, cannabis, ecstasy, amphetamines, LSD and cocaine – a rise of 41% on the previous year – as several other pubs on Tyneside and Wearside were targeted by police. They warned that 'the participation of prominent criminals in the sale and supply of controlled drugs continues and there are indications that some are combining their resources to formulate highly effective distribution ventures,' which obviously meant that the availability in the nightclubs was massively increased.

Being a gay club, in the early days Rockshots wasn't that easy to get into. One Saturday night Ian was knocked on his arse by a well-known doorman at the club and on another Saturday evening Mike, Adie and the boss, long blonde hair, immaculately decked out in Gaultier and some of Milan's finest, were pulled up by the doormen at the top of the stairs.

"You're not going in lads, not tonight."

"Why the fuck not?"

"Look, I know for a fact you're not gay."

"He is, I've had him," quipped one fella going into through the doors behind, pointing at the boss. Unwise move, thought Adie, gearing up for what he thought would be the inevitable fist fight that followed.

"You couldn't afford me," replied the boss coolly, diffusing the situation.

"Get yourselves away down to club Afrika." Into a car and the tape playing early bleep techno as the street lights flash over the bonnet and through the windows driving around the city looking for action.

They certainly weren't the only ones that had been 'sent away down to club Afrika' and DJs Scott (Bradford) and Scooby, who had been running their Rebellion nights on a Friday at Rockshots that had championed piano-driven Italian House for a good couple of years, found themselves looking for a new home for their sound as hardcore became a dominant force in the city. Scott and Scooby went to club Afrika and launched their legendary Shindig house nights on a Friday and Saturday as a counterpoise for those having to make their way down to Middlesbrough and the Havana, then later the Arena, for House music on a weekend. But club Afrika closed its doors suddenly without warning in April 1993, and the Shindigs moved on to Bliss, where the duo teamed up Back To Basics on occasions with the likes of Alistair Whitehead, Slam, Jon Pleased Wimmin and Graeme Park appearing at their hugely popular Thursday nights. Shindig then moved to the Riverside where they were bringing in the likes of EFX and Digit from San Francisco, and big-name DJs Graeme Park, Sasha, Andrew Weatherall and Jeremy Healy in the spring of 1994.

"Rockshots is a jumble of memories for me," said Shirley.

"I started going there when it was still a mostly gay club. There was a stage in the back of the dance floor where the kids from the town were and then we would be in the high booth next to the dance floor - I took my first acid in there, a Smiley I think. Madonna's *Vogue* was playing and a man in leather was crawling across the floor like a cat. Sally would DJ playing Hi-NRG: 'It's your pal mega Sal at Rockshots' and Black Box *Ride on Time, Pump up the Jam* mixed in with *Sylvester* and *Born to be Alive*. God - I must have been 16 or 17!" she recalled with a beaming smile.

"Then as time went on it got more popular with everyone and we'd be there raving, absolutely packed out - I want to say Scooby DJ'd some nights. Teagan was pregnant but we'd still be out, carefully manoeuvring through the crowd - me tripping and on speed and her straight tells you how much love was there for the music. The back room where you could get food was packed too then (not for food) and we'd be dancing away in the crush of people."

"Off to the loo for a line - my friend May had speed in there for the first time, and was all: 'What's it like, am I going to be OK?' We were like: 'Of course, we'll look after you, you'll be fine' and of course she was, we really cared for each and made sure all our friends were fine and having a good time wherever we were."

The golden rave years in Rockshots were well under way by early 1991 with the likes of DJ Rod, DJ Marky, DJ Tosh and MC Buzz putting on a Saturday night 'Rave to the Grave' event that ran from 8-2.30am with guests DJ Morris and MC Tone. The nights were packed out and maintained their huge popularity throughout the year and the next with events every Friday in two rooms with the regulars DJs Tosh, Diane, Destroy and T.N.T. and MCs Buzz, Kix, Unknown and Del appearing in the Main Hall and Shaun Fearon and Steve Arrowsmith in the Back Room (The Hug Club). Shaun Fearon (MC Buzz), along with his mate Davey S, was largely responsible for bringing the early rave/dance scene to Newcastle, which exploded in the club.

"Davey use to come to our events down the 'Boro and booked us to come up this end in about '88/89. I didn't just DJ and MC, I used to organise them. I organised the first one with Davey S at Rockshots and the rest is history. However, we were doing different places up Gateshead and Newcastle before then. We use to do the Pelaw ballroom, but outgrew that and that's why we went to Rockshots, and before that we used to do events at the Blackfriars Hall in Byker and few other places," said Shaun.

He was part of the *Underground Promotions* crew with mates from his home-town, Middlesbrough, and Gateshead and Newcastle that by the September of '90 were holding fortnightly 7pm-12 midnight raves at the Broadway Ballroom, the distinctive old Grand Cinema building, with around 500 packed in and a couple of hundred more unlucky punters getting turned away at the door as it was full. This success led to the approach to Rockshots to hold a monthly 'Euphoria' event in the club on a Saturday night, where they were keen to maintain the Underground 'street' vibe. In the July of 1990 MC Buzz, with Manchester hip-hoppers Dee Lawal & Cool T and GFX had played an early event at the Riverside in Newcastle on a Sunday night.

"I started DJing in 1989 in a club in Middlesbrough called Blaises on a Friday night and did the illegal parties at the Greenway after hours on Saturday nights with MC Buzz to form 'The Good Peoples Ball' where we went on to do clubs and gigs in the North East in 1990 before settling in at Rockshots," said DJ Tosh.

"We did once a month events to start with, then changed to every Friday due to popular demand. I also did guest slots at local clubs - Meltdown in Middlesbrough, the Eclipse in Stockton, After Dark in Sunderland, Energi House in Newcastle and the Venue in Spennymoor before hanging my headphones up from the club scene in 1996."

Former Philmores DJ David Strangeways recalled the explosion in the rave scene around Saltburn and across Teesside by 1989 and told the local press: "I DJ'd in barns in Warrenby and all over. I remember parties in Redcar in a kung-fu joint above a garage. It was a crazy time really."

By capturing that outlaw warehouse experience and authentically bringing both it and the crowd that they'd built up with them into a formal city centre nightclub setting, Buzz and Tosh, along with the likes of Andy Baxter, were also generating street hype around their early 'Powa Sound Session' Saturday nights. It hadn't been manufactured and was an organic growth in the music from bedroom mixers and illegal settings into the clubs, much as what happened shortly after with the Stanley crew and the Eclipse in Stockton. There was also plenty of competition between the clubs, and the Rockshots crowd were pleased to poach DJ Destroy from the Eclipse.

"Rockshots on a Thursday was mint and had some of the best House DJ's on from all over. The amount of times we were sat in the pub and someone would come up with the bright idea of getting the last bus through was unbelievable. Buzz was canny on a Thursday as well," recalled Tom.

"Rockshots was always the death of me, sniffing poppers and having blackouts most of the night. That and Shindig were proper sweat pits," said Smiler, who also remembered being followed around the club by a gay man that had gone to kiss him one evening. The club retained a high number of homosexual clientele on nights that were nominally 'straight' which gave the place an atmosphere of tolerance and a hedonistic sexual cool. But it could, at times, still retain the power to shock and test the limits of your Balearic-inspired decadence and nonchalant exterior.

"On another occasion, when the lights came on at the end, there were six blokes with their cocks out stood next to me - not the best feeling when you were off your face," he grimaced.

The other main nightclub that was instrumental in bringing the hardcore rave sound to Tyneside on a weekly basis was Walker's. The club had opened in 1984 on the site of the famous old La Dolce Vita on Low Friars Street, just around the corner from the Mayfair, and by the December of 1990 was promising '5 hours of non-stop house/rave/techno' from Bass Generator - DJ Guy from Trax - Mista C and guests. GFX played a live PA at a Spektrum night at Walkers in February '91 and a typical Thursday night that year saw Hardware Records running an event across two floors with live PAs from PSI Division and Ecstasy Club. The first floor DJs playing hardcore were Bass Generator, Smokey Joe and Massive C (from the PSI) while Floor 2 featured Happy House from S.L.P., Craig 'E' Mac and Blasta, the heavy smell of Vicks hitting you as soon as you got into the place.

But Walker's received some negative headlines and press in the May of '91 when there was a petrol bomb attack on the club. The bombs were thrown at both the front and back doors of the packed venue on a Sunday morning at around 1.25am. The club was evacuated and a number of fights and scuffles broke out on the street outside as five fire engines were rushed to the scene. Police, including dog handlers, were dispatched to control the disorder and one man had his jaw broken as the fighting spilled into Clayton Street and Westgate Road. The back door suffered the worst damage, being burnt and charred from the flames, but nobody was seriously hurt. There had been a gas bomb attack on the nearby Mayfair earlier in the year, which had exploded across the front doors and left them blackened and scorched.

A spokesman for Northumbria Police said of the Walker's attack that: "Potentially this could have been a very hazardous and life-threatening incident indeed. This was a two-storey nightclub full of young people enjoying themselves. ...fortunately, the only difficulty was getting the crowds, who were milling around outside, dispersed quickly and safely."

The PSI Division were back at Walker's in June with T-99 and Destroy, Andy Baxter, M. Jack and Nick & Temple at an Exposure night and on Friday 23rd August the Havana crew rocked the club with Hooligan X, Zero B, Collin

Patterson and MC Lee, Simon Gibb, Newcastle DJs Andy Baxter and Andy Lee being joined behind the decks by top London stars Darren Price, Stacy Tough and Simon Doward.

Bass Generator was a regular resident DJ at Walker's and on the 20th September, 1991, he was joined on the decks at the 'Outrage Spiritual Storm' night by Sasha, Fabio, Grooverider, Swan-E, Fingers, Woodstock, Eastie, Total Recall, Andy Baxter, and Howie with MCs Screechi D and Ron Jon, where records like Cubic 22's *Night in Motion*, M-D-Emm's *Get Down* and Praga Khan's *Injected with a Poison* would bring huge roars of recognition and absolute pandemonium. Shades of Rhythm and Unique 3 also played lived PAs at the 'Outrage' Friday nights.

Paul 'Gazza' Gascoigne was famously knocked out in the club in the October of '91 and Walker's was fined £20,000 for packing 1,117 people into the 600-capacity venue that December. One person collapsed of heat exhaustion as the heaving dance floor resembled something more like a football terrace with people literally swaying shoulder to shoulder as the warped sounds pulsed around the dark space that was drenched and dripping with sweat.

Eris started going to Walker's when she was just 16, though she admits that the thought of her own daughter going to clubs at that age freezes her blood stone cold. She was swept up by the swirling nights and heavy bass vibrations rumbling around the room, shaking her long dark hair off her face with eyes blackened by smudged liner, stifled by the heat and intensity inside the venue.

"It was quite literally the most exciting thing in the world to me. All week would revolve around planning for the evening, either a Thursday or a weekend night, if I remember correctly. Myself and my friend would save money and do chores all week just so we could go to the club and, usually, drop some acid," she said, the weird hallucinations and time-lag movements of other clubbers chopped up by a strobe as they grooved in their own little space, packed tight in the blackness.

"Suddenly, I wanted to dance all the time. I loved it. I didn't care how I looked and no one else did either. It was all about enjoying the music and losing yourself in the rhythm and the atmosphere."

"Once we had planned how we'd get there, we really didn't care how we were going to get back. We'd usually meet up with other friends we knew there and would, inevitably, bum a lift home from someone. We had no fear though. We were so caught up in the excitement of the time that we would have slept on a park bench afterwards if we couldn't get home – which I did myself a few times."

"I always remember Walker's as being very dark, very loud, very busy with water, probably sweat, condensed and dripping from the ceiling. Dancers would get soaking wet but no one cared. This wasn't a time to be worried about make-up or hair, it was all about the feeling and the experience. Other nightclubs we frequented included Rockshots, The Tunnel - where I have a memory of dancing all night on a massive speaker wearing a swimming costume - and The Blue Monkey, although I think Walker's was always my favourite."

The club was closed in the February of 1992 for a number of incidences of serious disorder and violence, including a fatal stabbing in November '91. Newcastle was described as a 'Wild-West town where 80 percent of young men were armed with knifes and some carried guns' at the subsequent murder trial at Leeds Crown Court.

Although Absolute Leisure took over Walker's and renamed it Planet Earth in 1993, it never really regained the legendary status and popularity that it had enjoyed in the early '90s and it was closed permanently in 2002 with luxury flats being built on the site. Another fatal stabbing at Liberty's nightclub in Birtley, the victim having a blade plunged into him eight times in the December of '91, highlighted just some of the gangland influence that was becoming increasingly high-profile on the North-East's lucrative nightlife market. The violent downmarket image that the hardcore scene was being perceived by in the media by May 1992 saw DJ Tommy Caulker of the Bigbird crew state in the local press that: 'They're completely missing the point with druggies taking over the whole thing which has inevitably led to violence and gangster intervention – just as in 1989 in Edinburgh."

Tommy was bringing in his monthly Dance Expo '92 nights at Rockshots and damned hardcore, continuing: "It's like the Emperors' new clothes situation now where young people feel they have to be drugged out of their heads and all they want are records with loads of bleeps to say it was a really good night."

"They don't realise there's loads of great new dance music coming out which has a lot more soul – the rest of the country has now caught on to the new stuff and realise there's a lot more to it than the commercialised hardcore stuff but the North-East as usual is way behind."

By the following month Surfers in Tynemouth had started their Subculture nights which promised to 'lock the doors on hardcore and bring in the sounds of summer' featuring the Rockshots crew DJ Tosh and MC Buzz, Destroy and DJ Diane. They had also brought up Andy Carroll from Liverpool and DJs Houseman and TC from London to Rockshots as their club nights continued to evolve. Andy Carroll was a resident at the legendary Quadrant Park in Bootle and went on to become one of the founders of Cream.

DJ Nick Detnon had been down in London but came back up to Tyneside where he hosted and played at a one-off *Lost at Sea* night on the Tuxedo Royale boat in the August of '92 with DJs Dave Seaman, D.O.P, Scooby, Blasta and Scott Bradford, and he claimed then that hardcore was 'a limited genre that had gone as far as it could go.'

"There's not a lot more you can do with it because there's only X amount of breakbeats that they use in the records and X amount of noises that they can get out of a keyboard, so people have reached saturation point in the music," he said.

"I've found that they've either diversified into progressive house or gone into stomping up-tempo Belgian Techno which is harder."

Ironically, by the July of '93, the boat was featuring hardcore on Friday nights as the Logic Sound System crew – Rod Richardson, Mark Dawson, MC Poetry, DJ Roppa and Surf-E – brought their sound up from Brannigans in Houghton-Le-Spring for the *Stowaway Club* and their first night featured a live PA from Odessy 2, while Madison's were holding *Unity – Increase the Peace* nights featuring their house DJs such as Mason, Monty, Cooper, X.P.R.E.S., Flashback, Ashes and Pike.

Detnon had continued: "There is a bad element at a lot of the big raves up here and there's a lot of muggings going on and that's obviously why they (the boat) were careful about venturing into dance events before...it is vital for club goers in Newcastle that this breakthrough has been made."

Local DJs Scott, Scooby and Huey were asked by the local press the following month why they felt that the North-East's electronic music scene wasn't making an impact nationally when others from the likes of Liverpool, Manchester and London were becoming household names. Scott, who was involved in the 'Mango' House nights running then at the Mayfair, said: "The North-East has got such a bad name for itself up till now for the clubs that have been going on. There are no clubs that are willing to give their DJs a chance to prove themselves, they either want chart music or they want hardcore, and even then there are only a couple who play hardcore. And the people who are little bit different have got nowhere to go, they've got to travel to Middlesbrough. The Arena is one of the biggest clubs around at the minute and we went down to Back to Basics in Leeds and it's no different to what we are doing. We could do exactly the same sort of thing up here. All we do around here is import DJs from London who play the same music when they don't need to. Look at Andy Baxter, he's deserted Newcastle, now he's down in Middlesbrough all the time. No-one will get up off their backsides and do anything, they would rather travel somewhere else just because it's the trendy thing to do."

His long-term musical partner and collaborator Scooby said there had been 'a massive change in the music style up here.' "When you stand in Trax, people who used to come in and buy hardcore are buying different types of music. You can see though that people are going far afield because they are sick of Newcastle and the way it is and the people that are going in the clubs, you know the charver in a shell suit. No-one is prepared to change and do something different. So it won't change until promoters at the bigger clubs realise that they have to get attention and people from, say, Leeds to come here for a club."

DJ Huey, whose Back to Rhythm nights at the Arena with MC Lee were going down a storm with NE clubbers, added: "It's a self-consummating society up here, I've found. You give someone your hand to get the chains around and they chop it off. I think it's the mentality of the people up here and their attitude. DJing was a sound profession in the first leisure club, long before 1989, long before rave DJs, now there are guys who walk around with a portable phone. He's always been a brickie or something but he plays records. But when people get that attitude, that it is work, that you do get up in the morning and you do conduct your business, then the work will be there. But most people are just like 'yes, well, it's a good excuse to do something. I couldn't be bothered to stay at school so I'll be a DJ.' It's the same with the clubs, it's a mentality. They know the score, but they're winding people up. It's down to the gangsters combined with the mentality and requirements of the people. And people don't need what they require. The demand is growing for the new stuff, but it just turns out to be a tailor-made prefabricated solution which is exactly what all the other ones in other towns are anyway. So essentially it will never catch up with its tail. I've thought about this before. I regard myself as a Northerner, I don't restrict my personal perspective to one back street. To that end Newcastle is a self-consummating society."

Bringing up big name DJs from London was a formula that had worked, however, and the queues ran around the block, literally closing off the street, when Danny Rampling came up from the capital to play at Rockshots in October '92 and again in '93.

"I have much love for Newcastle and visa versa - love the energy and vibe and realness of the Geordies," said the legendary producer, club owner and DJ, who is credited with launching Acid House into the UK after returning from a holiday in Ibiza in 1987 and bringing the Balearic vibe back when he opened *Shoom*, which ran for three years.

A new night was introduced on a Saturday in the club at the time with *Sugar & Spice* being started up by the Petrucci brothers, who owned the Tucci clothes shops, and Andrew Horsfield. They also complained that disillusioned Newcastle clubbers were having to travel miles to Leeds or Middlesbrough for a decent night out and were attempting to rectify it as the city nightlife reached something of a crossroads.

"Newcastle is one of the biggest cities in the country but it's got a dance scene of about 100 people because there are no decent clubs. Saturday night is the real key to it," Giancarlo Petrucci told the local press.

"It's going to be mellow, it's not going to be full of drugs and nutters. If I go to a rave now, I'm looking over my shoulder every two minutes. There's loads of muggings at places and it isn't funny anymore, it's just pathetic."

"You can go to and have a laugh in Rockshots, everyone knows that it is not a heavy club. The club itself has loads of atmosphere because it is small and the way it's done out, and it's got a kicking sound system that never distorts," he said.

Andrew Horsfield reckoned that there was nowhere decent to go on a weekend at that people had to travel at least 40 miles to 'let their hair down and have a good time.'

"We want to create a club where people can have a really good time on the doorstep at least once a month, with good dance music right across the spectrum in the way Walkers used to be two or three years ago. A night shouldn't just go for one kind of music, it should be everything."

"Rockshots has got that little room that we also want to build up with Garage, Soul Hip Hop, etc. I hope that in two- or three-months time people will be coming to the club to spend the night in there," he said.

Producer Mark Richardson from Washington in Tyne & Wear also began a new label, Hypa, in 1993 and released his own hard acid trance track *Arabic* under his artist name the Producer in the January. Further releases followed including Shindig's *Spunky Manmaba*, Hazi Hazi *Alien Temple*, Interlect 3000 *Future*, Habuba *Life Line*, Mabyus *Teknification* and *Miracle of Life* and Coloured Vision *Violet Rain* as the North-East continued to make its own music to be spun on the turntables in the clubs.

Scott Bradford and Scooby also teamed up with Mick Clarke from SR2 to release the techno track *D'addario* as Alicante on Hardware Records and the same label put out the progressive house sounds of *Baby Right/Viva* from Static Experience, who were Alun Peter Young and the Little Rascal.

Despite the innovation, the North-East generally still failed to make a big impact on electronic music on a national level and it remained very much entrenched in the underground and club scene, where DJ Huey started up his Kinky Disco Friday nights at Scirrocos in Washington. The policy at the club was for 'hot, horny House, gorgeous groovy Garage and illicit kinky Disco,' according to the flyers. But Tyneside's nightlife was dealt a massive blow that October when a licence to open a new 3,000 capacity venue based on London's Ministry of Sound complex in a factory unit on the Hawk's Road Gateshead East Industrial Estate was turned down. Hillstone Entertainments from the capital wanted to offer a dance floor, lounge, and cinema from 11pm-9am on Fridays and Saturdays.

"It will be modelled on our club in London, which has an excellent reputation," David Lawrence of the company said. "We will play serious music for dancing – not rave music. There will be no queuing outside, only inside the club. Security will be very tight. It will be as hard getting into the club as boarding an American jet." The police strongly opposed the plans and said it would act as a 'magnet for drug dealers.'

An attempt was made to recapture the old warehouse atmosphere in early 1994 when the Energi House nights were started up down on the Quayside in a 1,500-capacity warehouse at Forth Banks, but it soon fell foul of council officials and police. 100 ravers who turned up for an all-nighter in February were turned away from what was deemed an illegal warehouse party at the venue when the council was granted an injunction to stop the £10 a head event.

Energi House was another organisation that had attempted to exploit the members-only loophole and promoter Rob Walker said: "The music is garage and soul-oriented and everybody comes for a good time. We've already held two all-nighters and will continue to do so."

Energi House was raided by over 100 police officers in March and the future of the club was put in doubt as they seized cannabis, amphetamines and wobbly eggs and looked to strip the organisers of an entertainments licence. However, The Warehouse Concept ran every Saturday in June with Diane, Tosh, Carlos, and T.N.T. appearing regularly and a PA from MRX (*Feel So Real*) at one of the events.

World Headquarters opened up on Marlborough Crescent in May 1994, the same month that Rockshots was refused the renewal of an entertainments licence by magistrates on the recommendation of Northumbria Police, who listed 41 incidents in and around the club. The Police were still trying to close down Rockshots that November by trying to prove that the club boss was unfit to run it. They gave court accounts of drug use and immoral acts at the venue and a detective said he'd been offered ecstasy and cannabis in the club. The court also heard that the club stayed open after hours, and that the taps had been turned off in the toilets. It seemed that the Law was determined to stop the people dancing – and with the backing of the controversial Criminal Justice & Public Order Act, they were being guided by the very corridors of power in Downing Street.

Around 50,000 protestors had marched and raved against the Bill in Trafalgar Square that summer. Police in black riot gear with helmets, shields and batons moved to intimidate and mounted officers on horseback were dispatched onto the streets as the gates of Downing Street were shook by crowds. Mobile Sound systems pumped electronic beats of all varieties out of the backs of trucks as shirtless kids with dreadlocks grooved their way down the road holding placards and blowing whistles.

But it was a long way away from the back streets of Newcastle, where the police also raided the Riverside in November '94. Undercover officers had spent weeks dancing alongside unsuspecting clubbers when they put the nightspot under surveillance in Operation Quasar. Ecstasy and amphetamines with a street value of £3,000 were seized and 33 people were held after being told to stand with their hands on their heads as they were searched. It wasn't just the clubs where raves were taking place and a pub in Wallsend that had been 'specially reinforced' for an all-night party was raided a month earlier. 12 men were arrested and 6 charged with drugs offences (LSD and cannabis), obstructing the police and possession of an offensive weapon. On another evening, a man had been at an illegal rave in the same pub and was picked up in the city centre brandishing a sword.

A 34-year-old Northumberland man was also arrested by Spanish police for possession of a large amount of cannabis in a raid on a villa in the Costa del Sol that week, while a series of busts for the class C drug had taken place at homes throughout the region. Earlier in the year four men had been charged at Sunderland magistrates with importing Eve (MDEA), amphetamines and ecstasy in the North East's then biggest drugs seizure to date, and two men were pulled over by the Cleveland drug squad on the A19 and MDMA worth £150,000 was captured. Another £12,000 worth of ecstasy pills were captured in a raid on a Cramlington house in October 1995. The following month a kilo of amphetamines was recovered from a garage in Murton as a huge wave of designer drugs flooded the region.

Despite the controversy surrounding the club, Rockshots II was re-opened in November '95. The club might be back, but Hardware Records was no more by then; the electronic squelches, bleeps and bass lines of hard Geordie Techno had crashed and burned. The North East's first electronic dance label, which was highly instrumental in starting off the Rezerections in Newcastle, was gone.

Geordie Techno didn't die, however, and is still being produced today by the likes of John Rowe who runs his labels Hypnohouse Trax and the acid Hypnotek909. John played in numerous bands and took a music technology course in the late '90s, which led to a string of hard acid techno releases by the mid '00s. He regularly performs and DJs at festivals, raves and clubs and his music can be heard pulsing and throbbing around dance floors all over the world. Darkmode is another techno and electro artist from Newcastle who keeps the Geordie sound alive with his Biotech Recordings label, which was founded in 2011. Otherwise known as Davie Dodds, Darkmode's first release was *The Data EP* on Testin Out Records in 2005 and he's gone on to make a big name for himself playing at a wide range of parties, raves and festivals in the UK, as well as his producing. His tracks such as *Fields of Calantha* and *2049* wouldn't have sounded out of place in a warehouse rave in 1990 – but Davie is from another generation inspired by the Detroit sound all over again.

"I was too young to go to raves in Newcastle in the early '90s, although I did listen to the music and the mix tapes from the raves in those days. I can't remember Hardware Records so I can't say they had an influence on me," he said.

LAX (LaptopAcidExperience) is another Geordie producer from Whitley Bay 'still inspired by the DIY philosophy of early Chicago and Detroit producers (where the limitations of cheap machines defined house and techno)' who started out in the early '90s after being inspired by the Rezerections. His experimentations with low cost syths, drum machines and computer record-ing have led to a string of releases from *Dumpsville* in 2007 to the old skool inspired *Acid Terrorist* in 2016. He also releases as Hotface, weaving strange little apocalyptic visions into his EPs ranging from 'acid-fused housey techno' to 'spacey Ghetto house,' while Paul Lancaster took his lead from the acid house and techno sounds that he heard on Wear FM back in the early '90s. The old scene continues to have an impact on his Progressive house tunes such as *Bad Girl* and *Night Vision*. The times change, the clubs change, but the music goes on.

7

Club Havana

Sleeping down on the beach, the sea rolls in and crashes into the shore with a comforting rhythm to compliment the House music that drifts up on the hot air from the distant clubs in town. The sand is sometimes overwhelming as you lie there, feeling it run through your fingers, getting lost in its sugary softness, amazed by the vastness of the black night sky that engulfs the island as oppressively as the blazing sun through the day. And the sea, warm as a womb, constantly rushing in and whispering to the sand with a brown, shimmering coastline off in the distance. You feel very isolated and far from home.

Wandering back into town and watching the stoned, blissed-up, hugging clubbers turned out of sweaty venues with bright and wide eyes beaming from their tanned faces, the chemicals and loud electronic tunes still boring deep into their minds. Rounded clay-red and black volcanic hills rising ominously past the shady green palms, dated buses blowing up dust as they carry holidaymakers in Union Jack shorts to their holiday complexes further along the coast. Looking on in the oppressive strength-sapping heat at passing beat-up blue Opel Corsa Joys from a bar with a flashing green neon shamrock sign, working on the tan, supping an ice-cold bottled beer and lifting your dark glasses trying to remember just who the fuck you are. The Middlesbrough lads who left the industrial Teesside of steel works, furnaces and ICI factories behind to go clubbing on the Spanish islands of Tenerife and

Ibiza during 1987 and 1988 were some of the real innovators of the North-East rave scene and they brought that Balearic and Canarian vibe back with them from places such as *Paradise Lost, Bananas, Amnesia* and *Pacha.* Although the White Isle has retained the legendary status and reputation, probably from its affiliation with the big London DJs and media, in the North-East at least Tenerife was just as big an influence on the electronic dance culture. Perhaps even more so, as DJ Collin Patterson was a major player in bringing the sound to the area when he jetted back across from the island to provide the professional expertise and music to get the club Havana and Butterloggie rave projects really up and going.

"The island had a lot to do with the start of the North East rave scene, I think, as I discovered when I played at Butterloggie and then the Havana as I found out that the tapes I had been giving to Lee Harrison had been doing the rounds for all the time I was in Tenerife," said Collin, who was also legendary at the Arena, the Londoner going on to become known as 'perhaps the most individual of all the house DJs' as he played around the world in places as diverse as Portugal, Hamburg, Ibiza, back on Tenerife, Madrid, Germany, Ibiza, Italy, Croatia, New York, Slovenia, Japan, Russia and most of the big UK clubs and festivals. "I took up the residency at Havana as I hadn't been home for a while and was curious," he continued.

Coco Ariaz was one of the local Tenerifian DJs who played Chicago and acid house alongside the Brits during the late '80s and went on to become a break-beat hardcore DJ of repute appearing alongside the likes of DJ Randall, Joey Beltram, Mr C, Simon Bassline Smith, DJ Swan E, New Class A, Bug Khan & the Plastic Jam, Darren Jay and others at parties around Playa de las Americas. He opened up his own club K2 on the island in 1993. Newcastle's Andy Baxter had also DJ'd out on Tenerife; the buzz of motor scooters flying by on the narrow streets as groups do the rounds to the likes of the Paradise Club, Bananas, Fever, Cactus Park, Veronicas, Bobby's Bar and Busbies with the neon illuminated fronts flashing in the dark.

There always a big North-East presence on Tenerife with a number of Tyneside's underworld criminal faces having residence out there and being involved in the dodgy timeshare business, while three well-known Newcastle gangland characters – two from the West End, and one from the East End - were arrested by the Guardia Civil on Tenerife in April '89 after being nabbed at the airport when jetting in to the sunshine island with a large amount of cash, a small amount of cannabis and 26 ecstasy tablets in their possession. They were released from a detention centre after a week. A Sunderland man was taken to a Spanish prison in the October of that year after a raid on a property agency on the island netted two kilos of cocaine hidden in a safe in his office in the resort of Los Cristianos.

MC Lee was holidaying on the island with friends again that summer when he went back to watch Collin Patterson DJing in Bananas. Obviously impressed with the sounds that the DJ was spinning and sharing with him on those tapes, Lee went over and asked him to come and be a resident at the Havana. When Collin returned home to the UK he headed north and teamed up with MC Lee to form the legendary PA Hooligan X, while fellow innovator Huey Carr was the other DJ who was instrumental in the club Havana project. So just as Keith Flint's death in 2019 provoked an outpouring of love and compassion for the Prodigy dancer and occasional singer as it brought home mortality to a generation that looked up to the 'Firestarter' as a hero and legend of electronic dance music, similarly in the North-East there was a sense of shock and uncomprehending when MC Lee tragically died in Lebanon in 2016. The inquest into his strange death heard that Lee had possibly been murdered by hanging with terrorist groups Hezbollah and ISIS being mentioned along with rumours of a 'drug deal gone wrong' at the inquest. Legendary Rez DJ Howie also died in sad circumstances in 2017.

Club Havana had opened on Linthorpe Road in May 1989 and quickly became the cutting-edge Mecca for dance music in the North-East with DJs such as Mike Pickering making early appearances; Havana was way ahead of the curve. At a Bank Holiday Rave on Monday 28th August there was PA by Dionne *Come Get My Lovin'* with mystery tour buses leaving from the club at 12 noon for an event that ran to 2am and featured a free BBQ as the sounds of that golden summer really got going. The legendary New Yorkers Frankie Bones and Tommy Musto were at Havana on Monday 4th September 1989 to play a 2-hour live session of Break Bones, 1,2&3, Techno, and Loony Tunes while on Friday 22nd September E-zee Posse were in town to do a live version of *Everything Starts with an E*, which the club were calling 'Middlesbrough's new anthem.' And as the big opening chords and Hendrix-style guitar kicked in, lads in bright Ciao t-shirts and Gio-Goi tops reached for the sky and cheered, their hair-cuts starting to lengthen, girls with tight perms and hairspray in shorts and swimwear dancing without a care in the world, the faces all literally glowing and beaming in that initial innocent intense rush as if a little piece of sunshine had been dropped on the narrow back alleys, faded '30s gable-end advertising and disused chimneys of the often wet and gloomy North and landed in that low-ceilinged and tightly-packed sweaty venue.

"Apart from certain illegal substances the other explosion has occurred in 'street fashion,' baggy, light, bright and sweat absorbent garments have overthrown all the designer gear, making the restrictions within some club door policies a joke," noted Huey at the time.

"Club Havana is in fact the region's pioneer in '90s culture. The Brothers of Islam (the techno band) have in effect brought the N.E. up to date with the South, Europe and America in music and fashion. Introducing a blend of international rhythms, practical and multi-racial fashions within the context of an enthusiastic and harmonious atmosphere," he continued. Huey was always an intelligent and eloquent exponent of the DJ craft and club culture.

Manchester DJ Mike Pickering was soon back at Havana to bring the Hacienda sound by popular demand, Philadelphia's Bas Noir played a live PA and at the monthly Hip Hop connection event there was also a PA by Silver Bullet.

On Monday 25th September 1989 the club hosted a 'Mental Warehouse Session' with Eddie Richards – he hadn't become 'Evil' yet. Eddie was promoted as London's top rave DJ and he'd been playing to 17,000 at the famous Sunrise parties. He also did a PA as Jolly Roger featuring E-Mix. It was a hugely important moment that brought one of the biggest players in Acid House from the capital to the region and surely began to sow the seeds for the legal Butterloggie raves in MC Lee and Huey's heads. You would pick up the free music and events magazines in Trax or one of the clothes shops on High Bridge and see adverts for Havana and wonder at the line-ups. Havana was where it was at. Coaches were travelling down from Newcastle to the venue and people would come back with tales of just how amazing the nights there were.

"Initially people weren't that excited, especially because it was playing the soul and jazz funk that everywhere else was playing. But when the summer of love happened, that's when it all changed. We'd always played underground house music when we were at places like Bennett's in South Bank. Havana was very special - it was our first home where we were really welcome and people of whatever race, colour, creed - everybody was 'one'. People came from across the country. Acid house was like the punk rock or rock n'roll of its day - the kids embraced and understood it. It was our music and still is," Havana and Eclipse DJ Appo told the local press in a later interview.

"At that time, there was a big problem with violence in clubs. But then acid house and ecstasy came along and overnight, everybody was everybody's best friend. I'm not saying it's right or wrong - but that's what happened. And especially in the early days, the police didn't see it as an issue because there were never any problems."

By 1990 the club's flyers were loaded with the colourful daisy age imagery of peace symbols and flowers like a De La Soul album cover promoting 'Happy House and Hippy Hop' as people in little hats like the shopkeeper from Mr. Ben and Mexican panchos grooved to the sounds of 808 State, Seal, Adamski, and T-Coy. The club was only licensed to hold 250 but there was regularly up to 600 crammed into the place. MC Duke also appeared at the club, as did the likes of Brothers of Islam, Blacksmith, Richie Rich, and Doug Lazy and Razette.

"Havana was sweaty, dancing at the back dying for the loo but waiting for Candi Staton and the Source *You Got the Love* to play; sure enough the minute I head for the toilet I hear the intro and back I scramble to where Amy is, dancing all the way and loving every minute. Big smiles and rushing, off it on acid and speed," said Shirley.

"That song will be played at my funeral - almost 30 years on it still gives me chills. That's how the music gets you - you feel it, it's part of you and no matter how many times you hear it it's like the first time all over, that's when you know the music is good." Loved-up tunes with big vocals like that and K-Klass *Rhythm is a Mystery* that brought goose bumps, waves of joy and an outpouring of total adoration, tactile touching and stroking. Rub up with a stranger, as the E-zee Posse famously declared.

"We met Mr. Sweat in Havana, under the low ceiling at the back, at least that's how I remember it. A big bloke, not muscley-muscle but carpet-carrier type, sweaty as, shirt off and always with a huge hug whenever little Shirley and I would bump into him," she said.

In the March of 1991 residents Hooligan X featured every Saturday and Unique 3 every Wednesday, while the club was bringing up DJs such as Craig Walsh from London Limelights and Ibiza, The Doctor (Centreforce radio), Phil Perry of London- Queens - Ibiza, Darren Price (London), Kelly and Kenneth Matthews (Manchester).

On Friday 31st May Hooligan X appeared as usual alongside Asterix & Space from Sheffield, Rhythm Creator and DJ Russ (Seduction/Welly Club Hull.) Zero B played a live PA in September that year while the Scottish STREETrave crew, DJs Andy Carroll from Quadrant Park, Scott Gibson, Simon Gibb and Andy Baxter all rippled the room with pulsating waves of acoustic pleasure on renowned Saturday nights that would go down in legend.

"Club Havana in Middlesbrough and Jason Bushby's Big Beat at Philmores in Saltburn rivalled each other but had different followings - they were both fantastic clubs with unique atmospheres that I've never witnessed since," said legendary North East MC G-Force.

"Philmores didn't really have an MC of note but Club Havana had MC Lee, a bloke called Lee Harrison and a huge influence on me picking up a microphone. I remember going to Club Havana and having to queue for hours, it was one of the biggest club nights in the country at this time but only had a capacity for about 400 at most, the place was tiny, but fuck did it rock."

"I used to just stare at MC Lee. It seems weird now after MCing for so long but makes you kind of realise why people act the way they do when you meet them. To me I'm no different to anyone else, but people look up to you for what you do and that sort of thing always embarrasses me, but thinking back now, I was exactly the same."

"I first got on the mic at an under 18's night at Macmillans in Yarm, which became Tall Trees. My mate from school, DJ Marcus, was running the night. He was only 17 but was knocking about with the DJs from Club Havana and was getting pretty good himself. The nights were packed out, and one particular night a little black kid called Leroy from Middlesbrough was there and went on the mic and copied MC Lee. He was only about 9 years old but fuck could he rap and dance - he actually danced live on stage at an all-nighter in Cramlington in front of about 10,000 people, he was 10 then. Anyway, I thought that looked easy, it wasn't, I was crap, but there was no-one else so I kinda got away with it," recalled G-Force, who also noted MC Man Parris as another big influence on him in the early days.

In 1992 Havana moved to the Arena in 'Boro. That year also saw the popular House club To the Manor Born open up at Hardwick Hall in Sedgefield, the constituency of the MP Tony Blair, who would go on to become Prime Minister in '97. The Hacienda's Graeme Park made regular appearances at Manor Born, along with other House DJs such as Allister Whitehead and Mike Johnson. Whitehead also appeared at the Arena, where Simon Gibb, Collin Patterson and Andy Baxter were the residents. Lisa Loud came up from Milk Bar and Steve Lee from Boy's Own, while 808 State, Moby and DJ Fabi Paras, A Guy called Gerald, Normski and Tricky were all other acts that played the club.

While Spain had been hugely influential in bringing House music into Britain initially, the hardcore sounds of the UK were also being exported in the other direction at that time and when Mike ended up on one of the Spanish Islands for a spell in early '92 he recalled that The Prodigy's *Your Love* was the big tune in the clubs. Mike was working as a tout for one of the bars, standing in the tolerable soft evening heat and setting sun in shorts and sunglasses handing out free drink tickets to tourists. But he was given a shock one evening when the Guardia Civil pulled up and bundled him into the back of the car then drove him out to a remote, dusty spot in the hills.

"This was before you could move around and work anywhere in the EU – I wasn't sure what the hell was going on. They dragged me out of the back of the motor and slapped me around with their gloves. 'No visa, no work,' they said. It could have been worse, I was panicking what the hell they were going to do with their truncheons!" he said.

"One night a British DJ leapt over from the booth and stabbed a Moroccan with a steak knife that he kept by the decks. He punctured the fella's lung and the police came down and cordoned off the place. That was the end of that night. I knocked around the clubs with Stevie and gangs of lads that came down from Aberdeen, Bedfordshire...there were loads there from London at one point. There was a blonde lass with them called Lisa, and I'm sure she was the DJ Lisa Lashes! Hardcore was the main sound, the music was pretty much just like home."

But striding down the main strip on the dimpled pavements with green parakeets screeching overhead and the beach and sea just over a low volcanic wall was miles away, both physically and psychologically, from the darkness that was permeating the British scene by then.

"I used to put on buses from Sunderland to the Arena in Middlesbrough until one of our fellow organisers was threatened to stop by a bloke in a black BMW outside his house," said Tall Blonde Phil. Serious gangsters and low-level street dealers alike were muscling in to take over doors and control distribution. Houses were raided by dozens of officers armed with battering rams to take the doors off hinges in unsettling late-night busts all around the region. As the nightlife profits increased, so did the velocity of the weapons on the street. When doorman, heavy and former boxer Viv Graham was gunned down in Wallsend on New Year's Eve 1993, the shooter used a high-powered Magnum pistol. An AK-47 Kalashnikov assault rifle was seized during a cannabis and amphetamines bust on a house in Darlington in '92, and an unlucky drugs runner from Birmingham was pulled at Newcastle airport when his flight to Tenerife from Manchester was diverted due to bad weather and he was caught in possession of 1,000 ecstasy pills in three sealed cigarette packets after he triggered a body scan alarm in the May of '93.

The region's biggest LSD bust also happened that year when an undercover drugs operation named 'Billygoat' caught a Longbenton man as he pulled up at a suspect's house in Tynemouth with 2,000 squares of acid in sheets on him. They also found a different batch of 12 trips and £600 cash when they subsequently searched his home.

LSD valued at between £6,000 to £10,000 had been seized by the police in September 1990 from suspect packages containing jigsaws sent from Amsterdam to addresses in Scotswood Road and Gateshead. A 26-year-old Walker man was arrested.

The House scene definitely had a less menacing edge and atmosphere with fewer violent lunatics knocking around and a more loved-up vibe that was reflected in glowing favourable reviews in the regional papers.

"The Mangos in Newcastle were amazing - light and airy kind of sounds, even though they were in the Mayfair it was a totally different feel to the Rez," said Shirley, with DJs such as Sasha, Mike Pickering, Fabi Paras, CJ Mackintosh, Phil Perry and Connie Lush appearing at the nights. A newspaper report at the time stated that: "The best thing about Mango is the atmosphere, everyone is so friendly, no rough people, everyone just out to enjoy themselves." The writer also stated that: "The girls were dressed to kill in their sexy long skirts and blouses and the lads in their designer tops and trousers. One thing – everyone had dress sense."

That designer gear included clothing such as fine cut Valentino shirts and Armani jeans, the faint waft of Paco Rabane as people with tidy haircuts and immaculate shaves sat sipping at expensive imported bottled lager in booths and snorting cocaine off the coin in the toilets; it was an atmosphere of exclusivity that was at odds with the 'anything goes' feeling of the acid house and early rave scene. The availability of the Columbian marching powder was on the increase and in November '93 a courier with half a kilo strapped to his body was intercepted at Newcastle Central station. He had travelled by rail from Holland and was due to meet a 64-year-old Gateshead man who had been remanded in custody accused of smuggling coke worth hundreds of thousands of pounds along with a 40-year-old Scotswood man in April '92.

With the face-numbing buzz and swagger, clubbing suddenly seemed to be about looking cool again. About being a face around town, frosty and aloof, chopping out white lines with a credit card as slower almost elevator musak throbs around the space with an over made-up girl who looks like a page 3 model on your arm. Bars were done out in chrome and brass and had DJs spinning from booths as the weekend was elevated into an event all of its own.

No longer did you have the anticipation of waiting for a monthly or quarterly rave to come around, as the sounds, the flashing lights and glitterballs, the hustle and bustle were all there up for consumption every Thursday, Friday, Saturday and Sunday night.

"Frankie Knuckles and Dave Morales DJ'd in Whitley at Rogues – that was a class night," said Shirley. The Bronx-born Knuckles – or Francis Warren Nicolls Jnr., to give him his proper name - was often been dubbed 'The Godfather of House Music' before – and following - his death in Chicago in 2014. Frankie was just 59. He'd been in Chicago since moving there in the '70s and was developing something different to the acid sound that was coming out of the city as his electronic music embraced something warmer and more soulful.

"I wanted it to sound as big and beautiful and timeless as Philly (Philadelphia Soul). We did *Your Love* in the DJ booth at the Power Plant on a four-track, but it sounded big," Frankie told the Guardian in 2011. In 1987 he had helped to put out *Your Love* and *Baby Wants to Ride* as vinyl records after these tunes had been regulars on his reel-to-reel player at the legendary Warehouse nightclub for a year.

"Most young guys playing now think house music is supposed to be all four-to the-floor, 130bpm, hands-inthe-air. And it really isn't. It's a wide crosssection of music," continued the legendary Knuckles.

The popular sounds at the Havana combined just that eclectic mix of tunes as Chicago came to Middlesbrough and Detroit to Newcastle. Despite the links to heavy industry in all of those cities, the mellower house sounds just seemed more suited to sands, sun, sex, hot sweaty bodies, girls with full sleeve tattoos and dark glasses and pink bikinis sipping cocktails on a strip of neon lit bars.

The success of venues such as the Arena saw the rise of the mega-clubs with Leeds venues Back To Basics and Hard Times drawing a large number of North-East revellers into making the journey down into Yorkshire. Tall Trees opened up in Yarm in November 1995 in a stylish hotel and conference centre with large roman columns at the entrance and a 3,000 capacity. Big names in House such as Pete Tong, John Digweed and Paul Bleasdale appeared at the club in association with the Arena and Back To Basics. With a coned off

VIP lounge, champagne, dress codes and high ticket prices, Tall Trees had something of a feeling of decadence that was again a world apart from the original underground warehouse vibe. The Sugarshack at Middlesbrough Empire, another big old music hall with amazing acoustics, was another highly regarded and respected house venue by the mid '90s.

"It's genuinely one of my biggest life regrets that I didn't smash the arse off the raves.

I was massively into my indie dance like the Inspiral Carpets at the time and thought it was all annoying MCs and whistles. Then I realised what I was missing and that I was wrong! So it was more the house clubbing scene for me from '93 onwards," said Nicky Smooth. Others had drifted into House when the atmosphere began to change, and one former raver said that: "For me, in about '94, the music changed when it went to happy hardcore and very, very dark jungle and drum and bass which I wasn't keen on, so I started going to the house music clubs which I thought were amazing. Even the pills started going downhill around '93 - '95," he said - a popular view which has often been echoed around the North East.

The Ibiza club scene obviously exploded massively into a more commercial product around that time too. Manumission had moved from Manchester out to the Spanish island in late '94 following trouble between drug dealing gangs in the North-West city. Cream arrived in '95, the same year that Ku was renamed Privilege. Space, Amnesia, and Pacha, who were linking up with the Ministry of Sound, had a corporate glamour and global appeal. It was the time of the DJ as God, travelling the globe on private jets and with sparkly glitter, feather boas, tall boots and drag queens abounding, as the level of debauchery in the sunshine at pool parties around the cafes and in the darkness at night reached legendary proportions. The dull throbbing bass reverberating above the cicadas in the softly shaking palms with the sea setting orange on the sea. Others travelled further, taking in the hard trance at Full Moon parties on sandy beaches in Goa or Thailand, a mystical hedonistic time on the New Age Hippy trail around South East Asia, smiling at the recognition of a fellow Geordie accent in some busy street as you peruse the counterfeit goods. Pushing deeper into consciousness expansion and necking snake blood shots for the experience, asking where you can get a connection for some hallucinogenic yaje, feeling the sun nipping on your back with the strange vibrational echoes of native chanting embedded in the mellower head-spinning hypnotic tracks.

Maybe meeting a beautiful Indian girl who worked a call centre in the street buzzing with mopeds and beat-up cars with doe-eyed white cattle in a haze of purple dust and hand prints like ancient cave paintings up its side, neon bar and red coca-cola signs on peeling painted fascia boards, her big brown eyes wide, hair black as a raven's wing and shapely coffee-coloured breasts pressed full against her silk sari. As you knock back vodka 7ups she wants to know all about London and you can't tell if she is really interested in you or wants the crack for her work, so you have to tell her you're from Northumberland, all green hills a grey blur of burst rainclouds and gurgling burns cutting down a sharp scree-filled valley and not from the Smoke, the tall concrete skyscrapers of the capital as alien to you as her. You tell her to forget her headset, computer keyboard and sales targets as the heady spices from street food sellers permeates your table and you're unshaven and red-eyed sat in old skool acid house smiley t-shirt and shades pondering what lessons you've learned in this life and come up with compassion for animals, empathy with your fellow humans and judging by the smouldering look in the Indian girl's eyes it seems like you might be about to learn a good few new positions from the Kama Sutra, her full dark lips parted hungrily as she rolls a joint of strong weed thick as your finger and when you get her back to the hotel room under the cooling steady whip of the ceiling fan she's wet as a British summer and it's all good karma. Or feeling the golden sands squeezed gently between your toes with the sun starting to set and lighting the sky all pink and purple as the DJ begins cranking the south coast Big Beat music out of a giant stack of speakers and you dance away in a daft white floppy hat and surfer shorts with a stunning petite blonde Danish girl with sexy blue eyes and sand in her hair that you've been chatting to in and around the ramshackle bars for a couple of days, watching her snaking through the day-glo painted bodies and glow sticks towards you with a big smile of recognition on her face in a tight black swimsuit that shows off her beautiful body as the nearby palm trees rustle in a soft wind and you spin her some line like how we're all just stardust.

They are all just fading postcards on a fridge, snapshots in time. Getting people to open up and talk about a period in their lives 30 years ago when they'd been a sweaty mess involved in recreational chemicals in warehouses and clubs at home or chewing green cocoa leaves on an Aztec trail is difficult. They stare off into the distance, smile at the hazy recollections, avoid the gaze of the bearded sportswriter in a deck jacket and think now on their responsibilities and regret the loss of the seeming invincibility of youth and the sheer wild spontaneity of the 1990s. Jetting in planes round the world but always ending up back home eventually, back to the bridges hanging over the Tyne, back to the local villains squeezed tightly into leather jackets standing around on corners with their hands in their pockets, scanning the street through tightened narrow eyes with pit bull terriers on chain leads. Back to wild young lads in baseball caps pulling wheelies on BMX bikes racing around, but it's home and it's comfortable as a soft pair of old Levi's.

Despite the attraction of exotic sunshine jaunts, the North-East was generally more connected culturally, spiritually and musically to the Northern Hemisphere via the North Sea anyway and those links brought thousands of Scandinavian shoppers to the region at the Metro Centre on the Bergen to North Shields ferry in the early '90s.

Glenn Carlsson, Magnus Nordin and Thomas Norling are better known as the Swedish rave trio MDA and their absolute classic *Take an E* on BTech Records in 1991 was a massive tune that not only rocked the clubs in Stockholm but was regularly reverberating around the Rezerection. Further hardcore Nordik Beats came from the likes of Hypernature *Kaos* and Mindbender's *Energise,* an acid mix of bleeps and bass from the time, while by '95 the Norwegians were holding massive Hyperstate raves at Spektrum in Oslo with acts such as the Chemical Brothers and the Prodigy headlining. Further up towards the green shimmering Northern Lights and the Pole, Agzilla was one of the young pioneers of the underground rave scene in Reykjavik, Iceland, in the early '90s who was experimenting with breakbeats and drum and bass sounds.

The early hardcore techno of the frozen North was gradually giving way to more accessible sounds, however, and by the time Tall Trees had opened up Newcastle itself was gaining a huge reputation as a party city and had been named the 8th best in the world by an American holiday firm. With nights such as Hullabaloo and Arcane (which had been running since 1992) at the 3,000 capacity Newcastle Uni and DJs such as Graham Park from Hacienda, Dave Seaman, Gordon Kaye, Sacha, Ian Ossia, Phil Perry, Paul Bleasedale, Digit, Efx and Rasoul from San Francisco putting in appearances, Scott and Scooby from Shindig at the Riverside's reputation was going from strength to strength. Shindig had teamed up with Liverpool mega-club Cream for a night in '94 and also brought up Terry Farley, Pete Heller, Ashley Beedle, Rocky & Diesel for a Junior Boy's Own Party in the January of '95. NICE at Planet Earth was also featuring the likes of Jon Pleased Wimmin' with the sounds of Josh Wink being big at the time. Kevin Hurry and Kevin Swain, Lofty & Boomshanka live, Craig Walsh & Digs & Woosh, Dean Thatcher and Simon Dk all appeared in the city around March '95 and Scott Bradford recalled in a later interview that those Shindig days at the Riverside had been the best in his career.

The city was undergoing a project of regeneration and the Quayside was absolutely buzzing as Tyneside suddenly became a respectable and cool place to visit. The Quayside area alone boasted 36 restaurants, 27 pubs and seven nightclubs as the nightlife pound became huge for the economy and the introduction of door registration schemes made them harder to infiltrate. Even Newcastle United were on the up and with a team dubbed 'The Entertainers' that contained the French flair of David Ginola, mad Colombian Tino Asprilla – who once told Lee Clark that he and the cocaine drug lord Pablo Escobar picked the national team - and the stylish Belgian defender Philippe Albert, they came painfully close to taking the Premier League title.

Tall Blonde Phil had been introduced to the dance music scene when Tom Morgan gave him a tape of a DJ set from Rockshots.

"It was like nothing we had ever heard before. This was the summer of 1990 and dance music was still underground. A rare track would make it to the charts, but nothing that captured the spirit of the time. This was my first ever insight into a rave – it was pure gold, liquid gold in fact," he smiled.

"The tape made the journey with us on our first lad's holiday, five 17-year-olds rich with the currency of youth; mortal on cheap cartons of Sangria, sweltering in Spanish tents. We were entranced by the music which signalled this brave new world of rave."

That was just the beginning of a journey into sound that would see Phil mixing, DJing and clubbing around some of the biggest house venues on the globe over the next three decades including being a massive regular at the Arena in 'Boro. He was also a regular face at Café del Mar on Ibiza, in both his younger carefree days and as he grew older, sat relaxed in a designer polo shirt, knee-length sorts and shades on the chrome rail outside in the sunshine, the sexy, cool bastard.

But with the rise in House culture, hardcore had been increasingly forced underground and demonised in the media since the middle of '92 where it was portrayed as urban, Northern, cloth-cap with a gritty edge. Conversely, Ian felt that a lot of the house scene was just hype and fashion which didn't really have the same street credentials that hardcore had earned, and he preferred to remain within the ranks of the more up-for-it ravers.

"I was having a drink in the Printer's Pie with Mike and Adie and we decided to head down to a Shindig to check it out. We had an argument with the bouncers but got past them and inside, did a once around then left. The music was shite, the crowd were just standing around, and as we walked out you could virtually feel the sigh of relief. I was like 'fuck this, get me to the After Dark,'" he laughed.

Another night, with the fog hanging on the Tyne, Ian and Adie found a packet of tights in a club and decided to go and kidnap Mike from his girlfriend's apartment after for a laugh. As they walked up the empty streets at around 3am in black leather jackets with the tan nylons pulled over their faces, noses squashed flat, a police squad car pulled up alongside them.

"Where are you off to, lads?" asked the officer.

"Errr...emm." Explain that.

The house scene wasn't entirely without an edge and Dodger recalled an encounter outside the Newcastle Riverside in '98 when he was down with some other boys from the Aberdeen Firm on a stag do.

"Four of the party had left to go Greece for their hols and me and a couple of pals went to the Riverside. I was all Stone Island'd up, and came out of the club to be met by about 50 Stone Island-clad lads. Ooops, I thought, but they were sound and just asked where I was from and that. A lucky escape fae the Gremlins!" he grinned.

Similarly, while most of Ian's trips down to Middlesbrough had been with the football, rather than clubbing, he had some hair-rising recollections of visiting the ground back in the day. Journeys to the old Ayresome Park, where a cold mist in the white gleam of the floodlights cut through the deep purples with the breath of the crowds rising in plumes as they walked through red brick streets. Those floodlight pylons that you used to spot as a kid from miles around to pinpoint the grounds, the four tangles of metal struts towering above the slate rooftops.

"I was talking to Bill Gardner down in London years later and he told me that 'Boro was one place the ICF didn't enjoy going. The Teesside lads had a real reputation as absolute nut cases -I've seen them battling on the terraces, in the streets and in nightclubs and I had to agree with him," he said with a smile.

Back in September 1989 West Ham and 'Boro were on a North Sea ferry taking England fans to a World Cup qualifier in Sweden which was turned around and brought back to Harwich after brawls broke out and a former Commando died after going overboard while tripping.

"The whole boat was controlled by West Ham and Middlesbrough support-ers who had a deck each. The West Ham lads were dealing in drugs on a large scale. It was like a floating chemist's shop," one man told the press, with the heady mixture of LSD and alcohol being blamed for the chaos on board the Tor Britannia.

Two decades later and you're stood on the white Saharan sands at Corralejo, a spectacular pink full moon rising high in the sky as the music thumps at a free beach party with Spanish, German and British kids in bikinis and long shorts crowding around the DJ with their arms raised high, smiling and excited. Others sat around in groups cross-legged in the soft, crushed shells and rock talking, drinking and smoking, the cool house music drifting off into the warm evening air as the waves roll in with a regular, comforting whoosh. Your wife, her skin tanned and sunglasses perched up on her head, puts an arm around your waist as she sways to the tunes.

And all the while, in the back of your head, you're thinking: 'drop a banger, play some bloody Old Skool hardcore techno, man,' while suppressing the secret urge to lob some plastic chairs and bottles around. House music was all about the sunshine vibe and holiday feel, and Havana had blazed the trail.

8

The Blue Monkey

When a snooker ball landed near the car and bounced down the pavement just beside them, Mike knew it was going to be an uneasy night. They were filling the motor with petrol at the nearby garage when the object was launched at them from out of the large queue of people standing about waiting to get into the popular club with its strip of four yellow lights on the canopy above the door and blue monkey neon sign.

Looking across, he couldn't immediately see anybody that looked like they'd thrown it, and was a bit surprised that nobody else that was stretching their legs from the journey down looked too perturbed. Maybe they just didn't see it, he thought, as he glanced at the girls in their tight leggings and black puffa jackets and the lads in their Destroy tops as the driver held the nozzle into the tank.

"Did you not see that?" he said, slightly incredulous. "Someone's just lobbed a snooker ball at us, man."

"Don't be daft, Mike," one of the girls replied, brushing it off. But they bloody did. Welcome to Sunderland. The wrong side of the river. He didn't make a big deal of it, just raising his eyebrows, but it was the kind of small incident that could put you on edge ahead of a rave in Seaburn Casual country.

While the atmosphere inside the Bedford Street club could be electric, by '92 there was a slight undertone of menace outside and especially down at the docks after; for Geordies anyway. There had been a load of bother between

Newcastle and Sunderland in the semi-finals of the old Second Division play-offs in the May of 1990. It is most famously remembered for hundreds of Newcastle fans invading the pitch and lobbing coins and advertising hoarding in a riot which led to 52 arrests and seven policemen getting injured, but the Mags' thugs were also picking off pockets of Sunderland fans around the ground before and after the game. There had never been any love lost between the two cities with a rivalry stretching back to the English Civil War, if you believed the stories.

"There was a tea van down at the docks and we were sitting in the car with steamed up windows around dawn when this lad who looked smashed off his tits with rolling eyes came knocking on the window and asking: 'are you lot coppers?'" said Ian.

"When he got to the next car they started smashing up the windows and it sped off. They hated the coppers and after all the raids and were looking for undercover. If he hadn't got off the docks, they would probably have killed him – it was that frenzied."

Going down to the docks after the Monkey as the sun came up was a regular ritual for dazed clubbers and Mike recalled that although the ambience was great in the club itself, he always approached the early morning trip down to the mouth of the River Wear with some trepidation.

"There was a grass verge up to the top where the cars were parked up and the docks were spread out along a long strip of concrete. There would be a couple of hundred there in little groups standing against the railings, people sitting smoking joints, bits of low music here and there – lads you recognised from Washington or the Toon, and others that you didn't. I just never felt very comfortable down there," he said.

"The atmosphere was hanging like a mist over the river, man. There were people knocking about with baseball bats and all sorts. Maybe it was just me, but it wasn't a nice experience – people saying they were going to black-out, coming down heavily off Slammers. One night it sounded like everyone was talking to me in a lisp. I was coming down and I thought: 'they're doing it on purpose; they're trying to fuck me up, the bastards.' I was with two sisters and they were just full of non-stop chatter – lads who were coming down were just walking off. There was a mix of people including lots in floppy hats and some canny folk, but there were also some nasty fuckers. The Monkey was really good, but going down the docks after wasn't."

The former shipbuilding town had produced some real hard-men and, ironically enough, Mike's granda Bobby had been a little game-as-owt Mackem in a red and white tea-cosy hat himself. The Seaburn Casuals had formed in around 1985. They made national headlines when they played a major part in the infamous England riot at Lansdowne Road in Ireland in 1995 when they travelled over on the ferry with 'Boro and Carlisle's BCF (Border City Firm).

The old ground was famous for the huge roars and chanting that echoed around the cavernous roof space in the Fulwell End on a Saturday and the freezing North Sea air that chilled you to the bones on the steep sloping terraces of the exposed Roker End opposite. October, 1992. Liam O'Brien coolly firing a free-kick over the wall and slapping into the corner of the net to send the Mags packed together behind the goal into absolute pandemonium. That pure hatred of a derby day, with sporadic fights breaking out all over the place, was in stark contrast to the chemical-induced bonhomie that had been enjoyed in the initial rushes just a year or so earlier.

Sunderland's rave scene had started out with Acid House being played in the likes of upstairs in Chambers and the 'little room' in Bentleys from 1988. There were also a number of illegal parties in the city during the following year, with one of the Sunderland lads recalling lifting flashing orange council roadworks lights to illuminate their early raves in factories, boarded-up houses and deserted business premises in an amber glow with LSD being the prevalent drug.

By the summer of 1990, Chambers was throbbing to the sounds of the likes of D-Shake *Techno Trance/ Yaaah* and L.F.O. with the club lights pulsing and the bobbing and grooving crowd clasping hands, cuddling, grinning and grinding their jaws in bucket hats and baggy T-shirts. When the Butterloggie brought their shows to the Blue Monkey later that year, it kicked off rave culture massively in the venue. On Boxing Day 1990, at a night called Nemesis, there were live PAs from Ariel and Hooligan X while Stacey Tough from Boy's

Own, Andy Baxter, Collin Patterson, MC Lee and Simon Gibb from Club Havana absolutely rocked the Monkey from 7 till late. The Oz nightclub in nearby South Shields was similarly bringing the sound in 1990 with GFX appearing live at the venue.

The Club Havana crowd were hugely influential in the early success of the Blue Monkey and the fantastic atmosphere that was generated in the club at the time. On the Bank Holiday Monday, April 1st, 1991, from 8-2 am, Hooligan X were back with Unique 3, DJs Collin Patterson, Krazy K/ G Man, Scott Gibson (STREETrave, Ayr), DJ Huey and Andy Baxter to start the series of massively successful Ruktion nights.

Ruktion 2 was held on the Bank Holiday Monday 27th May from 7-2am and featured Asmo, Craig Walsh, Hooligan X, and The Doctor (from Centreforce in East London) live on stage. The DJs were Collin Patterson, Simon Doward (London), Andy Baxter, Simon Gibb and MC Lee, while the flyers were boasting future monthly PAs from Zero B and GFX.

Ashton Martin remembered dancing at after-hours car park raves under the bridge in Sunderland when the Monkey had shut for the night where the atmosphere was almost as good as it had been inside the hot and sweaty venue.

"We used to buy speed from a lad a few years older than us and this one night we didn't have anything on, so him and his mates asked us if we wanted to go clubbing in Sunderland," she said.

"So we got in their cars a headed out to Sunderland and hit a couple of pre-clubbing pubs, took the gear in the toilets and then headed over to the Blue Monkey. We had an amazing night, totally happy and dancey and didn't want to leave! We heard that there was a place to go to after, down at the bottom of the Queen Alexandra bridge. It was fab, the boys drive us over and cars were parked all the way up the hill leading down to the base, where cars had packed in a huge circle with their lights on and music blasting."

"The atmosphere was incredible but the guy who was driving us was coming down and wanted to go home, but we managed to convince him to stay. He went back to his car to get more stash but he got jumped and they nicked his drugs and car radio and beat him up. We didn't know what was going on till he came back down to where the party was happening with blood streaming down his face. He had to go to hospital so we found other friends to take us back home."

"We went back to theirs and partied well into Sunday getting stoned. The following weekend they asked us over to theirs again and they'd give us rides over to Sunderland to the Monkey. They had drugs but no cash to pay to get us and them into the club. So they went out and came back with a load of pound coins. I found out they'd turned over the phone box. We must have thought we were invincible and just used to get in a car with anybody who said they would take us clubbing. Bloody mental," she said, shaking her head slowly in reflection. Others made their way down to Hendon beach in their cars with the music blasting from a van's sound system as the sun came up pale on the cold North Sea.

The 8-2am format at the Blue Monkey was still in place for Monday 12th August when 'Fantasy Phase 1' launched a night of outstanding hardcore with Carl Cox, Asmo, Devious D, DJ Howie, Andy Baxter, Bass Generator, MC Crisis, MC G, and Adrian, as strobes and lasers lit up the darkness and dry ice billowed heavily from machines, faces suddenly appearing in front of you then getting lost in the fog again by the bare metal railings leading up to the balcony where shirtless men in American flag bandanas clambered up and stood with arms aloft. Bedlam; tightly packed onto the heaving main dance floor dancing with your head down, long hair flicking sweat that stings in your eyes as you stomp and punch out your moves with the hoover sound taking you higher and higher. Looking up to see a forest of lit-up arms, girls chopping the hot air with their hands out and jerking their bodies in thin black tops with a leather bodice underneath, whistles blasting rhythms. The centre of the cyclone and the frenzy, shards of light spinning off a glitterball, the wall of sound that hits you in the chest and threatens to stop your heart, feeling it beating in your throat.

"Inside the club the subs were about 4 foot across and there were two stacked on top of each other either side of the dance floor. They were so powerful that no matter how packed it was no body would stand within a few feet of them as it actually hurt!" recalled one of the Newcastle lads that used to frequent the club.

"I got the shock of my life the first time I went in there," said Ian. "It was an old music hall with three balconies and the atmosphere inside was absolutely brilliant; nice people, a lovely crowd. One of the lads I went down with tried to sell some lads some magic mushrooms. He hadn't dried them or prepared them or anything, they were still wet in a plastic bag with cow shite on them! I couldn't believe it - I thought 'what are you doing?' Adrian Street has just played a blinding set, the place is buzzing, and you're trying to sell mushrooms that are stinking of shite! The Blue Monkey was the perfect place for a rave though. It had a big spiral staircase up the middle which was a bit difficult to navigate when you were spaced."

The police raided the Blue Monkey in November 1991 and made nine arrests, but it couldn't bring down the buzz that was being generated and the Butterloggie crew were putting on raves at the Blue Monkey again the following month which featured twin-head lasers and balloons to add to the party atmosphere.

Smiler recalled hallucinating pulling balloons off the ceiling which were 70 feet away with his hands while everybody was stood still. "It was so real," he said.

"The same night one of the lads was trying to get into his work van in the middle of dance floor in the Blue Monkey, or that's what he thought he was doing – we thought he'd lost his mind! The things that went through your head while you were off your face were mad."

The mood was changed seriously, however, when there was a fatal stabbing outside the Blue Monkey in January 1992 as a fight broke out while crowds of people were flooding out of the club at around 2.15am. The police launched a murder investigation and a senior officer stated: "It was a violent fight. There may have been more than one person involved in the fracas. Hundreds of people were leaving the premises at the time of the fight."

Ian recalled being stood in the queue outside the club on another night when a transit van pulled up and some Geordie villains armed with baseball bats jumped out and piled inside to smash up the doormen. But the party went on.

Hardware Records head honcho Shaun Allan was very much aware that the weekly club scene was taking over from one-off raves or warehouse nights at the time and told the local press that: "Yes, I guess people are going into clubs more. The whole thing is a lot more exciting than regular gigs. It's got to be really because it's like a whole new field. The type of DJs we've got today are pushing their music to the limits making it altogether exciting, there's a lot more experimentation in dance than people give it credit for, quite honestly."

"You're always going to get some muso types who say 'oh, it's just machines, it's just computers,' but they all remember the day when it was just a guitar. What you get now is youngsters and not-so-youngsters pushing it as far as it will go, pushing the technology in areas that people would have never thought possible in a million years. Like the use of sound within records as opposed to the use of chords and musical arrangements," continued the Neo-Technik man.

"The music industry at the minute is finding its own little areas, there's room for everything and likewise there is good and bad in everything as well. There's good Techno, bad Techno, people dabble around with Techno the same way they are dabbling around in any other field of music that they're not particularly 100% into or behind. You can tell that with whatever field it is."

Dream 3 took place on Monday 17th February '92. Digital Orgasm were the live PA while John Da Silva, Nipper, Jam MCs, Smokey Joe, DJ Adrian and MC G also featured at the night. Wendy Wolfe shook her curly dark hair as her head bobbed to the music while she danced, her big brown eyes wide with pure joy and her beaming face lit up blue by the UV lighting. Raising her arms in the air as a piano break elevated the whole club in a mass of cheering and whistles.

"I wish I had more memories, but by the time I got there I was always smashed," she laughed. "But I do remember that night was the night that I had to climb out the bathroom window and jump off the garage roof to get out as my mum had locked the front door." Just 18 and with a world full of possibilities ahead of her, Wendy was caught up in that very moment where the rave was the only thing that mattered. It was a feeling shared by the vast majority in there; just get down, get into the place and feel the music drowning everything else out. It felt important and you didn't want to miss anything - you had to be there every week. The fluttering in her stomach as she held a little white pill between her thumb and forefinger and tasted it bitter and dry in her throat, washed down with a slug from a bottle of water in some dark corner.

In early April the London hardcore techno sound was brought to the Monkey by a number of top DJs including Grooverider, Fabio, Face and SS with the organiser Seamus Conlon, of Axiom Promotions, telling the local press beforehand that he believed the rave scene was becoming staid. "The trouble is that businessmen are now getting involved and taking the dance culture away from its roots. We want to bring back the enthusiasm and kick the scene back to where it began," he said.

But a crowd of only 300 turned up when the club had been expecting to be packed out by 1,000. Only a few ventured onto the dance floor and a number of others danced away in front of the massive speaker stack. One clubber told the *Evening Chronicle*: "Tonight there is hardly anyone dancing, mainly I think because they are not rave-goers or because they are not into the really heavy hardcore which is being played tonight."

Another said: "The music here tonight is brilliant, really top-notch, but it is the atmosphere that is wrong. There is just no comparison between raves held in nightclubs and those held outside or in warehouses. The really big raves, where you have hundreds and even thousands of people dancing, are brilliant."

In an effort to bring that 'big rave' feeling into a club setting, on Sunday 19th April 1992, the Blue Monkey held one of the first legal all-nighters in the North-East to be staged a nightclub. Spin Masters (basically 808 State) Sammy B, Wear FM's Smokey Joe and MC B featured and a live PA from Hardware's PSI Division gave a first taste of the TWOC EP. The PSI had been invited to the New Music Seminar in New York City around that time and it was a big deal for the Geordie techno outfit. Adrian Street, Pez and Nick, formerly of POGO, and Chris and Danny G from Images were also on the bill.

Allnighter 2 went off on the Bank Holiday Sunday May 3rd from midnight to 8am and had a top line-up including DJs Slipmatt and Lime, Spice, Dangerous

Brothers and MC G, Adrian Street, with live PAs from SL2 and Bass Value. In an attempt to freshen things up on a weekly basis, the 'Massive' nights were started up every Saturday from 8-2am with resident DJs Adrian Street, Smokey Joe, Andy DB, MCs B/Jam, MC DC and LJ Richie, while Allnighter 3 was held on Bank Holiday Sunday 24th May from midnight-8am and was another huge show with the likes of DJ Massive, DJ Swan E, Smokey Joe and Adrian Street with PAs from Eskimo & Eygpt and Destroy.

What the clubbers didn't realise was that the Blue Monkey had been under surveillance by undercover police for months and in June the club was swarmed by officers in a sting known officially as 'Operation Peanut,' or simply as the 'Big Raid' to anyone who was there. The lights were flashing in the club, the smoke machines belching and the tunes booming out at high volume as the atmosphere was starting to peak at around 10 o'clock on a Saturday night. What those inside the venue were unaware of, however, was the revolving blue lights of 13 vans that had congregated on the street outside. The vehicles hadn't turned their sirens on in the approach, just the lights that glinted off cars and shop fronts and windows as they descended. Around 200 people were still queuing to get in and they scattered as 170 black uniforms started to climb out the vans and get organised to go in.

Confused clubbers looked on in shock as the police swarmed into the building, stopped the music and turned the lights on with an officer taking to the microphone to tell everyone to stand still with their hands on their hands. Sniffer dogs, held back on their chains, edged their noses around nervous ravers and people were being handcuffed when any substances were found. Although the police seized 300 Es, 200 wraps of speed and a significant quantity of LSD, about half of that had been thrown on the floor along with bundles of bank notes. There were estimated to be around 750 people in the club and 35 were arrested and taken away to various stations around Sunderland for questioning. "One person was arrested for a public disorder offence and the rest for possession, possession with intent to supply and the supply of drugs," a police spokesperson told the press after. The club owner said that the Blue Monkey had tried to combat the drug problem in the past and they had approached the police for help, but their response had been very negative.

"Our doormen come from a national company and search people as they come in but there is only so much you can do. You can't ask customers to strip. Drugs are a potential problem in any successful club and I'm not surprised by the number of arrests because we had almost 1,000 people on the premises," he said, while insisting that the club would be open again the following night. There had also been a large-scale drugs raid on the Tunnel nightclub in South Shields three months earlier which saw 13 arrested and thousands of pounds worth of LSD, amphetamines, cannabis and ecstasy seized as the police started to crack down and crack down hard.

When it came to court in the October, Sunderland Licensing Magistrates were told that 'the dance floor was a seething mass of young men stripped to the waist and dancing wildly to the rave music,' and an undercover cop said: "You had to duck, dive and dodge as arms were being flung about and it was getting wild."

The undercover operation had totally infiltrated the club and the officer had bought two grams of speed from lads on the balcony that overlooked the dance floor inside. "One man said he was there every Saturday and if I wanted to sort any of my friends, he could get speed, ecstasy, or any type of drug," he said while giving evidence. The officer and a colleague had been approached in the queue outside and asked: "Are you sorted yet? which I took to mean did we have any drugs. They said they had drugs with them and if we wanted any we should go inside." The Blue Monkey was stripped of its drinks licence as a consequence with the magistrates claiming that the chief shareholder was 'unfit to hold a license and had allowed the club to become disorderly.'

Just a week or so after the raid, on a Tuesday night, Dream 4 took place from 8-2am with Dream Frequency being the PA, and DJs Ali Cooke from Back to Basics in Leeds, JM Easy, Jam MCs from Konspiracy in Manchester, Kaygee, Smokey Joe, and Adrian Street. As well as DJing in the club, Smokey Joe, along with Mickey C from SR2, were also the producers *Two Bad Boys* on Hardware Records' new label SDI (Strategic Dance Initiative) which was launched that November. Mickey C (Mick Clarke) was heavily influenced by spacey 'Krautrock' and had released a solo synthesiser album in 1975 on a German label. *Games* was released in 1978 and is a superb electronic musical journey with a Kraftwerk feel; Mick's innovation in sounds was another massive key to the development of North-East Techno that can't be underestimated. He was in one of the earliest British synth bands *Naked Lunch* down in London in 1979, played a minimoog in the band Baby Patrol in the early '80s and by the early '90s released a couple of SR2 (the Hendon postcode) tracks on Hardware – *Compulsion* being more of an early bleep, klonk and spooky choir pads Geordie Techno sound in the Detroit style, and *The Crunch* more hardcore - and played a live PA at the first Rezerection, which he later described as 'basically a showcase for Hardware Records.' One of the acts at Rez 1 that wasn't signed up to Hardware was the Scientist, who was another excellent exponent of bleep techno. The Scientist was Phivos Sebastiane, from London, who cited the Dr. Who theme music and BBC radiophonic workshop stuff as early influences and you could hear that spacey, futuristic sound in his records. He got his first synthesiser, a Yamaha CS01 MKII, in 1984 aged 11. The Scientist's 1990 releases on Kickin' Records included *The Exorcist* and *The Bee*, which contained some of the earliest breakbeat techno sounds, while *Spiral Symphony* and *For Those Who Know* came out just before that legendary night at the Mayfair. Without the likes of the Scientist and SR2, there's no hardcore techno as we know it.

Mickey C produced the 1992 single *'It's Brill Up North'* with Bill 'Blaster' Watson of Ignition Records as a response to the KLF's *'It's Grim Up North,'* and Adie Scott recalled listening enthralled to the track in the dark on a bus up to an Edinburgh Rezerection as the car headlights flashed by up the A1. Mickey C was also part of the influential Wear FM crowd with a Monday night show called 'Elevation,' reading the shout-outs on the station with his fellow SR2-er Ian Wright, who occasionally DJ'd at the Monkey. Boss Shaun Allan said that the label was set-up to 'handle more of the ravey, jungley type of stuff that we couldn't really put out on Hardware.'

"The main reason we're setting up SDI is that it's a fresh start for the business side of things. But also because of the way the whole dance thing has splintered off into different fields, we wanted to be more specific about what we would release on Hardware. It's now an out and out Hard Euro Techno label whereas SDI can handle the more London-type sounds," he said.

"As always, we will carry on using local people – the new TD production series of tunes is being done by DJ Massive C, Jussy, Paddy and all the Mad TD lot, and the only thing that isn't locally based and we are putting out on Hardware is a tune from Finland that should be out by January. The thing with doing SDI was that we didn't want to mislead people by putting other styles on Hardware as it expands as a record company if you like."

The great irony was that while technology was advancing the production of electronic music, it was also starting to change the way in which that music was received; CDs had been launched a decade earlier in 1982 and were just starting to make their mark in the market – CD sales overtook vinyl in 1988 and had overtaken the cassette by 1991. While jukeboxes in pubs were still predominantly playing 7" vinyl singles in '92, the number of CD jukeboxes was steadily increasing. But for a small indie dance label on Tyneside it was obviously still an exciting time to be involved in the pioneering production of the sounds that were being played at a high volume in clubs such as the Monkey.

"If we've got an SDI camp doing their stuff and a Techno camp doing Euro Trance and Techno stuff and we're also dabbling a bit in so-called progressive stuff with Scott Bradford and Scooby working on a tune, it means you get a bit of crack going and people doing mixes for other people," continued Shaun.

"We're all here in Newcastle and we're all getting on a bit better and helping each other out more. If that wasn't happening, I just wouldn't do it because it's not done for money, by a long way. The good thing as well is that you can trust someone if they say that a record has a bad mix, you respect their opinion and it puts a different perspective on the tune which only makes it better."

Regular Monkey DJ and North Londoner Smokey Joe (Joseph Brodie) produced his first track *The Hard Way EP* on Labello Blanco Recordings in '93, and Mick Clarke helped him write the drum n' bass tune *Wha' Dat (Gimmie My Gun)* on therecord. His *Crimewatch EP* was also out on SDI that year and he went on to become a Jungle artist of some repute as he embraced the more ragga-influenced southern sound.

DJ Massive C was responsible for some of those harder and darker SDI sounds which included the *Count Zero* and *Inner Fury* mixes. Former PSI Division member Massive C (Alan Clark) was also known by the aliases Burning Chrome, and released a hardcore techno track *How Long Must I Wait* on Huxley Records in 1992 before continuing his jungle/drum 'n' bass as Al Massive with *Getting' Busy* on Rude and Deadly Records in '96 and 5th Element – where he put out *Call on Me* on Urban Gorilla recordings in '97. He is also famous for working with Justin Maughan on the aggressive underground filthy beats from Elementz of Noise. The Junglists started their own nights up in Newcastle in '98 with Turbulence at the University Student Union with resident DJs Phobia, Piper and MC Mike-E-Rider, but it was still all something fresh and new when Massive C's moody hardcore tunes were first coming out during 1993 where the Blue Monkey was open on Saturday nights from 8-3am and was again putting on its Bank Holiday Sunday special all-nighters. On Sunday 2nd May '93 there were PAs from Terrorize, Inner Seduction and Indiana 99 while DJs Adrian Street, Jason Bushby, Bass Generator, Destroy and X-DC tore it up on the decks.

The troubles continued at the Monkey, however, and an explosion shook the four-storey building at around 11.30pm on Monday 24th May with flames and thick, black smoke ripping through the club. Nobody was hurt in the incident, which was dealt with by Tyne and Wear fire brigade, but the damage was enough to knock the following weekend's all-nighter on the head where there was meant to be PAs from Sunset Regime, Baby June, Love 4 Sale featuring B-Buzz, and DJs Adrian Street, Jason Bushby, Bass Generator, Destroy and X-DC. Worse was to follow as the club was boarded up and closed for a year the following month. The Blue Monkey returned in the June of 1994 but had only been open for 45 minutes when it was hit by a third drugs bust.

Police seized £3,000 worth of gear, including ecstasy, in a two-hour operation that saw 20 people arrested. But the club's management remained defiant and claimed that they would open up again the following weekend as a workers' co-operative for non-alcoholic drinks and dancing for members in a clever legal move to get around the stiff licensing laws. The police denied that they had a vendetta against the Blue Monkey and a Chief Inspector insisted that: "If we receive information that drugs are being taken on the premises, then we will act accordingly."

Just a few days after the raid the Blue Monkey was burned to the ground by an arson team who also took a security guard prisoner at gunpoint. The two-man squad poured petrol all over the building and held a gun to the head of the guard before handcuffing him to a pole. The pair removed the cuffs and bundled him into a car before igniting the petrol which exploded into an inferno of orange fire and black smoke. They drove off at high speed and kicked him out of the motor in Wardley. When 70 fire fighters were rushed to the city centre club they found two butane gas cylinders inside and had to evacuate nearby buildings, including the petrol station, as they battled the ferocious flames.

"It may have some thing to do with rivalry and all sorts of other things that have gone on behind the scenes," a lawyer told Newcastle Crown Court.

Tall Blonde Phil could feel the heat from the inferno tightening the skin on his face as he picked at the meat in his kebab and watched on from the street in a gathering crowd something akin to bonfire night, watching his memories of the club turned to ash.

The Blue Monkey brand was moved to club Fiesta in Stockton but the troubles followed it out of Sunderland and in the October it was closed again when Stockton Borough Council took out a High Court Injunction. Although the Monkey was re-opened, in December gunshots were fired outside the club in what police described as a 'war between two gangs for control over doormen and the drug trade in Cleveland.' One man was charged with threatening to kill the manager.

The police were keen to do everything in their power to get the Blue Monkey shut down for good and a senior officer said: "We will do whatever we can to ensure its effects on the local community are minimised, through appropriate policing. I put the organisers on notice that we will not tolerate an establishment that attracts violence, disorder or other criminal behaviour to Stockton."

The club was re-named the Colosseum soon after.

9

Eclipse

The PSI Division headlined at the Eclipse on Saturday the 11th January 1992 where they were billed as 'Newcastle's only Techno band' and played their exclusive new release the *TWOC* EP to an enthusiastic crowd. The keyboards up on the stage with cables snaking around the floor, looking out into the darkness to see faces illuminated by the rapid chop of a strobe light, arms raised and girls lifted up on shoulders nodding their heads, chewing their lips and grabbing up-reached hands. DJs Craig E Mac, Smokey Joe, Massive C from the PSI, and Diane from Rockshots were also representing Newcastle and lined up with house residents Appo, Juckie G, Johnny P and Tosh. Behind the partying the PSI Division were a heavy-duty outfit with strong principals and they played a gig in aid of the Anti-Nazi League in the Cumberland Arms pub in Byker that August alongside Urban Sound System and DIG, while Alex Martin of the band volunteered his services as a humanitarian aid worker across in Bosnia during the brutal conflict out there.

"The horrors of the war have been transformed into unsettling soundscapes and twisted dark Drum 'n' Bass tunes in my studio on the North Shore of Sydney," said Alex, who shipped out to Australia shortly after the band was dissolved in around '94.

The Eclipse had opened on Brunswick Street in Stockton-on-Tees on Saturday 7th December 1991 with Bass Heads, PKA, DJ Ralphie and guests, while the following weekend Unique 3, Rave Nation, DJ Martin Lever, and resident DJ Adam rocked the building. With the club's flyers promising feature appearances from the likes of Grooverider, Sasha, Carl Cox, Fabio, Jumpin' Jack Frost and Mike Pickering, Eclipse was a huge instant success with hardcore clubbers looking to get a weekly music fix.

Bass Generator, Smokey Joe, DJ Adam, Binni, MC G-Force, DJ Dom, Destroy and MC Crises were the behind the decks on Saturday 18th January 1992 and DJ John, Morris, Scott (Rockshots), Roppa, Scooby, Rod, Diane, Tosh and MCs Buzz, Saucy, Kix, and G-Force the following Saturday as the biggest names in the North-East's techno/rave culture all made appearances making the Eclipse one of the premier rave clubs south of Tyneside. Hanging around as the lights go up chanting 2 Bad Mice *Bombscare* bah-bah-bah...bah-bah bah-bananababa; not wanting to let it end, got to keep the party going as you filter out of the venue and are hit suddenly by the cold morning air, ears ringing from the high volume inside.

"I used to stand on the stage dancing with a friend in my big furry hat - how I didn't get heat stroke I don't know! It used to be so funny to come out of there on a Saturday morning and all the market lads would laugh at the state of us, but I knew what a night I'd had, and I was on my way to bed while they had to work all day," said one of the girls who was a regular at the club.

"Eclipse was my favourite ever rave club. I spent many an hour in there dancing my ass off to Smokey Joe and Destroy," added another.

By the May of '92 the Eclipse was running for 12 hours from midnight to mid-day every Friday and Saturday but the party ended abruptly when the club was raided by police that summer. The manager was charged with allowing the supply of drugs and also with supplying ecstasy and amphetamines.

The Eclipse in Stockton closed soon after and was moved to George St. North in Monkwearmouth where they upped from the capacity from 450 to a 1,200 in a square white standalone building next door to St. Benet's Catholic Church. The move proved controversial straight away and 2,000 people signed a petition against it opening.

The parish priest was also concerned and told the press: "We have the integrity of the church as a place of worship to protect. Rave clubs should not be within spitting distance of churches. We are very worried rave people will be coming out of their parties on Sunday mornings when parishioners are going to church." The club planned to open on Thursdays, Fridays and Saturdays, charging £7.50 or £15 entry depending on the night.

The Eclipse in Monkwearmouth opened in the July, was damaged by a suspicious fire and then faced a High Court injunction to shut it down in the first month. However, the club could still draw top-name line-ups and on Friday 7th August Jason Bushby, Adrian, Smokey Joe, Orpe from Amnesia House, Daz Willot and the Lethal MC from Fantasia all played, while the following night saw Jason Bushby, DJ Excel, Tosh & Dianne from Rockshots, DJ Destroy and MC G-Force take their turn at spinning the sounds.

The police and the council moved to shut the club again in September 1992, and the following month it didn't open on one night after the power supply to the building was cut off. The Eclipse was then ordered to close and its drinks licence was revoked. It was claimed by Sunderland licensing magistrates that the capacity of the club had been increased without permission, Northumbria Police said that 'the illegal increase in numbers had affected how they policed north Sunderland at weekends,' and local residents had continued to object because of the proximity to the church, a school and a monastery. However, the club was re-opened as their lawyer exploited a legal loophole and said 'if the club was not run as a profit-making venture it did not need to be licensed' and it was re-named After Dark.

The opening night on 17th October 1992 ran from12pm-8am and had live PAs from Terrorize and Bass Value. The DJs were Excel (Chambers) MC G-Force, MC B-Jam, Jason Bushby, Smokey Joe, and Adrian. MC G-Force, who had been the promoter and was responsible for booking the DJs and live PAs at the Eclipse, wrote on his Mixcloud page: "I started MCing at 16-years-old at a time when MC's were few and far between up and down the country, never mind the North East. I've MC'd all over the country and Europe for the legends of the scene from Carl Cox to Joey Beltram, Nipper, Sy, Stu Allan to name but a few. It's in my blood and always will be."

G-Force had originally been part of the Hysteria crew and went on to form the bouncy techno band NeuroTek with DJ Excel, Franky Tully and Scott Brown. They are still producing and releasing to this day with their latest album *Together* featuring G-Force and being produced by Excel, as the links between the Scottish and North-East happy hardcore acts ran deep – Stewart Brown's Bass-X, Mallorca Lee's Ultra-Sonic and a number of others producing a similar sound across the Border.

The Hysteria had ran every Saturday night from 7-12 at The Stanley Inn (Buffs) on Durham Road in Stanley with G-Force and DJs such as Destiny, Detonator, and Technique. The other MCs included Rhyme, Sub Zero and Trix. They later ran all-nighters at the Top Hat in Spennymoor. Excel had started out DJing at venues such as Chambers in Sunderland and The Tunnel in his hometown South Shields before going on to be a big name around the rest of the region's rave scene.

"During one night in Philmores I was approached by a guy called Stevie Lloyd wanting me to MC in his new club in Stockton called The Eclipse, which was ironically the same name as my favourite club in Coventry. He told me he was opening the first all-nighter in the North East, and he wanted me there - I was as happy as a pig in shit and readily accepted," laughed G-Force.

"The Eclipse opened, but the first night was surprisingly quiet and it was for a further few weeks after that, it wasn't really advertised properly. I asked Ste if I could do the flyers and the promotion myself to see if we could get it busier, I was only 17 but loved the thought of running the night myself. I put together a line up of DJs that I'd always dreamt of working with, and also the best DJs from each area. I called it the North East Elite - I had Smokey Joe and Bass Generator from Newcastle, DJ Dom from Darlington, Jason Busby, DJ Adam from the Havana and a young lad who had never DJ'd anywhere before but reminded me of DJ Sasha called DJ Destroy. The night was rammed packed, from 400 we got 1300 and the job was mine," he continued.

"It was unreal, I was booking all the big DJs I'd always dreamt of working with from up and down the country and having them on my night, and I was MCing for them, it didn't come any better. By this time I was getting work all over the country and did the Galacticas at York Racecourse and Ripon Racecourse in front of 10,000 plus, and I was still only 17/18. That was crazy."

"From then on I was involved in the opening and running of every all-nighter in the North East and gave many of the 'old skool' DJ and MC names you hear today their first breaks."

Despite High Court writs, injunctions and contempt of court applications, the Promobots were in the club on the 31st December 1992 as the club's New Year's Eve party ran from 10pm-10am. But the venue was another that could see the atmosphere change into one of violent intimidation if your head wasn't in the right place with gangs of lads looking to isolate people and mess with their minds.

Mike recalled the After Dark hanging heavily in clouds of dry ice and a strobe light flickering the scene as blinding hardcore vibrated from the speakers. Ian was getting increasingly paranoid that some lads had pulled a blade on him and was convinced that they were going to waiting for him outside with baseball bats.

"You couldn't see for the smoke machine, it was that thick. Then all of a sudden a nasty face would appear, coming out of the mist. 'Just watch and he'll come around again,' Ian was saying. Sure enough, the same face would come around, again and again, turning to look back menacingly over his shoulder," said Mike.

"One of the Washington lads agreed and said 'there's some nasty fuckers in here just out to fuck you up, that's what they get off on. It's like a competition for them.' I didn't see the razor, like, but Ian had me convinced. I said 'howay, let's go' – but when we got out in the coolness of the morning there was nobody there waiting, of course. Nothing happened."

1993 was a weird time. The After Dark was open every Friday and Saturday from 10pm-8am, wandering around the space lost in the pounding bass and the lights gleaming hallucinatory and strange with an unquenchable thirst. Nights that blended into one long repetition, gangs piling into cars and ending up in after parties with a crowd you'd met in the club. Before you know it, the Sunday dinner time has arrived and you're all getting a bit sick of the Colonel. He sat in the corner with his stupid aviator shades and green uniform on, smoking a bifta that he never passed around. He had an umbrella and a rubber duck. He made daft quaking noises and fell about laughing. They weren't giggling, though. Not now. Ian still was, like. He had a skinhead and a broken nose and the Colonel was pals with him instantly. They were sharing cans under the table. But as the Colonel had a pistol on his hip holster, they didn't say anything. There were just eyes rolled skywards, tutts, shrugs and shaken heads. Ian was telling the Colonel rapid jokes, thick and fast as a machine gun. He'd had another wrap of speed. Everyone else was coming down, deflated, the low menacing acid house on the tape deck twisting their irate, angry and frustrated heads. It was daylight outside and normal people were starting to go about their business. Shutters being raised with a metallic screech. Laughing, whistling, greetings being shouted. Adie felt like a zombie, totally detached from it all as he looked on out of the flat window. The rave seemed such a long time ago. Could it really have just been last night when they'd bumped into the Colonel on a dance platform waving a green neon glow stick above his head?

The techno was thumping and lasers span in green and blue smoke-filled tunnels before clicking into a grid of squares that descended over the silhouetted hands reaching for the sky. Adie'd had a couple of Es and was in the full grip of a euphoric rush when he saw him grooving away in his uniform with a military peaked cap on.

"Top uniform, mate," he shouted over the tunes as he dipped his head in closer to hear, then nodded in time with the pumping tunes and flashed him the thumbs up. Adie didn't realise that he was a real dictator from some tin-pot regime. I mean, you don't expect to bump into dodgy leaders who may have committed genocide in a sweaty club in the north east of England.

Throughout the night Adie found himself bursting for a piss, but when he got into the urinals, the music reduced to a dull repetitive throb and thump through the walls of the glaring white toilets, he could only pass a few dribbles. No matter how hard he squeezed, there were just a few drops. And he was shocked to find that his cock had shrivelled away up inside his body, he was so high.

But the white tiles felt good and cold as his sweaty head touched them. His tongue hung out loosely and his eyes rolled in his head as waves of tingling pleasure washed over him, mingled with a strange feeling of unease and apprehension that vibrated around his body. The bright glare of the strip lights seemed so unreal away from the darkness and his hands felt jittery.

160

The only answer seemed to be to get back out into the sweaty, hot crowd and start pounding away with his feet again, trainers sticking to the floor tacky with chewing gum. As the door swung open, he was hit by a wall of heat and sound, the lights spinning in the blackness and dark shapes of arms reaching for the sky like a football crowd celebrating a goal.

He got back out and he was there again. The Colonel. Maybe he was always there. He tagged along when they were all going up the steps of the club being handed flyers at the end with bodies vibrating so hard from the noise that they felt shaky and he was there when they were getting into the taxis, chewing on their cheeks and lips with the MDMA still sending rushes down their faces.

He was there as the street lights flashed across the windscreen when they drove through the urban streets to the flat for a party, twisting his fingers in front of his face as he tripped on acid. Adie didn't invite him. Neither did Miah, or Mike, or Wendy or any of the others in the gang. But he was there anyway.

Adie watched him from across the room, smoking a Regal king size. He was getting paranoid. The Colonel and Ian were plotting to get him. They were going to pin him down and force ten black microdots down his neck for laugh. Adie tried to giggle along with the others, but it was false.

He would have to get them before they got him. Some kid in a tracksuit was putting his head around the top of the kitchen door and another was kicking his leg around. It looked like there was a huge man in there. It was a fuck-up, and Adie knew it was a fuck-up, but it still did his head in. His smile was forced. As soon as he got the chance, he'd make a grab for the pistol and smash the fuck out of anyone that tried to stop him. The night's sweat was dry on his skin and he felt washed-out, heavy eyed and lethargic. Somebody else that he didn't recognise kept flashing his hand up so you could see him do it out of the corner of your eye, but when you looked at him, he'd shrug and aggressively ask what you were looking at.

Adie had to sit on his hands because his time was coming. He was definitely going to go for the gun. When his mind was made up, he began to relax a little. He was still aware of things going on just out of his periphery of vision – cupboard doors opening and shutting quickly, pictures flipping off the walls and back. And he was convinced that Miah fancied the Colonel. She was joining in with the laughter and sat down to smoke with them, flicking her hair out of her face. But everything would be alright when he grabbed that little black metallic gun. He'd take it and shoot every fucking one of them. Blam! Blam! Blam! Suddenly his grin didn't feel so forced.

The Colonel and the gun weren't real, of course, but the sense of paranoia very much was. Noticing the holes punched in the plaster board walls and kicked into the plywood-fronted doors as you sit uncomfortably in a house with people that were awesome last night but are rapidly becoming strangers. Feeling the tension mount then the relief as you step blinking out into an unfamiliar street in some County Durham former pit village not knowing where the hell you are as you look around for a newspaper shop to grab a drink of milk or Lucozade, still detached from reality but slowly coming around. Finding the cars and getting the hell out of there but knowing all the while in the back of your mind that you'd be back for more next week. Bumping into a lad who you'd lost in the club the night before and him admitting: "I got bored so I drove to a rave in Blackpool." A 250 miles round trip at 2am. The madness never ends. *Insomniak – I must sleep.*

On Sunday 1st May 1993 the After Dark's Bank Holiday all-nighter featured The Rhythmic State, Full Effect, Richie P, and Jason Bushby. A year later, on Sunday 29th May 1994, just three weeks after nine alleged members of the Seaburn Casuals had been arrested in a series of dawn raids on houses where drugs, knifes and replica guns were seized, the ever-popular Bank Holiday all-nighter featured two live PAs from Bass Reaction and Technosis while Jason Bushby, Full Effect, Surf-E, Excel and Mal were on the turntables. MC's G-Force, Rhyme and Attack took turns on the microphone. But it feels nothing like a Rezerection for some and there's none of the buzz of '91. The gears have changed. It's the infamous cold rush. Dopamine-depleted and gaunt in a Stone Island coat, lost in a twilight world where the weekend can't come back around quickly enough. Chasing something that you feel you can't ever reclaim, that eternal hedonism with everything revolving around the beats. People were drinking alcohol again and knocking back vodka colas while the street price of cocaine had halved from around £60 to £30 a wrap. Ecstasy had been a connecting drug, an empathogen where people had felt together, whereas with coke more freely available the atmosphere took another dip away from the joyous innocence of the early days into insanity; a neon man leaping from the walls to attack while people complained of chest pains and heart worries. Strangely enough, way back in April 1988, two South American gentlemen had been arrested in a dawn raid on the Grand Hotel in Tynemouth and taken to Glasgow for questioning after six kilos of cocaine were seized from a ship docked in Greenock.

The cold rush – Marc Acardipane captured the feeling and likely coined the phrase with the Cold Rush Records label that launched in January 1993. Dark and spiky tunes on EPs like *Doom Supporters*, *Doomed Bunkerloops* and *The Last Judgement*. The unsettling heavy off-key sound on his *A New Mind* featuring Rave Creator in '96 dived straight into the disjointed thoughts of the nocturnal nightmare prevalent in the burned-out ravers that were occupying an eerie zombie zone of sleep deprivation and chemical comedown.

After Dark's final event took place on Friday 24th June 1994 from 10pm-8am and featured a live PA by NeuroTek. The DJs were Full Effect, Excel, Jason Bushby, Destiny and DJ Mal with the MCs G-Force and Attack.

The club was closed for good after a series of lengthy legal battles when the church bought the land on which it was situated. The battle also led to a change in the Law in January 1995 – as the After Dark weren't selling alcohol, the loophole meant it was beyond council control. The new law said that any entertainments premises needed a licence if profits were made. After Dark 2 opened as a happy hardcore club in South Shields in 1996, running from 10 at night to 12 noon, featuring the likes of local favourites MC Techno T, MC Stompin' and DJ Selector C and would go on to champion the Spanish 'Makina' sound that was coming out of the Barcelona club scene. The Hysteria crew were also back to take over After Dark 2 on Friday nights from November '96 with Detonator, Destiny, Technique, G-Force and Rhyme adding Excel and Full Effect to their ranks as they 'came back to sort things out' and 'bring techno home' with their Phase 3 events. Things certainly needed sorting out as Euro happy hardcore descended into a commercialised product aimed at a youth market with the likes of the Vengaboys, those Bonkers compilation albums and Scooter hitting the airwaves. Watching Ian Van Dahl doing an awful, tuneless live PA of *Castles in the Sky* while Scooter were probably everyone's secret guilty pleasure; who couldn't hear the German band and not want to do a little jumping dance in a square with a daft grin? They had actually been around since 1985 in various guises before hitting it big around the continent in the mid '90s as they became synonymous with the happy hardcore genre; the bleached blonde hair of H.P. Baxxter shouting into his fuzz distorted microphone as they had 23 top ten hits and sold over 30 million records. Someone was buying them. Embarrassingly enough, the North-East's most commercially successful dance record was probably Lindisfarne's 1990's *Fog on the Tyne* novelty remix that featured a grinning, rapping, dancing Gazza in a shell-suit that reached number 2 in the UK singles chart.

The Venue opened up in Cheapside, Spennymoor as a Private Member's Dance Club in 1992 with its Twilight Zone running every Saturday from 10-8am for £10 entry. It was burned down in 1995. The resident MCs in the club were Stompin', Fresh and Techno T, and the resident DJs were Morris, Lix, Roppa, Richie P, Charlie, Marty and Fosta. Zero B, Love Decade, and DEA performed live PAs at the club on Saturday 12th December 1992 and the following year saw 'Big Beat' every Friday which kicked off with the likes of Jason Bushby, Excel, Destroy and Adrian Street. DJ Tripp (Galactica), Smokey Joe, Mark Dawson (Utah Saints) also appeared at the event which ran from 10pm-6am. The live PAs were a big draw at the 12-hour Twilight Zone which started out as a 10pm-10am event then moved to 12-12 every Saturday and Zero B, Vertigo, Bass Value, Love Decade and Rhythm Quest, In Frantic, The Rhythmic State, Elite, Suburban Delay all performed at the Venue in 1993.

Other live acts appearing alongside the DJs in the May and June of '95 included Anticappella, Rhythm Response, Sharada House Gang, Reach and the 49ers while Frantic, J.X., Rhythm Response and QFX starred at the club in the July and August of that year. The club was a massive space in a majestic old music hall with a priest hole way up high where the DJs played, and you could get water, fruit juice or even a cup of tea - "Loads of sugar in a hot, milky cuppa at around 3am. It was smashing, man!" said Ian. "Italian House was the main sound at the Venue. Lots of pianos and up-lifting vocals."

The first raves in Rome had been promoted by Chicco Furlotti at Euritmia in 1989 and by '92 DJs and producers of Italian techno such as Paolo Zerletti *Re-Activated* and the Colombian Alex Quiroz Buelvas, who was the sound of Paraje and Ramirez, were making catchy yet hard tunes with a Mediterranean flavour that were hitting dance floors right across Europe, not least in Spennymoor.

The Venue was another club that suffered an arson attack though, and in September 1995 the club owners were ordered by Sedgefield magistrates to pull down the fire damaged building within 10 days because of its dangerous condition.

Heavy black smoke that had poured out from the heat-shattered windows stained up the white walls outside, with metal fences erected on the street and the interior blackened and charred from the flames as the close ties of clubland to gangland were again very publicly on show.

The LOGIC nights at Branigans in Houghton-Le-Spring were big around '92/93 with Bass Generator, the Wear FM crew and Rockshots' Subculture posse Tosh, TNT, Destroy, Dianne and MC Buzz all appearing, while Power-house at Manhattans on the Sea Front at Redcar was another popular rave venue around '95 with the sound being provided by the likes of DJ Morris and MC Stompin', Rhythm Response, DJ Technique, DJ Full Effect, MC Attack, and Ultimate Buzz. Bourbon Street in Sunderland was also playing happy hardcore sounds at the time with DJs such as Adrian Street, Excel, and Full Effect also playing at the nightclub. 140 police stormed the club in September '95 and made 29 arrests for drug and public order offences while executing a warrant under the misuse of drugs act.

Three months earlier, nine men and a woman were charged with drug offences and a doorman with possessing an offensive weapon when police raided Oz nightclub in South Shields, while the massively popular and influential Philmores at Saltburn had been unfortunately tied up in hardcore's increasingly bad reputation when a man had died after taking ecstasy in the club in 1992. Another man died in 1994 after taking amphetamine sulphate at a rave in the Monkey Magic club in Stockton.

The Colosseum on Norton Road in Stockton was previously known as the Blue Monkey and was in a former 1930s cinema building, a huge venue with two massive balconies and the standard rig up of lights and lasers. It was another alcohol-free member's dance club to get around the licensing laws and in 1995 featured the likes of Q-Tex, Mikey B, Full Force, Bass Reaction, Ultimate Buzz, Jason Bushby, Full Effect, NRG, Crossfade, Techno T and MC Attack at the legendary all-nighters which ran every Saturday from 11pm-9am.

The club had originally been called Fiesta and had opened up on Saturday 30th July 1994 with Rhythmic State doing a live PA at the 10pm-10am venue with Jason Bushby, Adrian Street, G-Force and Full Effect being the residents. When the club took on the Blue Monkey name, they were putting on Sunrise all-nighters every Saturday from 10pm-8am where the likes of Shades of Rhythm and QFX appeared live. The grand opening night for the Colosseum was on Saturday 22nd April 1995 and starred Clock (Axel F) with support DJs.

"I was reading the graffiti on the doors as I sat outside to get some air and have a cigarette one night and someone had scrawled 'This club is dedicated to those who run from the Law to rave' – I thought that captured the place perfectly, it was that kind of a club," said Ian.

"It could get wild and violent, a bit of an outlaw feeling. We were driving back up the A19 one morning when a car full of Sunderland lads flew past, closely followed by a car full of 'Boro hanging out of the windows with knifes and muckle machetes. It was like something out of the Wacky Races, man," he continued.

"There were stories of lads getting their teeth knocked out with hammers and I saw a bloke getting a right kicking in a dark corner one night. It was all to do with rival drug gangs in the place. There were some very shady people knocking about."

A huge early morning raid on the club in February 1996 saw 200 police in riot gear seize cash and 700 Ecstasy tablets, 150 wraps of speed and 30 pieces of cannabis resin. The club owner Gary Robb disappeared abroad and his brother spent time behind bars following the bust, which involved around 20 vehicles, undercover detectives inside the club, unmarked police vans, dog handling teams and a police helicopter. 35 people were arrested.

The Colosseum was a major happy hardcore venue and as well as the regular resident DJs, the club brought in a number of big names for special nights and guest appearances with the likes of Marc Smith, Scott Brown, Bass Generator, Technotrance, Davie Forbes, Slipmatt, DJ Stompy, Paul Elstak, Mikey B, Hixxy, DJ Demand, M-Zone, DJ FX, and DJ Smurf all putting in appearances at some time. The club was also big on live acts and Sonar, Bass-X, Active Force, System-X, Ultimate Illusion, Cytronix, Delta Nine, and NeuroTek all appeared at Norton Road.

"I was never that keen on PAs," admitted Ian. "One came up from the South Coast to play the Colosseum one night and everyone just went and sat down or wandered off to the toilets. It must have been awful for them, the dance floor just cleared. They could totally change the atmosphere that the DJs had been building up if they didn't get it right."

But it was the MCing that the club was really famous for. MC Stompin', from Gateshead, got his break at just 15-years-old when he was going to the Venue every weekend and was handed the mic for five minutes here and there. He was determined and persisted. "Eventually I got the job and I never looked back," he said. Stompin' was big into rap and bouncy techno, and named *Bomb da Bass* as his favourite tune. MC Hype, also from Gateshead, was another who appeared at the Colosseum and other events around the North East including the After Dark and Judgement Day while MC Attack hailed from Sunderland and said: "You only get out of MCing what you put into it; don't go on, say what is relevant and keep it short, sharp and powerful."

From their high vantage point in the club overlooking the dance floor in crews of three or four, or stood up on the speaker stacks, the MCs spat out the rapid rhymes that they'd penned down in notebooks and gone over in bedrooms, practising getting right into the flow with the 4/4 beats. It was lyrical street poetry, pure fast to keep up with the tunes. MC Ace from Leam Lane giving it some with his lines like: 'Padded up inside a cell with someone next to me, say I had possession of a drug called XTC, I said is it false or is it true, is this just a deja-vu, in fact this thing was just a dream, wake me up before I scream.'

So just as the earlier hardcore rap from the likes of NWA had spoke of their reality on the streets on Compton, the MCs in the North East clubs had their own distinct voices being played out over a pounding happy hardcore sound as the lasers flashed in the darkness, the rumble and grind of the tunes. Some sat around the sides, others making their way through the almost Spanish-style arched doorways to the bar, the main dancefloor stomping with girls in small tight sparkly dresses and lads with shaved hair in Adidas, Fila, ski hats, white gloves and glow sticks, jaws grinding. G-Force was the main man on the region's MC scene, and he himself gave the breaks to all of those young lads, just as he'd got a break himself from Jason Bushby back in 1990.

"The first time I met Jason Bushby, my good friend, whom I've known right from the start, was at his night in Saltburn, the Big Beat at Philmores. I was told by a friend that his nights were wicked, and that they didn't really have an MC, so I thought I'd have a look down and just try and blag my way on. Fuck, I was keen back then," he laughed.

"Anyway, Philmores in Saltburn was miles away from where I lived in Yarm, and I didn't have a car, or anyone to go with, but that wasn't going to put me off. I remember getting a bus from Yarm to Redcar, it took about an hour and a half but it was the only bus on a Friday night going anywhere near Saltburn. I got off the bus in Redcar and just ran down the beach for two miles until I got to the club. By the time I'd got there the queues were massive, coaches had arrived from Leeds and Sheffield and I was certain I wasn't going to get in. Luckily, I did, eventually, and that night changed my fortunes forever," smiled the modest and likable G-Force.

"I got into the club and it was packed to the rafters, both floors, but I remember thinking that it wasn't exactly kickin' like I was told, but there was a reason for that, and my initial worries were answered later. I remember having a blast on the fruit machine and winning about £15, so I thought I'd buy myself a 'little fella,' and I'll never forget what happened after that."

"I was sat down talking to some girl who was getting her tits massaged with Vicks by some complete stranger, and I was starting to love the place. Then the little fella kicked in like an orgasm of the brain, I was fucked, totally smashed and then it happened; Jason Bushby, as a trademark, would play an old air-raid siren at exactly 12 o' clock, or maybe 11, either way he played it.

He did it to indicate that the night was about to kick off, and fuck did it."

"Everybody stood up and got up on tables and chairs, and waited for the air-raid siren to end, as soon as it did, he dropped the huge club anthem of the time *Rofo's Theme*, and the place went beserk. By this time I was off it, and game enough to try anything, so I walked up to Jason Bushby, told him I was MC G-Force, DJ Marcus's MC, and could I have a go on the mic. Anyway, the blag worked, I got on, and was invited down every week thereafter, or should I say I just turned up every week and he let me in for free and I went on," he grinned.

"It was an unbelievable buzz, and something you only get when you first start, luckily for me it was right at the beginning of the 'rave boom', so I was laughing."

MC G-Force became a massive and integral part of the region's rave club scene and was involved in just about every project, including the Eclipse, After Dark, the Venue, Colosseum, After Dark 2 in South Shields and the Judgement Days.

"Over the years I did pretty much everywhere, and although the buzz wasn't quite the same, I still enjoyed it. At one time I was working at least 3 nights per week and up to 5 nights on Bank Holidays. I was doing two or three clubs a night but all the main ones. I've been there and done it all over the years, there is nothing left to do, I've worked with all the biggest names in the business, and for me personally it will never be like it was years ago," he said.

"As for my MCing, technically I won't get any better, I've reached the pinnacle, it's like anything - the longer you do it, the more you learn. I'm not big headed, far from it, I don't see myself as anyone special but what I do know is there is nothing you can tell me about the art of MCing. I was the first in the North of England to really make a name for himself bar MC Lee, I've done it the hard way but I've paid my dues, and I'm still around today."

The Colosseum put on a special 10pm-8am Fusion Genetix night on Friday 16th May 1997 which featured the DJs Slipmatt, Marc Smith, Hixxy, Stompy, Force, Dougal and Unknown, and Krazy-G with a PA by Force & Styles and MCs Storm, Techno-T, G-Force, Attack, Junior and Westwood as they brought in the big names from the happy hardcore scene that had been appearing at the

Rezerection. The Judgement Day crew also appeared at the Colosseum in July, August and September when Newcastle University was closed as the students went home for the summer.

"They were all-nighters and with no backstage or booze they were pretty boring for me," said DJ Smurf. "Delta 9 was the main guest at one of them. I'm not 100% sure I was at that one - I may have had a gig somewhere else. For one of these all-nighters, I played a set of early French hardcore, stuff on Epiteth etc. All the relentless kick drum tracks with not many breakdowns. After my set, one guy asked me: "What was that trancey stuff you were playing?" OK then," he said, with raised eyebrows.

"Loftgroover played one of the Colosseum all-nighters. Now Tony Loft Collins doesn't really drink that much, but he managed to polish off almost a full bottle of Jack Daniels and was hammered at the end of the night. Me and David 'Boony' Brownlie had to carry him out the club, and we put him on Boony's coach back to Stirling in Scotland. He got a shock when he woke up 200 miles away," laughed the Geordie prankster.

The club was finally shut down in November that year. Ian was there at the Colosseum's final night, leaning over the metal railings on the balcony and gazing down on the dance floor at the end.

"Well, that's the end of that," he said, turning to the mate he'd gone down with.

"I don't remember too much about the night, but Techno T was devastated and sounded like he was going to start crying. He kept saying things like 'It's the last night, it's the final chapter' over the microphone. A belting tune came on at one point and the place went mental, it was absolutely bouncing. The needle leapt on the record and Techno T shouted: 'even the records are jumping in here tonight!" laughed Ian.

"I'm sure he even did an 'oggy, oggy, oggy,' at one point. I thought he'd lost it and was in bits. My sides hurt with laughing. But that was it. That was the end. It was over."

10

Geordie Gabba Mafia

Harder, faster. The Dutch gabber sound was huge at the Rezerection event 'The Nightmare' in July 1995 at Edinburgh with the lights going up like something from *Close Encounters of the Third Kind.* Thump, thump, thump...no place to hide from the constant, relentless audio attack that hits you almost like an air-raid with bomb blasts, sirens and the vibration of low-flying plane engines. The frequencies in sound vibrate at different levels and create geometric patterns known as cymatics. If sand on a speaker can make these shapes, then hard techno must mess with your mind the same way on some molecular level – the repetitive warped bass drum and almost military sound taking you into a trance-like euphoric state. It felt like Armageddon.

Rotterdam Records held a Live Showcase at the event featuring Euromasters, King Dale, Bald Terror, Hard Attack, Evil Maniax, and Rotterdam Terror Corps. The Feyenoord brand of Hardcore got more intense and darker as it continued to evolve around the street fashion from the terraces, where the Dutch had a similar problem with violence to the UK. In one notorious incident in the Netherlands in 1989, a Feyenoord S.C.F. hooligan lobbed two home-made nail bombs at the Ajax F-Side crew at the De Meer Stadion in Amsterdam and injured 19. It drew terrifying parallels to nine years earlier when a Newcastle fan had chucked a petrol bomb in among travelling West Ham fans. Popular Dutch DJ Paul Elstak hails from The Hague, where local football side Den Haag were similarly followed by a substantial hooligan element. The Ultras at clubs around the continent were drawn to the hard sounds and unfounded accusations of links to neo-Nazi groups were made in the mainstream press, who were terrified by the image of skin-headed men in black scooter jackets and boots attending events in Italy, Holland, Belgium and Germany, while Scotland's ravers were going for more of a baseball cap and Burberry check, CP goggle jackets, gold chains and Kappa tracksuits kind-of look. Both Elstak and the Terror Corps would celebrate football hooligan culture with later tracks like *You're a Hardcore Hooligan*, which featured samples from the movie *Football Factory*, and *Rotterdam Hooligan*. Rotterdam was all about speed – both in the beats per minute and the chemicals.

Mainland Europe had long been leading lights on the hardcore scene. German DJ and producer Marc Acardipane's *We Have Arrived*, under the name Mescalinum United, is often cited as the first ever hardcore techno record. Planet Core Productions released the track on an EP named 'Reflections of 2017' back in 1990. Acardipane started hanging out in bunkers as a place he could listen to loud music as a teenager in his home city of Frankfurt where he'd been trained in classical guitar from the age of 8 and the electric guitar from 12. By 16 he was interested in football – he's an Eintracht Frankfurt fan - and had started buying drum machines and synthesizers, inspired by his electric guitar teacher who played in a bad punk band and had got an 808 and an MS-20 8-track recorder. He had been into Hip Hop at the beginning with NWA, Run DMC and Public Enemy his big personal favourites, and was mixing breakbeat sounds but soon realised: "OK, I'm white, not from Compton, and we need our own street music from Frankfurt, and that is how hardcore techno was born."

We Have Arrived was pioneering and Acardipane recalled that when the first time he played it live, the sound engineer ran to him complaining that he was destroying his PA. "He didn't know that the whole track was already distorted. Nobody had heard that before," he said. By 1993 his tracks like PCP *We are from Frankfurt* were the hardest, most cutting edge around.

The Hardcore that followed was morphed and warped into the aggressive bouncy sound that was being played by the likes of Tango and Cash, Darrien Kelly, The Darkraver, Gizmo, DJ Rob, Petrov, and Mark Maclaughlan at 'The

Nightmare,' with further PAs from Neophyte and a Terrortraxx live showcase with Too Fast For Mellow, Two Terrorists, E-Wax, Body Lotion, and Brothers In Law.

DJ Rob of Rotterdam club Parkzicht fame, where the sound reputedly originated, said "I think Gabberz think differently than others generally think about them. They think 'when I'm out to party then I'm going out to forget my problems,' amongst other things, and not to be looked at, like what's happening at the mellow parties and in clubs. That's where people want to be seen. Look at how pretty I am blah blah blah. Gabba isn't about being noticed, some are just standing in a corner having a good time listening to the music."

Ruffneck Alliance records producer Patrick Van Kerckhoven twiddled knobs on a sound deck to add the 'panicky' feel to a record and said: "It's difficult to explain what darkness is. What is dark to me might not be dark to you," while trying to get across some of the thinking behind the hard Rotterdam sound.

"When we are making a dark record, you visually imagine how it will sound at the party. You've got to feel it. Create atmosphere with sound combined with the images in your head, imagine all the people, the sounds floating over them, you see all these lights and the total atmosphere. It's hard to explain."

The gabberz were a bit blunter in putting their views across. "Whoever doesn't like it can fuck off," says a young Dutch skinhead to a curious cameraman from Lola da Musica at a party over in Holland. "If you don't like it, fuck off. Gabba is ours. And it's the best thing there is."

Gabba could be looked upon as something like digital electronic grunge with the distorted and down tuned sound - it also had that kind of underlying introspective and alienated feel to it, while simultaneously being out there, loud, punky and in-your-face.

"Rotterdam hardcore was *THE* hardest music at that time. At around 170/180bpm I used to think it was mad. I remember Source Code on KNOR 1 - I thought that was the maddest thing I'd ever heard. Not to mention those mental Euromasters records," laughed DJ Smurf.

"The Rotterdam scene was huge in Scotland, with Bassy G being the main man. All the top Scottish Jocks at the time started playing the Rotterdam stuff, and the likes of Ruffneck Alliance and Human Resource were regular visitors to the Fubar and Rezerections," he said.

Guido Pernet of Human Resource said that their famous 1991 track *Dominator* had been put down in just three hours, and felt that the track had 'certainly contributed' to the later gabba sound. "Especially because of the sounds we used: that saw synth is one of the most copied sounds from gabber and hardcore," he told Alfred Bos of DJBroadcast. Pernet recalled producing the tunes in a tiny bedroom with a sloping roof so they couldn't stand up and a pile of basic equipment in the corner, which was somewhat magical to him. He also explained why he thought that *Dominator* had been such a massive hit in the raves and clubs.

"First: the song didn't sound Dutch at all. Larenzo's rap made it sound more American than American. Second: the lyrics. All rappers can say what they want, but this one was the superlative of everything on it. That moment was over. That's why it was also a text that people could sing along. Pretty simple in the ear, pretty easy to understand. I still meet people who found out that I worked on Human Resource and they tell me their story with that record, their reaction is often based on that text," he said.

"And then the sound: that sawing synth. That is also a different story. That summer *Mentasm* by Joey Beltram had been released, that was already loud. If it had not been there, we would have had that sawing sound too. That sound expressed a certain anger, that sound was louder than what was being made at the time. Those are the three key elements that make the track catch on."

Created using waveform oscillations, pulse width modulation and a thick chorus effect, the 'hoover' or 'saw synth' was a defining and enduring rave sound which was elevated even higher by the Belgian producer Fabian van Messen in his 1992 hardcore techno classics Defcon 1 *Defcon (Theme)* and *Brainwasher*. Van Messen had been part of the Bassline Boys with Marc Neuttiens. They provocatively wore Nazi uniforms on stage in 1989 with their controversial acid house track *Warbeat* sampling Hitler, Churchill and crowds chanting 'Sieg Heil.' The scandal didn't do them much harm, and their follow-up track *On Se Calme* went gold selling over 400,000 copies and being particularly popular in France.

The sound even made an appearance on Lady Gaga's 2008 pop hit *Poker*

Face. It was unsurprising, really, as the eccentric, arty New Yorker, with her flame thrower bra, told the crowd between songs at the Glastonbury Festival the following year that: "I used to go to festivals, get naked and take acid." Gaga was a raver.

The 8 'til 8 'United Nations of Hardcore' Rezerection at Ingliston on the 27th May '95 had been billed as the USA v Scotland and featured the DJs Omar Santana, Rob Gee, Adam X, and Ralphie Dee, who flew over from the States, with local talent Marc Smith, Scott Brown, and Davie Murray flying the flag for Scotland. The PAs were from Bass X, Ultimate Buzz, Bass Reaction, and Q-Tex with the MCs Madman and G. Lenny Dee's Industrial Strength label also had a showcase featuring Disciples of Annihilation and Temper Tantrum.

"It was an utterly amazing night. Rob Gee and then Disciples of Annihilation and Temper Tantrum live were something else," recalled DJ Smurf.

"The majority of the crowd stood still in shock while me and a few of my mates went nuts. Adam X came on about six in the morning and played some ear-piercing acid techno - that killed everyone, apart from us. Amazing set."

"When the event finished, we were walking in the car park and some guys were putting flyers on car windows. One of them was for the Nosebleed event I was playing at the next month. I picked it up and said: 'ee, that's me.' One of the guys said: "Are you Smurf? I'm David. I'm running the event," he laughed.

The dreek Scottish weather threatened to put a dampener on the big outdoor rave in autumn as it was pouring with rain for 'The Event 3 – The Equinox,' a mammoth 20-hour event that started at 12 noon on the 2nd September. 16,500 people packed two massive arenas at the biggest dance event held yet in Scotland, with a line-up of 47 DJs and live acts including the likes of Lenny Dee, Joey Beltram, Marc Smith, Scott Brown, Bass Generator/Technotrance, Loftgroover, Dave Angel, Jeff Mills, Producer & Scorpio, Colin Dale, Seduction, Tom Wilson, and Paul Elstak. It was wet and fairly miserable as ravers splashed and sank to the ankles in mud, but the music and atmosphere was again outstanding and Scott Brown later recalled that it was one of his most memorable gigs ever. "It was just incredible. Walking down the catwalk to the stage was one of the best experiences of my life. Ten thousand people roaring and screaming my name... just wow!"

Scott Brown had blown his student loan on synthesisers and samplers with some mates he met at Uni as they started out in 1991 writing music in the band Q-Tex. He had always been into techno and acid house then rave music and had a huge record collection, but said he didn't have any interest in becoming a DJ and 'just fell into the Hardcore scene which was massive in Scotland in the early/mid '90s.'

"I was becoming more known for my individual productions by around '93 and promoters assumed I was a DJ so kept asking me if I could play sets. One thing led to another and I started to play at events all over," he said.

Brown loved the sound coming out of Holland and was desperate to make music like that which he hoped to get it released on one of the Dutch labels.

"I went on a pilgrimage back in '93 to seek out some labels and hopefully have meetings with label owners. I took the bus from Glasgow to Amsterdam (via the Hovercraft crossing at Dover/Calais) – it took 24 hours and I was shattered, it was all I could afford at the time! I was armed only with the addresses found on the back of my favourite 12" records, no phone, no contacts, nothing. I literally just rolled up to places like Mokum, Combined Forces and Mid-Town with some DAT tapes of my music. Incredibly, some of my UK released tracks had made it across the water and the guys I spoke to knew who I was. That was the start of a great relationship with the Dutch," he continued, in an interview with Alive at Night. Brown also produced the Rezerection Anthem *Do What Ya Like.*

"The Scottish have always been lovers of 'big choons'," said DJ Smurf.

"Scott Brown and his many labels caught onto this and produced some huge bouncy techno anthems, based on the gabba sound of hard kicks and hoovers. This sound made its way back to Rotterdam and out came all those shitty pop-song gabba crap shit bog arse nonsense stuff. Rotterdam DJs were coming to Rez and playing Ultra-Sonic and Evolution Records! What the fuck!" he said, exasperated.

"This was good in a way because it pushed hardcore gabba underground. Only the hardest were left. Paul Elstak was responsible for most of the crap that came out, but I still respect him for starting the whole gabba scene back in the days. The harder Rotterdam sound was coming back in over in the UK in around '98. Some of the slower dark stuff was incredible, just as good as PCP stuff."

DJ Smurf continued to take his hard sounds around the clubs in 1995 with gigs at Stirling's legendary Fubar and a bi-monthly residency at Nosebleed in Rosyth, as well as the Judgement Days and his Dilated Pupil events at Whitley Bay and Newcastle, and he looks back at the time with some fond memories.

"Nosebleed was the best club in the world. The punters were amazing. Like all Scottish crowds, they are always up for a party, and the friendly atmosphere was great. I was always made to feel welcome up there," he said.

With his zany sense of humour and 'gabba' attitude, Smurf's sets were going down a storm and some of his antics included DJing naked and using his knob to move the X-fader, breaking his foot when he fell down the stairs at Nosebleed and had to play on one leg, dressing up as a Teletubbie, and as 'Smurfette' in his girlfriend's skirt, boob tube and a long mermaid wig. One night he stripped down to an Indian's head G-string on stage, and on another he dropped his mobile phone down the toilet when he called someone to listen to him throwing up. Smurf once cleared the dance floor at Diehard at seven in the morning, and on another occasion, he blew the ears off startled clubbers in a House room at MagicKingdom in Northern Ireland by blasting out 300bpm Gabba tracks. He also got on the local poteen that night when someone offered to buy him a drink, and advised him to try the rocket fuel.

"I'll have a treble," I said, 'whoah.' the fella replied. I downed it in one and asked for another 'wahhh, you don't want to do that fella,' he said. I downed that in one too. Five minutes later I was slumped against a wall and my legs gave way. Amazing stuff! Basically, I like to have a laugh, party and have a good time. I don't care what I get up to or how silly I look - as long as other people can have a laugh at me, I don't care. I like to think of a night of DJing as a night out, and make the most of it. I've had a great time partying over the years, and met loads of great people and hope to carry on partying until I drop," he continued.

Smurf went on to appear at some major gabba events around the globe – including Operation Nordcore in Germany, twice, Cold War 2 in Canada,

Together As One NYE 2002 in Los Angeles, Electrophonies in France, Underconstrucion and Hardcore Nation in Italy, and Hellgate and Hardcore Will Never Die in Switzerland, while he also took part in the Industrial Strength European Tour in 2002 in Italy, Switzerland and Austria. "I love playing everywhere. It's nice to get out, have a good time, and if I can DJ for an hour as well, that's a bonus," he said.

The term 'gabber' is reputed to come from Amsterdam's Bargoens, or Thieves Cant, a slang word for a 'gadgie' or 'charver.' The North-East's deep connections with the Faa Gypsy tribe in the 17th century, around the same time as the Amsterdam underground language was emerging, introduced a number of Cant words into the Geordie lexicon as well – words in common usage such as bari, cushtie, scran and deek all have the same Romany origin – gabba just comes from a Dutch version of the same language.

With regular events at places like Rosyth, Aberdeen, Falkirk and Dundee as well as in the Central Belt, the Scottish Bouncy Hardcore scene was absolutely massive and Ian recalled jetting out to Ibiza with the 'Tartan Techno' crew that summer.

"Slipmatt was DJing at an M8 foam party – I'd had a couple of pills and started getting messed up with all these faces appearing through the thick bubbles. You couldn't see what was going on, it was mental, man. It was a lass from Manchester who saved me. I don't know if she was an angel or what, but she took me up out of the chaos onto a platform. I was going mad dancing and she was loving it – then I turned around and she had completely disappeared. I was gutted because I was sure I was going to get my end away!" he said.

"I got a bottle of peach schnapps from the off licence on the way back to the apartment and knocked it back as I was coming down; exploded the bottle off the wall and sat with shattered glass everywhere. Another day we went to a beach party in a little bay with all the Glasgow lads. They gave me a pill when we got back and chucked me in the pool shouting: 'that'll bring your rush on.' It was a week of absolute carnage."

Relaxing on a plastic deck chair around the pool in dark glasses and an unzipped Henri Lloyd tracksuit top soaking up the sun with the condensation rolling down a glass of cold lager, Ian listened to the hardcore tunes emanating from the small outdoor bar and laughed along with the sunburned shirtless tattooed Scots stomping and splashing on the tiles as they geared up for another night in the famous clubs on the island. A Geordie? You're alright. *Just a Jock wi' his brains kicked oot.*

"The music was all bouncy stuff. Scotty Brown's *Now is the Time* was huge back then. But the scene was being ripped apart and categorised – people where taking tunes apart and analysing and classing them as Hard House, Hard Floor or Hard Bag, whatever. It was really the start of the big splits in musical genres," he said.

The first Judgement Day of 1995 took place at the Newcastle University Student Union on the 23rd February where N-Joi appeared, but a change was made the following month on Thursday 23rd March as the event was moved to Rockshots. The opening party of the 8-2am rave featured Hyper live on stage, with Bass Generator, Technotrance, DJ Obsession, Mason and MC Sneaky Eye in what was planned as a monthly event at the club. A week later Judgement Day 8 was back at the Student Union city centre with Human Resource bringing the Rotterdam hardcore sound to Newcastle with a live PA alongside Slipmatt, Brisk, Excel and Bass Generator, then on the 13th April Mickey B was a special guest DJ alongside the regular line-up. NeuroTek, Excel, Bassy G, Technotrance and Smurf played at Rockshots again on the 4th of May and the final appearance at the club on the 18th May saw DJ Seduction guest on the decks. Judgement Day was back at the Student Union on the 25th May and the 15th June before a Unity was held at the Mayfair on Thursday 27th July 1995 on the old Rez format, running from 7-2am. Q-Tex, Rhythm Response, Tom Wilson, Mickey B, DJ FX, Bass Generator and Adrian Street rumbled the old building with their hardcore sounds, and Judgement Day appeared back in the Student Union on the 22nd November and the 16th December.

There were some major concerns in Northumberland at that time that the former Rick's Bar in Amble was about to be turned into a rave venue, and it prompted a special meeting of Alnwick District Council to widen their powers over private clubs. The brothers Jimmy and Gary Robb of the Colosseum were reputed to be among the potential buyers for the venue and the council reacted by adopting the Private Places of Entertainment Act, which had been introduced in an effort to clamp down on 'alcohol-free private member's dance clubs.' Any existing private clubs in the area would be given three months to apply for a license, and heated public meetings were held over the future of the bar as the furore around rave clubs continued to stir up resentment in irate local government officials.

With the likes of High Rollers *Pump that Pussy* blasting out from souped-up GTIs cruising around packed with mean-looking kids with bum-fluff 'tashes and tracky bottoms tucked into their socks, or one of Bassy G's compilation tapes pounding from the open windows of a flat on an estate with a MC reeling off rapid lines, rapping into a microphone held firmly in his grip as he tries to keep up with the tempo, hardcore was being increasingly viewed as a social menace by the straight-laced suits and blue rinse brigade that ran things in the town halls. Ian laughed at the memory of the bowler-hatted Techno-T giving up one night as Tom Wilson kept increasing the sound to warp-factor speeds at one of the CountyDurham rave clubs on a night that would be captured and passed around on cassettes to be played at high volume in a haze of cannabis smoke. Among the Bass Generator Records releases in 1995 were DJ Technotrance *The Y.R.S. Stomp 2*, Water Pistol *Vol Two*, A.S.R. *Vortex / Overture* and *Power of Scotland*, NeuroTek *Crowd Control*, Scudder *The Kiss My Ass Motherfucker* EP, CJ Lehan's *Aftershock* EP and *Cytronix* Part 1, which were undoubtedly played in bedrooms throughout the region and will have led to a stream of parents screaming up the stairs to 'turn that bloody racket down.'

Marc Acardipane was correct when he said he saw music as a generational thing, and by 20 he thought rock was dead. He saw Techno as the rock 'n' roll of today. It should have been no real surprise then that the North-East should embrace the harder sound as the previous generation had been into Heavy Metal, the album covers from the likes of AC/DC and Slayer painted on the flap of their bait bags. So fine was the distinction between the genres that DJ Loftgroover was famous for dropping death metal tracks into his fast Gabba sets and Lenny Dee combined elements of punk/thrash/black metal into his speedcore sound. To give it another metaphor, it was strikingly similar to the intro in 808 State's classic *Cubik* – the electric guitar giving way to the sudden fat electronic notes and the cowbells kicking in. The blast delivered by *In Yer Face*. The spacey techno journey of *Sunrise* that set thousands of teenagers in Adidas trainers and terrace fashions off to seek the pleasures of the warehouse scene in the first place. The demise of the stringed instrument and the growth of electronic sounds also saw generational differences, however, as a younger crowd came through to start claiming the rave scene as their own. They'd been brought up on Sonic Hedgehog and Mario Brothers, better graphics, quicker loading speeds, more readily accessible internet and mobile phones, and were less burdened with the industrial heritage of the region. So by 1996 the Euro-influenced gabba was giving way to the increasingly popular big piano breaks, uplifting helium vocals and booming kick drum of happy hardcore at the Rezerection. It was a change in musical direction something comparable to 1992's venture into the Toy-town techno of *Trip to Trumpton, Roobard and Custard* and *Sesame's Treet*, for the purists at least, but Smurf continued to bring the harder sounds to Tyneside.

"Gabba continued to get a bit of a following in Newcastle, but there was nowhere to hear it. So along with a couple of mates, we started a night called *Hyper-Phonic* on a Thursday night in a bar in Newcastle - Donna Air was a barmaid there," he said.

"We had local guys on playing happy hardcore, bouncy techno and of course me, with the gabba. The nights were fun and ran for a month from the end of January to the end of February '96."

Rezerection teamed up with Dreamscape for 'The Arc' that April with MC Magika hosting for the MTV Party Zone cameras that filmed at the concurrent events. Magika had appeared at a few Rezerections and seemed to be the link, coming as he does from Birmingham, as the event looked to go south to the Midlands for the bumper outdoor Event 4 in June '96. The rave at Holly BushPark in Burton-on-Trent, Staffordshire, was to feature the likes of Charly Lownoise and Mental Theo, Slipmatt, Sy, Brisk, Hixxy, Stu Allen, Bass Generator, Scott Brown, Manu Le Malin, QFX and Q-Tex across two arenas with 25,000 in attendance, but once again the move into England apparently fell flat. Rez V in August was back in Scotland and featured another strong line-up including Marc Smith, Lenny Dee, The Producer, and a number of those that had been booked to appear over the border with 20,000 ravers turning up at the Royal Highland Showground with its fairground, fireworks, and five international arenas.

The final Rez of '96 was the traditional New Year's Eve show and featured the likes of Billy Reid, Davie Forbes, Hixxy, Technotrance, Tom Wilson and Bass Generator.

The Bass Generator records released during that year had included Bass Generator & Ryan Campbell - *Bug Boys*, Bass Generator vs. The Unknown Cheeser – *Burnin' Like Fire / Twisted*, Bass Generator vs. Cytronix - *God Damn It / Bust It Like* This and Bass Generator vs. Channel Zero - *Rusty Screwdriver*, Total Terror Force *Here to Do The Devil's Business*, NeuroTek featuring DJ Excel *Cocaine Re-Mixes* EP, CJ Lehan EP, DJ K2 *Gemini* EP, Ultimate Illusion featuring MC Badboy *Kickin' It Down*, DJ Obsession *What's Your Name, What Y'Had, Where D'Ya Come Fae?* DJ Technotrance *Ringpiece No 1*, Cytronix *Part 2* and *Part 3*, NeuroTek *Live and Direct* EP and Cytronix *Happy Series*, as well as the numerous compilations and DJ mixes put out by the label.

All the while the underground gabba scene continued to grow in Newcastle and in the November of '96 Loftgroover and DJ Freak appeared in Newcastle for the first time at DJ Smurf's Birthday Party rave.

"What a mad party that was. Kiss-o-gram for me, all caught on video, bahhh. At one of these parties, I DJ'd under the name 'DJ Imitation Beard' and wore a big black beard, long black wig, and had an elastoplast on the side of my face with 'Dolik' on it," said Smurf.

"Halfway through a hard set I played *Freedom* by QFX. The hard ends looked puzzled, and the cheesers got up to dance. I pulled the needle across the record, snapped the record, took off my T-shirt to reveal another T-shirt saying 'QFX are fuckin' shite.' The whole place went bezerk, ha, it was great. I got a phone call from QFX's manager a few weeks later going off it!" he laughed.

"I've met them since then and they're cool about it, nice lads and lassies. Anyway, with the small hardcore scene in Newcastle still buzzing, after much demand, the now infamous hardcore arena at Judgement arrived."

Judgement Day branched out that year and as well as its regular gigs at the Student Union, it began hosting events at the likes of Rixy's Complex in

Durham, the Commodore Complex in Stonehaven and all-nighters at the Doncaster Warehouse and After Dark 2 in South Shields. But just as the Judgement Days were growing, the Rezerection was beginning to demise. An Easter special on the 22nd March 1997 called 'The Bangin' Bunny Show' was held across three arenas at the Royal Highland Centre and Showground, and was again in collaboration with the big Midlands rave promoter Dreamscape. Production budgets had been reduced, but the music was provided by likes of DJ Brisk, Hixxy, Slipmatt, Dano, Marc Smith, Sy, Hype and Paul Elstak with happy hardcore being very much the dominant sound. The three-arena format was meant to be used again on Saturday May 31st at 'Event 97 - The Prologue,' which turned out to be the final Rezerection event of the era. An 8,000-capacity crowd turned up to pass through doors and hear the strains of Tchaikovsky's 1812 Overture as it opened, a sea of glow sticks raised, lasers and sweeping blue lights up, the energetic dancers on the stage in short luminous shorts and tops as the whistles blasted out and cheers reverberated around the roof space.

The plan was for the Dream Arena to star Force & Styles, Slipmatt, Sharkey & Druid, Seduction, Dougal, DJ Kid and MCs Gavsie and Odyssey. The main Rezerection/M8 Arena had Manu Le Malin, Billy 'Daniel' Bunter & Rob Vanden, DJ Pavo, Hixxy, Producer, DJ Noizer, Marc Smith, Scott Brown, Tom Wilson and the live acts Force & Styles, 4 Tune, Fairytales, Q-Tex, and Ultimate Illusion, with MCs Drokz, G, and Madman, while the Limbo/Lift Arena was to feature Billy Kiltie, Bhaskar Dandona, James Brolly, Percy X, Derrick Wallace, and Euan & Paul, but only the main hall was opened, leaving confused ravers looking around for the other stages. The music was still pounding, the venue was the same, but something had been lost along the way; one of the Exposure Dancers admitted that 'the vibe had changed massively by this point...it had become something else entirely and not what I remember the heydays being, for sure.' Some blamed the relentless intensity of gabba, others the cheesy uplifting electro nursery-rhyme riffs and melodic helium singing of happy hardcore. Some felt that the numbers of very young teenagers attending the events were taking it off in a different commercialised direction and others that the scene was becoming a parody of itself. The rave scene that had been all about unity was divided, splintered and fractured into sub-factions of sound. The magic was missing. It was just gone, lost in among the £2 Mitsubishis and Dollars, the cheap sportswear jumpers and baseball caps, the big over-excited staring eyes. The disastrous end to Rezerection was accelerated by the demise of ticketing agency TOCTA and the resultant loss of pre-event sales and money for the next planned event. It was cancelled and the Rez folded shortly after.

But Bass Generator was keeping the scene alive on Tyneside and Joolie Gee made the big mistake of knocking back a full bottle of vodka as she waited in the queue ahead of one of the continuing monthly Judgement Days at Newcastle University Student's Union. With her head intensely spinning in the darkness and the warped techno sounds pounding off the walls, Joolie raced to the toilet and spent the whole night spewing chunks into the pan; feeling the slight relief of the touch of cold porcelain on her sweating forehead, the horror as the pain and cramps in her stomach started again along with the seemingly endless heaving. The blinding pain of white light behind the eyes as the bass vibrations rumbled on relentlessly. "It's safe to say it was the first and last time that I ever drank at a rave," she winced at the memory.

On Saturday 20th December 1997 the Rotterdam Terror Corps appeared at the 6pm-1am Judgement Day at Newcastle Uni. The Terror Corps had been founded in Holland in 1993 by five DJs - Distortion, Reanimator, Petrov, Rob and MC Raw. Their shows featured huge pyrotechnics and famously had stunning scantily-clad female dancers in bondage gear and strippers up on the stage with them. The RTC were all about attitude. DJ Distortion told Electronic Beats magazine: "I would say that in Holland, the real boom in electronic music can be traced back to our infrastructure. Everything is really close here and public transportation is excellent. In fact, you can probably go by bicycle to most parties. That, combined with incredibly tolerant drug laws, helped to create a booming scene. Also, in around 1991/92, if you needed a license to throw a party in some public space, you just asked politely and you almost always got it."

Distortion was keen to point out that the darkness connected to the Gabba scene was all about image and an attitude, and continued: "All over the world, gabber is very much connected with images of terror and horror, like all the flyers and posters with devils, skulls, evil clowns, guns, knives...it's an image thing, and it's pretty strongly connected to metal too. Rob Gee, Delta 9, the Industrial Strength guys in America - they're all really into metal. And hardcore parties, like metal concerts, are also 80 percent male."

"Surprise, surprise. This isn't a Katy Perry concert. But the girls that do come get treated with total respect. After I convinced a friend of mine to go to her first gabber party, she was shocked: 'I thought I was ugly! I looked great and nobody touched me or even looked at me!'" he said.

Appearances from Lenny Dee, Sharkey, Bass Generator, DJ FX, Techno-trance, Soner, DJ Attack, DJ Bouncin', H.M.S., DJ Sass and the Geordie Gabba Mafia – Rob Saunders, U.E.P. and Smurf - along with XE-Cute and Sticky Fingers ensured that it was an unforgettable night of devastating noise for the enthusiastic crowd that was over way too quickly.

"The *Geordie Gabba Mafia* was the brainchild of DJ UEP, Rob Saunders and another guy called Dan. They printed off the infamous GGM circle stickers and made some T-shirts with the '*A Member of the Geordie Gabba Mafia*' phrase on them. These shirts became quite famous and guaranteed you would see the shirts at every big rave around the UK. One of the most popular ones back then was the 'Choose Life' text from the Trainspotting movie, changed to 'Fuck Life," recalled Smurf, who by late 1997 was playing hardcore gabba, noisecore, and speedcore in his sets, though he wasn't too bothered by the labels attached to the sounds that he span.

"I play stuff I would want to hear if I was out there on a dance floor. My sets have slowed down a lot - instead of just banging out insane 250bpm+ for an hour, I may start around 200 and build up, realising that you can still be hardcore and a slower tempo," he said.

"I wish some of the up-and-coming DJs would realise this. Every set varies, depending on the time I'm playing and who else is on the line-up. For instance, if Lofty was on the same event as me I wouldn't play many guitar tracks and just stick to the noisier stuff. It's all about variety on the night. Some up and comings just play to their mates, or to the 'big name' DJs of the night."

"I was also playing 'newstyle' Rotterdam sets at Judgement Day every two months at the time, back-to-back with Bass Generator, for 3 or 4 hours - none of the cheesy pop-rave stuff that had been around. This stuff was tough and dark. Spooky horror sounds and the like. The new sound around '98 was based on the slow, dark German Kotzaak/Cold Rush/Dance Ecstasy-type sound, of around 150bpm. Although I am more known for the harder stuff, and will only play a Rotterdam set when I am put on the flyer as playing that, I mainly prefer playing the harder, faster, noisy stuff."

Bass Generator had been there from the very start at Rez 1 at the Mayfair and the scene went full circle with a weird synchronicity to it as his Newcastle-based Judgement Day brought the bouncy techno sound back up to the Royal Highland Centre in Edinburgh for the Hogmany event on 31st December 1997 with 5,000 people in the venue. Ultimate Buzz, NeuroTek, System X, Dyme Brothers and N.R. Getik appeared at the 8pm-7am show, which the flyers stated would 'hopefully put an end to the ideas that the Scottish Hardcore scene was dead.'

"There was no gabber on the line-up, apart from me, and I was playing the first set," said DJ Smurf. "It was some buzz paying in the venue where the Rezerection all-nighters were held after attending almost all of them from 1992. At midnight, a few of us dressed up on Tellytubby costumes and walked about the stage. The health and safety people went crazy and told us to get off, because none of us could see out of the heads and we nearly fell off the stage," he laughed.

"A second room was opened, which was behind a huge curtain where the main stage was. For the last two hours of the night, myself and DJ Execute played a lot of gabber and speedcore (220 bpm+) which went down very well with the party people. Unfortunately, Uncle Tom Wilson (RIP) was playing at the same time and he wasn't too impressed, as he could hear the machine-gun music behind the curtain that separated the two DJ booths."

Although it was the end of an era, the evolution of underground electronic music in the North East continued and alongside the Geordie Gabba Mafia there came the rise of Makina culture, taking the art of MCing to the next level as the lyrics got increasingly meaningful and identity-led with people like MC Rockeye eventually becoming the new musical innovators in the area.

"I was looking for the next big thing – this Spanish stuff came in and it didn't really work at first," said DJ Scott in Rob Kilburn's cult *Two Monkeys* documentary, which you can find on YouTube. Scott was instrumental in bringing the new European sound to the area, which took off massively in the New Monkey club. He'd been out to Spain and brought a load of records back with him.

"You used to get a couple more every week to add on. That was late '97 and by '98 they started to get more and more and by '99 there was loads of it. But it was hard to get because obviously they were imports. You just had to go all over the country and get bits and bobs of it. You've got the North East rave scene here, which is only big in the North East – the Makina is only big in Barcelona."

"Scott Brown used to make bouncy Techno in the early '90s up in Scotland, and that was big down here, so it was kind of an advanced stage of that. That's what we love, and that's why the North East scene is different to everywhere else," he said.

Unfortunately, by '99, just as the Makina scene was starting to grow, the slow death of 'rave' had accelerated to leave little but a stinking, decomposing corpse.

"Attendances for events were starting to dwindle, ravers from 10 years ago were either too old, married with kids or in mental hospitals and record shops were closing all over the UK so it was difficult to advertise any events, as this is where the flyers for events were picked up," concluded Smurf.

"Judgement Day met its death in '99 too. The age restriction was always 16 and with numbers dwindling, this was reduced to 14. This was also the age of the 'charva' or chav. These young jerks started attending Judgement Day and causing trouble... robbing students outside, fighting, coming to events just to get off their heeds and generally being arseholes and not respecting the 'PLUR' (Peace, Love, Unity, Respect) of a rave."

"At the May event, some pricks kicked in the back doors of the venue and barged in and this got too much for the venue. Bass Generator and I had played early and were in a car on the way North to a party in Rosyth. Bassy got a call about the trouble and we had to head back. The next event, in June '99, was the last event at Newcastle University. The Judga did return later on in the year in December, at the After Dark II club in South Shields, but it wasn't the same."

Although the '90s were over, Geoff Waterston engineered the incredibly rare modular Orgon Drone 1 synthesiser around the end of the century and it is rumoured among the tech heads on computer forums that only six were ever delivered. His electronics work is talked about in revered, mysterious tones with the earlier '96 Orgon Enigiser becoming something of a Holy Grail among music producers, with some even talking about attempting to reverse engineer one.

"The Enigiser from Orgon Systems is a pure organic, fat, screaming, fuzzing, bubbling, gritty little monster!" wrote a fan called Alex, who marvelled that his machine was hand-numbered 0051 and was rare, difficult-to-find with no equivalent. Another wrote that his Enigiser was number 18 and was 'without a doubt the finest analogue synth that money can buy – it's done countless gigs, been beer-ified, dropped and abused and it still sounds like angels' flatulence. Geoff Waterston is a king among mere mortals (and I'm not even related).' Only 150 Enigisers were ever made, handcrafted in Whitley Bay by the GFX man, to create the unique bleep and bass of the original Geordie techno sound. A decade in dance and it just seems right that Geoff should retain some element of mystique and inscrutability; hardcore – you know the score.

Ravers at a Mayfair Rezerection

Inside a Butterloggie

Club Havana

The Hardware Records crew

The P.S.I Division

Blue Monkey

The Colosseum

Judgement Day

Rezerection at Edinburgh

Printed in Great Britain
by Amazon